D0044769

COVERING

# covering

THE HIDDEN ASSAULT ON OUR CIVIL RIGHTS

KENJI YOSHINO

MONTEREY COUNTY FREE

SALINAS
CALIFORNIA

LIBRARIES

RANDOM HOUSE

NEW YORK

Although *Covering* is a work of nonfiction, the names of certain nonpublic individuals have been changed.

Copyright © 2006 by Kenji Yoshino

All rights reserved.

Published in the United States by Random House, an imprint of The Random House Publishing Group, a division of Random House, Inc., New York.

RANDOM HOUSE and colophon are registered trademarks of Random House, Inc.

Grateful acknowledgment is made to Philip Levine for permission to reprint "The Doctor of Starlight" from *One for the Rose* (Pittsburgh: Carnegie-Mellon University Press, 1999), pp. 57–58.

LIBRARY OF CONGRESS CATALOGING-IN-PUBLICATION DATA
Yoshino, Kenji.
Covering: the hidden assault on our civil rights / Kenji Yoshino.— 1st ed.
    p.   cm.
  Includes index.
  ISBN 0-375-50820-1 (alk. paper)
  1. Yoshino, Kenji. 2. Gay lawyers—United States—Biography. 3. Japanese American lawyers—United States—Biography. 4. Gay rights—United States. 5. Civil rights—United States. 6. Assimilation (Sociology)—United States. I. Title.
KF373.A3Y67 2006
342.7308'5—dc22        2005046561

Printed in the United States of America on acid-free paper

www.atrandom.com

9  8  7  6  5  4  3  2

*Book design by Casey Hampton*

*For my parents*

It is a fact that persons who are ready to admit possession of a stigma (in many cases because it is known
about or immediately apparent) may nonetheless make
a great effort to keep the stigma from looming large. . . .
This process will be referred to as *covering*.

—Erving Goffman, *Stigma: Notes on the
Management of Spoiled Identity*

# PREFACE

Everyone covers. To cover is to tone down a disfavored identity to fit into the mainstream. In our increasingly diverse society, all of us are outside the mainstream in some way. Nonetheless, being deemed mainstream is still often a necessity of social life. For this reason, every reader of this book has covered, whether consciously or not, and sometimes at significant personal cost.

Famous examples of covering abound. Ramón Estévez covered his ethnicity when he changed his name to Martin Sheen, as did Krishna Bhanji when he changed his name to Ben Kingsley. Margaret Thatcher covered her status as a woman when she trained with a voice coach to lower the timbre of her voice. Long after they came out as lesbians, Rosie O'Donnell and Mary Cheney still covered, keeping their same-sex partners out of the public eye. Issur Danielovitch Demsky covered his Judaism when he became Kirk Douglas, as did Joseph Levitch when he became Jerry Lewis. Franklin Delano Roosevelt covered his disability by ensuring his wheelchair was always hidden behind a desk before his Cabinet entered.

I doubt any of these people covered willingly. I suspect they were all bowing to an unjust reality that required them to tone down their stigmatized identities to get along in life. Sheen says he needed to "get a name people could pronounce and connect with" if he "wanted to work commercially." Yet he now regrets having done so, and has exhorted his sons—Emilio and Charlie—to use the family name. One of them has not done so, signaling the enduring force of the covering demand.

In a supposedly enlightened age, the persistence of the covering demand presents a puzzle. Today, race, national origin, sex, religion, and disability are all protected by federal civil rights laws. An increasing number of states and localities include sexual orientation in civil rights laws as well. Albeit with varying degrees of conviction, Americans have come to a consensus that people should not be penalized for being different along these dimensions. That consensus, however, does not protect individuals against demands that they mute those differences. We need an explanation for why the civil rights revolution has stalled on covering.

Covering has enjoyed such a robust and stubborn life because it is a form of assimilation. At least since Hector St. John de Crève-coeur's 1782 *Letters from an American Farmer,* this country has touted assimilation as the way Americans of different backgrounds would be "melted into a new race of men." By the time Israel Zangwill's play of that name was performed in 1908, the "melting pot" had acquired the burnish of an American ideal. Only with the civil rights movement of the 1960s was this ideal challenged in any systematic way, with calls to move "beyond the melting pot" and to "celebrate diversity." And notwithstanding that challenge, assimilation has never lost its hold on the American imagination. Indeed, as our country grows more pluralistic, we have seen a renaissance of the melting pot ideal. Fearful that we are spinning apart into balkanized groups, even liberals like Arthur Schlesinger have called for a recommitment to that ethic. In the United States, as in other industrialized democracies, we are seeing the "return of assimilation."

I recognize the value of assimilation, which is often necessary to fluid social interaction, to peaceful coexistence, and even to the dialogue through which difference is valued. For that reason, this is no simple screed against conformity. What I urge here is that we approach the renaissance of assimilation in this country critically. We must be willing to see the dark side of assimilation, and specifically of covering, which is the most widespread form of assimilation required of us today.

Covering is a hidden assault on our civil rights. We have not been able to see it as such because it has swaddled itself in the benign language of assimilation. But if we look closely, we will see that covering is the way many groups are being held back today. The reason racial minorities are pressured to "act white" is because of white supremacy. The reason women are told to downplay their child-care responsibilities in the workplace is because of patriarchy. And the reason gays are asked not to "flaunt" is because of homophobia. So long as such covering demands persist, American civil rights will not have completed its work.

Unfortunately, the law has yet to perceive covering as a threat. Contemporary civil rights law generally only protects traits that individuals cannot change, like their skin color, chromosomes, or innate sexual orientations. This means that current law will not protect us against most covering demands, because such demands direct themselves at the behavioral aspects of our personhood. This is so despite the fact that covering imposes costs on us all.

The universality of the covering demand, however, is also a potential boon for civil rights advocates. I, too, worry about our current practice of fracturing into groups, each clamoring for state and social solicitude. For this reason, I do not think we can move forward by focusing on old-fashioned group-based identity politics. We must instead build a new civil rights paradigm on what draws us together rather than on what drives us apart. Because covering applies to us all, it provides an issue around which we can make common cause. This is the desire for authenticity, our common human wish to express ourselves without being impeded by unreasoning demands for conformity.

I thought I would make this argument in purely political terms. As a law professor, I have become accustomed to the tones of legal impersonality. But I came to see that I could not compose an argument about the importance of human authenticity without risking such authenticity myself. So I have written this book in a more intimate voice, blending memoir with argument. In trying to make the stakes of assimilation vivid, I draw on my attempts to elaborate my identity as a gay man, and, to a lesser extent, my identity as an Asian-American.

Yet this is not a standard "coming out" narrative or racial memoir. I follow the Romantics here in their belief that if a human life is described with enough particularity, the universal will begin to speak through it. What interests me about my story, and the stories of others, is how similar they are in revealing the bones of our common human endeavor, the yearning for human emancipation that stirs within us all.

# CONTENTS

part**three**

COVERING

sociable. I have never worked so hard, or been so happily appeti-
tive, as in those years.

Yet physically I remained a small dark thing altogether. I remember thinking during a soccer practice that I must have had a
lot of natural muscle once, to feel so punished as I watched those
boys scissor the air with their blond high school legs. Their bodies
hummed to a frequency not my own as balls sailed fluently into
nets. I sensed these bodies knew other bodies, as I knew calculus or
Shakespeare. That knowledge flaunted itself in the lilt of small
hairs off their necks.

I would not have been able to say I was gay and these others
were straight. I knew only I was asked not to be myself, and that to
fail to meet that demand was to make myself illegible, my future
unimaginable. I hoped time would soften the difference between
others and me, but knew it would do the opposite.

To evade my fate, I acquired a girlfriend. I have a memory of
my dormitory's stairwell, where boys would kiss girls good night
before curfew. I am standing on the bottom step looking down at
her. She is Filipina, a year older, her fluency in French standing for
her urbanity. The waver of shadow superimposes an ambivalence
on the sweet certainty of her face. I wonder what is more abject
than this—my brain urging the bloodrush and attention that
comes so naturally, so involuntarily, to others.

Of course, it was not wonderful to be her, either. Yet it was
many years before I would speculate about the other side of that
kiss. Only after I came out did I listen to the rueful stories of gay
men—how one picked fights with his wife to avoid sex, how another wished his girlfriend would turn into a pizza at nightfall. The
trials of those who love the closeted have yet to be told. I was
nowhere near imagining them then.

My rising anxiety gave me limitless life force in other spheres. I

# AN UNCOVERED SELF

"Send the beloved child on a journey," the Japanese proverb says. So when I turned thirteen, my parents sent me to boarding school. I could see they wished to keep me close, but worried about the effects of tenderness. Small for my age, not so much quiet as silent, I was tarrying at the threshold of adolescence. A singer, I was stricken when my clean boy soprano, that noise only boys can make, broke into a sublunary baritone.

So off I went, to boarding school and radical reinvention. The need for self-reliance called into being a self on which I could rely. As no one knew me there, no one could challenge the authenticity of this brighter self. Seemingly overnight, I became full of speeches, remember a biology lab in which we observed a spear-headed water worm. Like a starfish, it could grow back anything we razored off it, even to the point of generating multiple versions of itself. I saw myself in that gliding shape. Arrow-shaped, it never arrived where it wanted to go. But it knew, when cut, to grow.

As I moved from high school to college, my mill of activity became more frenetic, a way of keeping the world at bay. At Harvard, I took five or six courses a semester, and as many extracurriculars, foreclosing time for thought, for breath. Friends complained I was walled up, a Jericho waiting for its Joshua. Yet alongside my silence was a ravening urge to speak. So I began to study poetry—a childhood passion—more formally, finding solace in a language more public than thought but more private than prose. Instead of writing an analytic thesis to graduate as an English major, I petitioned to write a collection of my own poems.

Writing these poems gave me more pleasure than anything before. That year, the only reason anything had to be, was to be a poem—the icicles making their small clear points on the eaves, the broken gate that clacked double knuckled on its hinge, the bitter flesh star at the heart of a lemon. Poetry was my medium, as rigid and formal and obscure as its author. On Saturday nights, I would sit in my cement-block dorm room with my face lit green by my IBM's glow, agonizing not over women, or men, but line breaks. I thought myself happy, and in some sense I was.

The readers of my collection understood as much of me as I did. One grader took it on faith: "I cannot see what you have seen. But I can see that you have seen." The other did not. Impatient, he quoted Marvin Bell's line about how to become a writer is to become "less and less embarrassed about more and more."

Neither grader had license to say the collection was hard to read for a different reason: it was full of pain. The collection ends in crisis—the last poem, titled "The Infanticide of My Professions," was about the selves we had to kill in young adulthood. The word "profession" carried its double sense of façade and occupation. The poem expressed the hope I would destroy the selves I only professed to be, and be left with one with a natural vocation. That hope was smothered by the fear I might murder the real self or, worse, that I might find that self to be a tragic one. I still find this poem difficult to read.

Yet when I wrote it, I acted as if I could carry the world before me. My curricular and extracurricular frenzy had won me a Rhodes scholarship to England. (Perhaps the closeted should not be permitted to compete for these fellowships—we have the advantage of those Saturday nights.) But the carbonation in my veins when I won was less joy than relief. I had a new precocity to balance against my backwardness, this social acceptance to weigh against my refusal of life.

One person saw through me. The poetry professor who had supervised my thesis was a Pre-Raphaelite figure. A whippet-thin chain smoker, she had waist-length auburn hair and eyebrows sharp as circumflex accents. She was the best teacher I have ever had—she returned each poem marked up in three colors, one for each pass she had taken over it. She gave me a nickname: Radiating Naivete. "Radiating Naivete," she would say when we bumped into each other near midnight at Caffé Paradiso, "have you entered the realm of the erotic yet?" In a letter she gave me at graduation, she described sitting on a plane next to an emergency exit. There was an arc painted next to the handle, each end of which was marked with a scarlet word: "Engage" and "Disengage." The handle was on "Disengage." She said it made her think of me.

I was not ready when emergency came. Until then, I had been splendidly noncommittal: neither Japanese nor American, neither poet nor pragmatist, neither straight nor gay. But it seemed all ambiguities had to be resolved that year. I had to choose citizenship—the red Japanese passport or the blue American one, the two colors of blood. I had to choose a career—literature or law. Most of all, I had to choose—or choose to acknowledge—the sexuality that roiled the surface that summer when I fell bewilderingly in love.

The Japanese character for erotic desire is the same as that for color. Some say this commonality arises from the Buddhist teaching that desire, like color, distracts us from enlightenment by calling us to the things of this world. The world's colorless wave broke kaleidoscopically over me when I met Brian. We lived together after graduation while we attended summer school—he to complete medical school prerequisites, I to prepare for my time in England. Brian was the first in his family to attend college and was, like me, hungry to prove himself. But unlike me, he had directed his intensity outward, devoting his college years to ceaseless public service. This moved me.

One glittering afternoon, we walked along the Charles River. It was a Sunday—the riverside drive was hedged with sawhorses, closed to cars. The cyclists sheared the air. Dazzled by the needles of light stitching the water, I turned to watch him watch them. I noticed his eyelashes were reflected in his eyes, like awnings in windowpanes. As I tried to make sense of that reflection, I found I could not look away. His irises were brown, clouding into orange, with brighter flecks around his pupils. Then it became as important not to look as to look, as I feared I would be lost in a rush of bronze motes.

It hardly mattered that I knew he was straight. I experienced my desire for him, which was a pent-up desire for many men, as having an absolute absolved necessity. Just as the brain seems larger than the skull that contains it, so did my desire seem grossly to exceed the contours of my body. I thought if I could only make him experience the strength of what I felt, he could not demur.

I had, in one sense, chosen the right man. Brian responded with compassion. Yet my desire was now not only thwarted, but exposed. Brian made me acknowledge my knowledge; he made me own myself. I snapped back into my skin. And I felt something in me crack—like a safe, a whip.

Oxford was gray. The stone gargoyles simpered with their cheeks on their long fingers; the deer in the park outside my rooms were, in the college poet's phrase, "connoisseurs of the air"; genial professors overfilled our glasses with claret, encouraging us to "exploit the meniscus." But it seemed as if I spent the entire first year in my bed. I retreated into the one-seat theater of my mind, which unspooled images of Brian's orange eyes, the glittering river. I watched the sunlight that dappled my room gather into the coins of light passing cars would slide across the ceiling. I became so gaunt the tectonics of my face surfaced; I began to feel more a tenant than a resident in my body.

I would think, I wish I were dead. I did not think of it as a suicidal thought. My poet's parsing mind read the first "I" and the second "I" as different "I's." The first "I" was the whole watching self, while the second "I"—the one I wanted to kill—was the gay "I" nested inside it. It was less a suicidal impulse than a homicidal one—the infanticide of the gay self I had described in the poem.

My only consistent foray from my rooms was to the college chapel, where I prayed to gods I did not believe in for transformation. No erotic desire I had ever felt exceeded my desire for conversion in those moments. It is hard now to recall that young man at prayer. To see him clearly is to feel the outlines of my present self grow fainter.

An older American student tried to help. Arad was struggling to come out himself, but seemed, I thought enviously, much more self-possessed. He was the prodigy of his class—his intellectual feats, in medicine and philosophy, were reported in hushed and reverent tones. Tall and angular, he accentuated his forbidding demeanor with a black coat that billowed out like the wings of a predatory bird.

Arad was kind to me. I never named my malady, but he knew its ways better than I. I remember sitting in his rooms listening to him describe the deadlines he had set for himself—to come out to his parents in three months, to go to a meeting of the college gay group in six months, to begin to date in a year. It was important, he said, to be a creature of the will. Unable to meet his eye, I looked over his shoulder at the wall behind him, which was tiled with diplomas and awards. In the center were some framed black-and-white photographs he had taken. One caught my eye—a statue of a kneeling angel weeping with her head buried in her arms.

It was a portrait of abject perfection, a portrait of him, and it terrified me. I recognized the striving impulse in Arad as an attribute of my former self, and felt shame for having lost the discipline he still possessed. Yet I was also frightened by the harshness of that will. I thanked him and left, never to return. I could not help him, and I knew he could not help me.

In my second year, I met the woman who would. Maureen interviewed me for a job at a management consulting firm to which I had applied—in the mantra of my classmates—"to keep my options open." An expatriate American on the cusp of thirty, she was living in England with her husband, who was an Oxford don.

That day, I saw this contrast in her—flaxen hair against dark suit, slightness of build against stillness of carriage. I trusted her. When she asked me during the interview about a risk I had taken, I told her about writing my collection of poems, saying emotional risks often felt more real to me than physical or analytic ones. The day after the interview, she told me I had advanced to the next round, and offered to coach me through it. We scheduled a time to meet, and in a rash fit of trust, I sent her my thesis.

When we met again, she told me she disagreed we assassinated the selves we did not choose to live. In her view, while the chosen self lived in Technicolor splendor, the unchosen ones lived on in black-and-white. It would be easier, she said, if assassination were possible, as those unchosen selves became the demons that bedeviled the chosen one.

Not then, but soon thereafter, I learned of her unchosen selves. Maureen's first fealty was to art—to the cello, as well as to literature. She had broken that allegiance to escape the starving-artist existence of her musician parents. Yet she now regretted having done so; by that time, she had stopped playing music or reading literature. She saw me as a younger self she could save from the same fate, a rescue connected to her own redemption.

Maureen startled me with her access to so many selves, not only in herself but in me. She acted as my sibyl in the world of business, which, as my father's world, loomed in my mind as a sphere of temporal power. With her at my side, I became convinced I could master this world, a conviction that made it possible for me to reject it. Maureen also understood my more private literary self. Better read than I, she was an acute critic of my writing. I felt my isolation break, as if an audience member had walked through the fourth wall of a stage to put her arms around the soliloquist. Perhaps most important, Maureen understood the coexistence of these selves. Torn herself, she could frame the question of what I might look like whole.

The classical muse speaks poetry for the poet to transcribe. Maureen was a different kind of muse: she listened. In the writing I showed her, I still cloaked my meanings in poetic obscurity. Although I knew she had already guessed I was gay, I could not acknowledge the truth that hung between us. Yet this was nonetheless a literary convalescence: I wrote more in those few months than I had in the preceding eighteen. I wrote for the whorl of her ear.

My academic career self-destructed in slow motion, like a glass that bounces on the floor before it bursts. My tutors could no longer hide their contempt. But I no longer needed to be beyond their criticism. I had to trust that what felt right was as often right as what felt wrong was wrong. And what often felt right was the steaming water in the bathtub in my dormitory. The wall clock, whose Medusa face had paralyzed me, now ticked toward my recovery. I felt like a statue coming to life. It was my own warmth that startled me.

One Saturday, we wandered into a haberdashery on Jermyn Street in London. I found a vest—gold lions ramping through a cobalt brocade. I would not have worn it as an undergraduate, nor do I wear it now. But then, as I ran the brittle fabric between my thumb and finger, I experienced a jackdaw craving for it. I slipped it on. I could not decide whether it looked ridiculous. "It becomes you," the shopkeeper said gruffly through his waxed mustache. I realized it did become me, and that I could become it. It did the work outlandish clothes do for us—it drove my invisible difference to the surface and held it there, relieving my psyche of that work. The shop did not take checks, so Maureen put the vest on her credit card, and I signed away an alarming portion of my living stipend to her. By next mail, she sent back my pale green check, cut in half and folded into two origami cranes.

Toward the end of my second year, we went to the London Zoo. After we thought we were done, we saw signs pointing down to the "Moonlight World." We descended into a murk lit only by a green neon strip along the handrail. Here were the fragile fantastics that could not stand the light. Lorises glowered with their amber eyes; echidnas shambled through their holes; bats hung in the velvet bags of themselves. With their leaflike hands on the rails, the children and their grandparents were so quiet—closer, on either side, to speechlessness than we. I stared into the liquid eyes of a loris and thought I had lived like this for some time now—darkly, grotesquely, remarkably.

I surfaced back into my life. I made decisions with percussive efficiency. I chose the American passport over the Japanese one, the gay identity over the straight one, law school over English graduate school. The last two choices were connected. I decided on law school in part because I had accepted my gay identity. A gay poet is vulnerable in profession as well as person. I refused that level of exposure. Law school promised to arm me with a new language, a language I did not expect to be elegant or moving but that I expected to be more potent, more able to protect me. I have seen this bargain many times since—in myself and others—compensation for standing out along one dimension by assimilating along others.

I had been wrong to think there was no beauty in the language of law: the line of legal argument has its taut pleasures. But law school is not a safe place for poets. Eyes awelter with the Federal Rules of Civil Procedure, I wrote ruefully to Maureen that I had switched from being the Pied Piper of Hamelin to being its mayor. As the maples in New Haven changed like traffic lights from green to yellow to red, I felt my own life slowing again.

The German Romantic poet Hölderlin says, "The danger itself fosters the rescuing power." We are lucky when that line describes our lives. That spring, I needed a path into the law. That spring, a visiting lecturer named Bill Rubenstein offered, for the first time, a course titled "Sexual Orientation and the Law." At the time, he was the only openly gay person on the law school faculty.

In his mid-thirties at the time, Bill had worked as a gay rights litigator for the American Civil Liberties Union before making this transition into academia. Dark haired and rangy, he is Russian Jewry's answer to Mr. Darcy. His beauty helped me come out—I thought nothing could be wrong with a condition housed in a person so radiant.

At the beginning of term, I went to Bill's office hours. His office was almost bare, which I attributed to his visitor's status. My eye swept over his scattered effects, tracking the grit of his life. The crossword half done in pen. The untidily folded black glasses with their odd, hollow-looking stems. Behind him on the shelves, boxes and boxes of pens and pencils, stacks of sticky notes and yellow legal pads. Was this Yale hospitality, or was he an office supplies survivalist? Then I collected myself. I told him I was gay, still shuddering inside as I spoke the words. Nothing has convinced me of the power of words as much as the experience of coming out the first few times—one ends the sentence a different person. I confessed I was anxious about taking his course, as I feared it would out me to the law school community.

While I tried to speak calmly, Bill has since told me I failed. He said I reminded him of the dinner parties he was attending in those days. At the mainly straight dinners, his age peers would jabber on about their children. At the gay dinners, they'd jabber about their coming out. This made him think coming out is the closest many gay men will come to giving birth. The act of giving birth to oneself is miraculous and terrifying, but unlikely to be calm.

To my surprise, Bill advised me not to take the seminar, telling me to come out on my own schedule, not Yale's. He urged me to get the syllabus, to buy the casebook he had edited, and to read along with the class. He promised he would discuss the materials with me whenever I wanted, and would do so in the library if I felt uncomfortable meeting in his office. He said I could take a course from him the next year if I felt ready to do so.

I took his advice. I also took to sleeping with his book. I would read it before falling asleep each night, and settle with my arm around it. In this time when everything was changing, this text would not change. The print would stay fixed on the pages, the words would say tomorrow what they said today.

Last year, Bill invited me to join him as a coeditor of his casebook. I felt I was being called home. For that book—my book of hours—was where the law began to matter to me. I could see the difference the law made in gay lives—employees were fired for saying they were gay, parents lost custody of their children, people were denied, in gay activist Larry Kramer's words, "the right to love." The sinews of legal language began to seduce me. A court's saying, "You have no right to love," did not just describe, but actually created, that reality in the world. It was like the incantations of myth, this speaking things real: "It is so ordered," "We hold," "We reverse." In my second year, I began to speak myself more real as a form of resistance, coming out to more and more people. I signed up for Bill's "Queer Theory" seminar. And I began to think about becoming a law professor.

In the spring of my second year, I interviewed for clerkships—

postgraduate stints under a judge's tutelage. During one interview, a federal appellate judge noted Bill's "Queer Theory" class on my transcript and asked what the word "queer" meant. Still overawed by the federal judiciary, I assumed he knew the word and was gauging the subtlety of my grasp of it. So I said I understood it to be a derogatory term for homosexuals that had since been co-opted by the gay rights movement, like the pink triangle. I was about to continue when he asked what the pink triangle was. A beat. I told him the pink triangle was used by the Nazis during the Holocaust to mark homosexuals, but had since become a symbol of gay pride. He said, "I didn't know that."

Even as I tried to conceal my surprise, I tried to rationalize his authority. I reminded myself he belonged to an older generation, and that appellate judges could lead cloistered lives. But then I re-called this judge had recently decided a gay rights case in which he had denied gays the judicial protection afforded some groups—like racial minorities or women—under the equality provision of the federal Constitution. In determining whether a group merits this protection, a judge is legally required to consider whether it has suffered a history of discrimination. How could this judge have analyzed the history of discrimination gays had suffered, I wondered, without encountering the pink triangle? Might the judge have reached a different result in that case if he had under-stood the symbol and everything it means?

On the plane ride home, I worried at these questions. I experi-enced the judge's ignorance of the pink triangle as a *literary* offense, an offense against narrative. The pink triangle was the gay com-munity's bid to make its story known. How could the judge rule on those lives in such a consequential way without knowing that story? By the time I returned to school, I knew I would write an essay on gay symbolic politics that drew on both legal and literary theory. I wrote with a passion I had felt before only for poetry. I became a lawyer for the gay self I had tried to kill at Oxford, the poet I had thought to kill in law school. I wanted to reverse the infanticide of my professions and to resurrect those abandoned selves. If the law wanted to intervene in the intimate particulars of my life, I would ask it to know me intimately.

Some of the heat I put into this document came off it. The published paper was cited by progay judicial opinions. It also secured me a teaching job at Yale, where I have been a professor for the past nine years. I teach classes here in sexuality and the law, law and literature, Japanese law, and constitutional law. Contrary to my belief that I had to kill all but one self, it is the polyphony of selves that has been celebrated here.

The month I was hired, Arad killed himself. It would wrong the grief of his intimates to make too much of my own feelings. Yet I was shaken, especially when I read the eulogy his friends had written. Rather than continuing the narrative of perfection they thought had contributed to his isolation, his friends sought to humanize him. One detail was unforgettable—as a child at boarding school, Arad had been discovered in a broom closet with a bottle of bleach, trying to dye his skin white. As I read that story, I thought of Arad's absoluteness. I thought of the alabaster angel in his photograph and knew, with some combination of guilt and relief, that I was imperfect and able to survive.

For even that far out of the closet, I was still making bargains. While closeted, I micromanaged my gay identity, thinking about who knew and who did not, who should know and who should not. When I came out, I exulted that I could stop thinking about my orientation. That celebration proved premature. It was impossible to come out and be done with it, as each new person erected a new closet around me. More subtly, even individuals who knew I was gay imposed a fresh set of demands for straight conformity.

When I began teaching, a colleague took me aside. "You'll have a better chance at tenure," he cautioned, "if you're a homosexual professional than if you're a professional homosexual." He meant I would fare better as a mainstream constitutional law professor who "happened to be gay" than as a gay professor who wrote on gay subjects. Others in the vigorously progay environment in which I work echoed the sentiment in less elegant formulations. *Be gay,* my world seemed to say. *Be openly gay, if you want. But don't flaunt.*

For a short time, I acceded. When I taught mainstream courses like constitutional law, I avoided gay examples. I wrote articles on nongay topics. I didn't bring the men I was dating to law school functions. I chose my political battles carefully.

I soon grew tired of such performances. What bothered me was not that I had to engage in "straight-acting" behavior, much of which felt natural to me. What bothered me was the felt need to mute my passion for gay subjects, people, culture—as if this were the love of which I still had to be ashamed. I knew I would be breaching some pact with myself if I stopped writing on gay issues out of a desire to conform. I decided I would commit myself to gay rights, a decision that led me to this book.

My struggle to arrive at a gay identity occurred in three phases, which I could also trace in the lives of gay peers. In the first phase, I sought to become straight. When I went to the chapel at Oxford, I prayed not to be what I was. I will call this a desire for *conversion.* In the second phase, I accepted my homosexuality, but concealed it from others. By the time I talked to Bill about his class, I was no longer trying to convert. I was, however, trying to hide my identity from my classmates. I will call this a desire for *passing*. Finally, long after I had generally come out of the closet, I still muted my orientation by not writing on gay topics or engaging in public displays of same-sex affection. This was not the same as passing, because my colleagues knew I was gay. Yet I did not know a word for this attempt to tone down my known gayness.

Then I found my word, in sociologist Erving Goffman's book *Stigma.* Published in 1963, the book describes how various groups— including the disabled, the elderly, and the obese—manage their "spoiled" identities. After discussing passing, Goffman observes that "persons who are ready to admit possession of a stigma . . . may nonetheless make a great effort to keep the stigma from looming large." He calls this behavior *"covering."* Goffman distinguishes passing from covering by noting that passing pertains to the *visibility* of a particular trait, while covering pertains to its *obtrusiveness.* He relates how Franklin Roosevelt always stationed himself behind a table before his advisers came in for meetings. Roosevelt was not passing, since everyone knew he used a wheelchair. He was covering, downplaying his disability so people would focus on his more conventionally presidential qualities.

I read these passages in one of the cubicles in the Cross Campus Library. There, enclosed by walls marked with graffiti, I felt like Crusoe finding Friday's footprint. Someone had been here. This distinction between passing and covering explained why I wasn't done with conformity to straight norms when I came out of the closet. The demand not to write on gay subjects was not a demand to pass. It was a demand to cover.

I knew I would live with these three terms—"conversion," "passing," and "covering"—for some time. They described not only a set of performances on my part, but also a set of demands society had made of me to minimize my gayness. The conversion demand was the most severe, then passing, then covering. I had traversed these demands sequentially, and I believed many gay individuals had done the same.

These three phases were also phases of gay history. Just as I had moved through these demands for assimilation as an individual, the gay community had done so as a group. Through the middle of the twentieth century, gays were routinely asked to convert to heterosexuality, whether through lobotomies, electroshock therapy, or psychoanalysis. As the gay rights movement gained strength, the demand to convert gradually ceded to the demand to pass. This shift can be seen in the military's adoption in 1993 of the "Don't ask, don't tell" policy, under which gays are permitted to serve so long as we agree to pass. Finally, at millennium's turn, the demand to pass is giving way to the demand to cover—gays are increasingly permitted to be gay and out so long as we do not "flaunt" our identities. The contemporary resistance to gay marriage can be understood as a covering demand: *Fine, be gay, but don't shove it in our faces.*

What I found jarring about these histories—one personal, one collective—was that they cast assimilation in such a negative light. I had always associated assimilation with ethnic identity, and had thought of it as a benign force. The Japanese say children learn by watching the backs of their parents. And no one could have been more persuasive than my parents about the virtues of assimilation.

Both my parents were born in Japan. My father graduated from high school in 1950. He looked at war-ravaged Japan and saw no future. At the suggestion of a relative, he applied to foreign universities, and was accepted at Columbia. He left Japan with his high school English, telling his parents not to expect him back for ten years. He has, in small things as in large, always kept his word.

When he returned ten years later, he had finished a doctorate in economics. While back in Japan, he met and married my mother, a Tokyo native who had earned a four-year college degree in economics, a rare feat for a woman then. He began teaching at UCLA—my sister and I were both born in Los Angeles. Then he got tenure at an Ivy League university, where he taught until he retired a few years ago.

My parents are an American success story, and decline to tell that story any other way. When I studied American history in junior high, I began to ask my father questions. When you came to Columbia, wasn't that right after the Japanese internment? Wasn't there virulent prejudice against the Japanese? To this day my father will not answer, choosing instead to talk about how hamburgers cost just a nickel then. Part of me rails against the blanks this leaves in my family history. But part of me knows he is trying to protect us both by keeping his life mythic.

My parents raised my sister and me in both countries—we spent school years in the States and summers in Japan. They taught us to assimilate into both societies, to be "one hundred percent American in America, and one hundred percent Japanese in Japan." The day I won the Rhodes was a proud one in my father's life—the ultimate proof his son had made it in America. And who could blame him? Assimilation is the magic in the American dream—just as in our actual dreams, magic helps us become better, more beautiful creatures, in the American dream assimilation helps us become not just Americans, but the kind of Americans we seek to be. Just conform, the dream whispers, and you will be respected, protected, accepted.

That whisper came differently to my gay ear. Here, too, I had a motive to assimilate—I would be more accepted if I stayed in the closet. I also had more opportunity to do so—I could pass as straight, but not as white. Yet I experienced assimilation less as an escape from homophobia than as its effect. I also sensed that assimilation played this negative role in gay history as a whole. I firmly believed gays would be fully equal only when society stopped conditioning our inclusion on assimilation to straight norms.

Over time, this skeptical view of assimilation prevailed. In fact, it seemed the signal contribution the gay rights movement could give to civil rights as a whole. The gay rights movement is profoundly indebted to its predecessors, such as the racial and feminist civil rights movements. As we reach maturity as a social group, gays can repay that debt, contributing a critique of assimilation that will enrich the civil rights paradigm for all who take shelter in it.

The applicability of this critique is not immediately obvious. Traditional civil rights groups, such as racial minorities or women, have generally not been subjected to conversion or passing demands. Conversion and passing, however, do not exhaust the forms of assimilation. There is also covering.

All civil rights groups feel the bite of the covering demand. African-Americans are told to "dress white" and to abandon "street talk"; Asian-Americans are told to avoid seeming "fresh off the boat"; women are told to "play like men" at work and to make their child-care responsibilities invisible; Jews are told not to be "too Jewish"; Muslims, especially after 9/11, are told to drop their veils and their Arabic; the disabled are told to hide the paraphernalia they use to manage their disabilities. This is so despite the fact that American society has seemingly committed itself, after decades of struggle, to treat people in these groups as full equals.

We are at a transitional moment in how Americans discriminate. In the old generation, discrimination targeted entire groups—no racial minorities, no women, no gays, no religious minorities, no people with disabilities allowed. In the new generation, discrimination directs itself not against the entire group, but against the subset of the group that fails to assimilate to mainstream norms. This new form of discrimination targets minority cultures rather than minority persons. Outsiders are included, but only if we behave like insiders—that is, only if we cover.

I saw this shift as an undergraduate. When I arrived at college, in 1987, I thought I might want to be an academic, and looked for role models on the faculty. The preceding generation of civil rights had done some work—the faculty was no longer exclusively white, male, ostensibly straight, Protestant, and able-bodied. But when I looked at the outsiders Harvard had included, I saw covering at work, though I had no name for it then. "I'm more black than Dean X," my white dorm mate quipped, referring to the African-American dean whose demeanor was more patrician than any Boston Brahmin's. Women faculty members often muted their visibility as women, avoiding feminist scholarship and downplaying their child-care responsibilities. The rare gay faculty member who was out of the closet did not flaunt his sexuality, appearing to all viewers like a bachelor don. Alan Dershowitz writes that although he wasn't the first Jewish professor at Harvard Law School, he was the "first Jewish Jew." My only disabled teaching assistant, like FDR, was always seated behind a seminar table before class began.

This was progress: individuals no longer needed to *be* white, male, straight, Protestant, and able-bodied; they needed only to *act* white, male, straight, Protestant, and able-bodied. But it was not equality. The message for an Asian-American closeted gay student was clear: downplay your ethnicity and your orientation. Don't uncover yourself.

Of course, I cannot assume all these individuals were covering.

Dean X may just have been being himself, and if that was the case, I would be the last to press him toward more stereotypically African-American behavior. My commitment here is to authenticity, as experienced by the individual, and that authenticity would be just as threatened by an imperative to "act black" as it would be by an imperative to "act white." This is why I am equally opposed to reverse-covering demands—demands that individuals act according to the stereotypes associated with their group.

While I could be wrong about any particular individual, however, I knew Harvard generally demanded covering. Individuals in conditions of freedom will be diverse. At Harvard, the span of this diversity was truncated—either because the institution had selected individuals who naturally conformed to mainstream norms or because it had pressured them to do so. Like America as a whole, Harvard was still skewed toward traditionally dominant groups.

This covering demand is the civil rights issue of our time. It hurts not only our most vulnerable citizens but our most valuable commitments. For if we believe a commitment against racism is about equal respect for all races, we are not fulfilling that commitment if we protect only racial minorities who conform to historically white norms. As the sociologist Milton Gordon identified decades ago, the demand for "Anglo-conformity" is white supremacy under a different guise. Until outsider groups surmount such demands for assimilation, we will not have achieved full citizenship in America.

In my early years of law teaching, I searched for remedies. I had learned the language of power; it was now time to wield it. To my chagrin, I found our major civil rights laws—such as the Civil Rights Act of 1964 and the equality guarantees of the federal Constitution—do not currently provide much protection against covering demands. Courts have often interpreted these laws to protect statuses but not behaviors, *being* but not *doing*. For this reason, courts will often not protect individuals against covering demands, which target the behavioral aspects of identity—speaking a language, having a child, holding a same-sex commitment ceremony, wearing religious garb, or refusing to "correct" a disability.

American equality law must be reformed to protect individuals against covering demands. Yet our generation of civil rights will also increasingly need to look outside the law. Many covering demands occur at such an intimate and daily level that they are not susceptible to legal correction. Such demands are better redressed through appeals to our individual faculties of conscience and compassion. When my colleagues suggested I stop writing on gay topics, my best response was not a lawsuit but a conversation.

Law is also an inadequate remedy because the covering demand extends beyond traditional civil rights groups. When I lecture on covering, I often encounter what I think of as the "angry straight white man" reaction. A member of the audience, almost invariably a white man, almost invariably angry, denies that covering is a civil rights issue. Why shouldn't racial minorities or women or gays have to cover? These groups should receive legal protection against discrimination for things they cannot help, like skin color or chromosomes or innate sexual drives. But why should they receive protection for behaviors within their control— wearing cornrows, acting "feminine," or flaunting their sexuality? After all, the questioner says, *I* have to cover all the time. I have to mute my depression, or my obesity, or my alcoholism, or my schizophrenia, or my shyness, or my working-class background, or my nameless anomie. I, too, am one of the mass of men leading a life of quiet desperation. Why should classic civil rights groups have a right to self-expression I do not? Why should my struggle for an authentic self matter less?

I surprise these individuals when I agree. Contemporary civil rights has erred in focusing solely on traditional civil rights groups, such as racial minorities, women, gays, religious minorities, and individuals with disabilities. This assumes those in the so-called mainstream—those straight white men—do not have covered selves. They are understood only as impediments, as people who prevent others from expressing themselves, rather than as individuals who are themselves struggling for self-definition. No wonder they often respond to civil rights advocates with hostility. They experience us as asking for an entitlement they themselves have been refused—an expression of their full humanity.

Civil rights must rise into a new, more inclusive register. That ascent begins with the recognition that *the mainstream is a myth.* With respect to any particular identity, the word "mainstream" makes sense, as in the statement that straights are more mainstream than gays. Used generically, however, the word lacks meaning. Because human beings hold many identities, the mainstream is a shifting coalition, and none of us is entirely within it. As queer theorists have recognized, it is not normal to be completely normal. All of us struggle for self-expression; we all have covered selves.

For this reason, we should understand civil rights to be a sliver of a universal project of human flourishing. Civil rights has always sought to protect the human flourishing of certain groups from being thwarted by the irrational beliefs of others. Yet that aspiration is one we should hold for all humanity.

I do not mean discrimination against racial minorities is the same as discrimination against poets. American civil rights law has correctly directed its concern toward certain groups and not others. But the aspiration of civil rights—the aspiration that we be free to develop our human capabilities without the impediment of witless conformity—is an aspiration that extends beyond traditional civil rights groups.

To fulfill that aspiration, this generation of civil rights must move far beyond the law. While law can help us be more human in crucial ways, it will never fully apprehend us. We should not mourn this fact: it would be worrisome if law could capture us so handily. Law's inability to apprehend our full human complexity, however, means our culture must do that work.

This book performs the point that the new civil rights requires both legal and cultural action. My first passion was literature, which I left from the belief that "poetry makes nothing happen." Now I see Auden meant those words ironically, and find myself revisiting my old belief. Law wields a brutal coercion literature cannot approximate. Yet literature has a power to get inside us, to transform our hearts and minds, in a way law cannot. This book uses both languages, relying not only on legal arguments but on literary narrative—the stories of people, including me, who struggled against demands for conformity.

In telling these stories, I do not argue categorically against assimilation. Such an argument would be rash, for assimilation is often a precondition of civilization—to speak a language, to curb violent urges, and to obey the law are all acts of assimilation. Through such acts we rise above the narrow stations of our lives to enter into a broader mindfulness, and often, paradoxically, we must do this to elaborate ourselves as individuals. I argue here only against coerced assimilation not supported by reasons— against a reflexive conformity that takes itself as its own rationale. What will constitute a good enough reason for assimilation will be controversial, and I am for the most part encouraging us to have that conversation rather than seeking to impose my own canon. But one *illegitimate* reason is simple animus against a particular group—the demand that gays assimilate to straight norms, or that women assimilate to male norms, or that racial minorities assimilate to white norms—because one group is considered less worthy than another.

My argument begins at its source—gay rights. I retell the history of gay rights as the story of a struggle against weakening demands for assimilation—the demand to convert, the demand to pass, and the demand to cover. This history reveals the dark underbelly of the American melting pot and indicts any civil rights paradigm conditioned on assimilation.

I then argue that this gay critique of assimilation has implications for all civil rights groups, including racial minorities, women, religious minorities, and people with disabilities. In America today, all outsider groups are systematically asked to assimilate to mainstream norms in ways that burden our equality. These groups should make common cause against coerced covering, demanding an equality not staked on conformity.

In the end, however, I maintain that this quest of authenticity is universal. I argue for a new civil rights paradigm that moves away from group-based equality rights toward universal liberty rights, and away from legal solutions toward social solutions. I have a personal investment in framing civil rights in this way, as I sorely need, and often lack, the courage to elaborate the many invisible selves I might hold. It is because I have found my gay experience helpful in elaborating my other, nongay identities that I seek to share it. Told carefully, the gay story becomes a story about us all—the story of the uncovered self.

one

# GAY CONVERSION

A colleague once told me a story of a house full of books. The house belonged to an intellectual historian who had accumulated a library with tens of thousands of volumes. When he decided to move, a friend of his who was a civil engineer urged care. The house contained so many books, the friend said, that it had sunk and settled around them, becoming dependent on them for structural support. Unless the books were removed in a slow spiral from the top down, the engineer warned, the house risked collapse.

After my colleague finished this story, she noticed my wide eyes. She asked if I related to the historian.

"No," I said. "I relate to the house."

There are books around which our lives sink and settle—

the dog-eared, bath-warped books that line the shelves of home and memory. In my childhood, these were books of classical mythology, which told of men unfurling into birds, women melting into fountains. Then my formal literary education began—Shakespeare, Milton, Blake, alongside Shonagon, Murasaki, Kawakami. During law school, I reread these books to keep the law at bay. Then I found books inside the law, like Bill's casebook, that found their way inside me. On the first page of his *Confessions,* Rousseau says he will hold that book when he goes to meet his Creator. I do not think of the books I will hold so much as of those that will hold me, that will hold me up.

Almost all the books that are important to me give me pleasure. One exception is Jonathan Ned Katz's *Gay American History.* Published in 1976, when gay studies was a fledgling and fugitive enterprise, Katz's work is a seven-hundred-page compilation of historical documents. I discovered it as a second-year law student, about the time I read Bill's casebook. Yet while I read and reread Bill's book, I found Katz's book, with its scarlet covers, difficult to revisit.

The difficulty lay in the chapter titled "Treatment: 1884–1974," which gathers documents describing attempts to convert homosexuals into heterosexuals. Perhaps the most disturbing accounts involve invasive surgery. Katz includes the case history of Guy T. Olmstead, who voluntarily underwent castration in 1894 to overcome his love for another man, William Clifford. Olmstead states: "Since the operation there has never been a day that I have been free from sharp, shooting pains down the abdomen to the scrotum." Nonetheless, he deems the operation a success: "I have absolutely no passion for other men, and have begun to hope now that I can yet outlive my desire for Clifford."

Lobotomies, which present-day conversion advocate Robert

Kronemeyer says were administered "promiscuously" in the 1950s and 1960s, are also represented here. In a 1941 procedure, a needle inserted into the anterior part of the brain "was swept downward toward the orbital plate and upward toward the vertex." The procedure was "repeated in order to make sure that the pathways were cut." The doctors reviewing the operation observe the patient was diagnosed as psychotic in 1945 and demented in 1947. The absence of intervening factors forced the doctors to conclude the lobotomy had caused the dementia.

Electricity was an alternative to knives. A 1935 presentation before the American Psychological Association cautioned that electroshock treatment would not convert homosexuals unless shocks were administered at "intensities considerably higher than those usually employed on human subjects." A patient describes a 1964 electroshock treatment as follows:

> You're in your pajamas, and you just lie down on a table. Then you don't remember any more because they give you a shock. The shock itself erases anything you were experiencing before, any memory of it. I had seventeen shock treatments—I did have awareness enough to ask one of the nurses how many times I had had it, and she said, "I'll look it up." She said seventeen. . . .
>
> I do remember after my own shock treatment listening to other people having shock treatment. I don't think that should be allowed. I was in the next ward. You hear that horrible scream. There's one loud scream—"Ahhhhh!!!"—very loud, each time they give you a shock, as the lungs are being evacuated. You hear what sounds like hundreds of people having shock treatment. They always did it in the morning, it went on all morning, three hours of those loud, single screams, one person at a time.

I'm struck by the limits of the patient's resistance: what he thinks should not "be allowed" is his exposure to the shock therapy of others, not his own treatment. He can hear their screams more clearly than his own.

Gentler clinicians worked only on the psyche. A 1963 account of hypnotic aversion therapy instructs doctors to use the "fastidious" nature of gay men to forge an association between the patient's "disgust reactions" and the male body. A similar 1967 study contains the following sample instruction:

> I want you to imagine that you are in a room with X. He is completely naked. As you approach him you notice he has sores and scabs all over his body, with some kind of fluid oozing from them. A terrible foul stench comes from his body. The odor is so strong it makes you sick. You can feel food particles coming up your throat. You can't help yourself and you vomit all over the place, all over the floor, on your hands and clothes. And now that even makes you sicker and you vomit again and again all over everything. You turn away and then you start to feel better. You try to get out of the room, but the door seems to be locked. The smell is still strong, but you try desperately to get out. You kick at the door frantically until it finally opens and you run out into the nice clean air. It smells wonderful. You go home and shower and you feel so clean.

These are only words, not incisions or shocks, so their violence may be harder to see until we plug in our own best-loved bodies for the algebraic "X," with which the instruction begins. There are ethical reasons to desist from such acts of imagination, but images rise unbidden in my mind. A man's wrist lifts as he pours water from a pitcher, making it seem as if water, wrist, world, exist so this angle can be. A parallelogram of moonlight reads the bumps on his back as he sleeps in my arms. When I fix on these images, I know that to transform the desire they embody into loathing would be a violence as sure as a knife across a painting.

Much of the poignancy of these accounts lies in how many gays "voluntarily" embraced conversion therapy. In his introduction, Katz reveals he tried it himself: "I entered analysis, voluntarily I thought, with the idea that 'my' problem was my homosexuality, and my goal a heterosexual 'cure,' although even then I was wise enough to know that I never wanted to be adjusted to a society which was itself desperately in need of radical change." For much of American history, to be heterosexual was a condition of humanity. Anxious to join the human race, even questioning radicals sought to kill their gay selves.

There are books whose covers we wish to close forever. Yet as I began work on the gay struggle against assimilation, I was driven back to Katz's book and others like it. I wanted to understand how the gay rights movement had successfully retired the conversion demand. But I also wanted to understand my intuition that this retirement has been less than complete.

In telling that story of change and continuity, I focus on psychoanalytic conversion therapies. As Timothy Murphy observes, "Virtually every sexual orientation therapy ever formulated has typically passed into history along with its originators," but "psychoanalysis has proved one exception to this rule of obsolescence." The hardiest weed teaches the history of the garden.

The usual difficulty of knowing where to begin a history was solved here through stipulation. Both proponents and opponents of psychoanalytic conversion therapy agree its history begins with Freud. Their agreement ends abruptly there, as each camp brandishes Freud as its champion. I realized Freud's stance on conversion was complex, and went back to his *Standard Edition* to sort it out.

A fundamental question raised by homosexual conversion is whether homosexuality arises from nature or from nurture. Freud's answer was clear—he believed all human beings were bisexual. This innate bisexuality meant homosexuality (as well as heterosexuality) was culturally rather than biologically determined.

The belief that homosexuality arises from a cultural source has often raised hopes about conversion—as present-day conversion therapists say, "What can be learned can be unlearned." Freud expressed no such optimism. His famous 1935 letter to an American mother states:

> By asking me if I can help [your son], you mean, I suppose, if I can abolish homosexuality and make normal heterosexuality take its place. The answer is, in a general way, we cannot promise to achieve it. In a certain number of cases we succeed in developing the blighted germs of heterosexual tendencies which are present in every homosexual, [but] in the majority of cases it is no more possible.

In *The Psychogenesis of a Case of Homosexuality in a Woman,* he explains: "In general, to undertake to convert a fully developed homosexual into a heterosexual does not offer much more prospect of success than the reverse."

Freud also questioned whether gays *should* be converted, even if they *could* be. In his letter to the American mother, he contends that "homosexuality is assuredly no advantage but it is nothing to be ashamed of, no vice, no degradation, it cannot be classified as an illness." He put it more bluntly in a newspaper interview: "Homosexual persons are not sick."

Yet just as Freud never relinquished the belief that homosexuals could sometimes convert, he never surrendered the belief that homosexuality was a form of erotic immaturity. Usually cited for its tolerance of homosexuality, his 1935 letter also describes homosexuality as "produced by a certain arrest of sexual development." Even more disturbingly, Freud stated elsewhere that homosexuality should not necessarily be expressed in homosexual acts, but directed to more "social" ends.

Despite the ambiguity of his views, I find it hard not to cast Freud as the great white father raising his staff against the advance of darkness. I am not alone in my romance. Psychologist Kenneth Lewes's history of psychoanalytic approaches to homosexuality describes how completely contemporaries fell in with Freud's model in his lifetime, yet began to mold his teachings into a more sinister form before his body was cold. Insofar as homosexuality was concerned, psychoanalysis in 1939 "moved from the humane and cosmopolitan system of investigation it had been with Freud and his circle to a rigid and impervious set of values and judgments." The new generation of therapists—Irving Bieber, Albert Ellis, Sandor Rado, and Charles Socarides—challenged each of Freud's premises.

The year after Freud's death, Rado delivered a lecture that reads like an Oedipal tantrum against the originator of that concept. In it, he denounced Freud's belief in universal human bisexuality. His proof for the innateness of human heterosexuality was that male orgasm was simultaneously the most pleasurable and the most procreative sexual act.

In Rado's view, gays were driven from this innate heterosexuality by bad parenting. He believed antisex views expressed by parents could lead their daughters to fear the penis as a "destructive weapon" and their sons to fear the vagina as a symbol of castration. Other conversion therapists expanded on this theme. Bieber worked up the popular model that male homosexuality arose from close-binding mothers and distant fathers. (Bieber's model is presumably culturally specific—otherwise practically every Japanese man I know would be gay.) Socarides added that female homosexuality arose from malevolent mothers and rejecting fathers.

The therapists also rejected Freud's view that conversion therapy was ineffective. The most systematic study of conversion therapy for gay men was conducted by the New York Society of Medical Psychoanalysts in the 1950s. Published in 1962 under the primary authorship of Bieber, it cheerfully concludes that "a heterosexual shift is a possibility for all homosexuals who are strongly motivated to change." Through this typical move, the study defends conversion therapy by ascribing failures to a lack of patient motivation. Yet even this hedged conclusion is not well supported. Of the seventy-two exclusive homosexuals in the study, 19 percent converted to heterosexuality, 19 percent converted to bisexuality, and 57 percent remained unchanged. Why did those 57 percent put themselves through "conversion" therapy if they weren't "strongly motivated to change"? Despite such flaws, Bieber's is still among the most cited studies on the viability of conversion.

Finally, the conversion therapists assumed homosexuality was a mental illness. Rado declared it a "deficient adaptation." Ellis and Bieber described it as "psychotic" or "psychopathologic." In a crucial move, the American Psychiatric Association adopted this view in its 1952 taxonomy of psychiatric diseases. The first edition of the *Diagnostic and Statistical Manual of Mental Disorders* (*DSM*) classified homosexuality as a "psychopathology."

These therapists ushered in a "gilded age" of conversion therapy from the 1940s to the 1960s, during which gays entered therapy in droves. In his memoir, *Cures,* gay historian Martin Duberman recalls seeing three conversion therapists during this period. Like Katz, Duberman describes how he so internalized "the dominant psychiatric view that homosexuals were a homogeneous group, bound together by dysfunction and neurosis," that he thought of conversion as his "only hope for a happy life."

Other scholars raised dissenting voices. Entomologist-turned-sexologist Alfred Kinsey published studies on human sexuality in the male (1948) and female (1953) that showed same-sex sexual conduct was much more widespread than commonly thought. His studies tacitly questioned the abnormality of homosexuality—could an activity millions of Americans engaged in be so heinous? Psychologist Evelyn Hooker challenged the pathologization of homosexuality more directly, showing personality experts could not distinguish homosexuals from heterosexuals. (Hooker's test of clinical "gaydar" lives on in the Internet game of "Gay? or Eurotrash?" in which players are set the hopeless task of distinguishing gays from European urban hipsters.) Most radically, psychiatry professor Thomas Szasz argued the pathologization of homosexuality was a naked power grab by psychiatrists—an attempt by the medical establishment to wrest power away from the church.

The Stonewall Riots of 1969, of which more later, drew these and other strands of activism together, making a concerted challenge to conversion therapy possible. Gays began agitating for the deletion of homosexuality from the *DSM,* drawing on their growing sense that, as activist Del Martin framed it, "psychiatry was the most dangerous enemy of homosexuals in contemporary society." The patients had become impatient, and had turned to make diagnoses of their own.

This antipsychotherapeutic stance marked a sea change. Until that point, therapists and gays were ostensibly on the same side. Unlike law and religion, medicine sought to assimilate gays into society through conversion rather than banishing them through condemnation. Guy Olmstead, castrated in 1894, insisted that "doctors are the only ones who understand and know my helplessness before this monster." In fairness, conversion therapists also manifestly viewed themselves as nurturing advocates for their patients.

By Stonewall, however, most conversion therapists and most gay activists stood in opposed camps. Rather than seeking to convert to heterosexuality, gays sought to convert psychiatrists to their point of view. As professor of public health Ronald Bayer details, each APA meeting from 1970 onward signaled a progay advance. In the 1970 meeting, gay activists disrupted a psychiatrist's presentation on aversion therapy with the cry, "Where did you take your residency, Auschwitz?" Asked to wait their turn, they responded, "We've waited five thousand years!" Pandemonium ensued. Anxious to forestall such outbursts, the APA granted gay activists a place in the program the next year. The year after that, a gay psychiatrist testified "openly" on a panel for the first time, albeit from under a mask and cloak, identified only as "Dr. Anonymous." Finally, in 1973, gay activists like Ronald Gold and conversion therapists like Socarides and Bieber faced off. "Stop it," Gold said to the therapists. "You're making me sick."

Significantly, the challenge to the *DSM* classification asserted the validity of homosexuality. Rather than arguing they *could* not convert, activists argued they *should* not have to do so. Riffing off "Black is beautiful," they improvised the slogan "Gay is good." The efforts of these activists, along with their allies within the psychiatric establishment, led to the deletion of homosexuality from the *DSM* on December 15, 1973.

Law lagged far behind. A 1952 congressional enactment required the Immigration and Naturalization Service to exclude individuals "afflicted with psychopathic personality" from the United States. Everyone at the time understood this category to encompass homosexuals. When the APA depathologized homosexuality in 1973, its president urged the INS to stop exclusions based on homosexuality. The INS refused. Not until 1990, seventeen years after the *DSM* deletion, did it surrender the power to exclude homosexuals as psychopaths.

Today, conversion therapy grows scarce. The major mental health associations, such as the American Psychiatric Association and the American Psychological Association, have withdrawn their support for the practice. Conversion therapists bemoan their beleaguered status, claiming Americans have been "brainwashed" into accepting homosexuality. Responsibility for converting gays has devolved back to religious organizations, such as Exodus International and Quest. These two groups have had their own difficulties, as the "ex-gays" who led them have subsequently reemerged as "ex-ex-gays."

The world is changing; the stories I hear are changing. A colleague recounts how his friend, a gay man, was taken to a mental hospital as a teenager by his parents, who wanted to commit him. He struggled so desperately he smashed the windshield of the car, but they literally dragged him to a psychiatrist. The psychiatrist calmly told the parents he was more inclined to commit them than to commit their son. He told them to go home. I imagine the gay teenager's ride back behind the broken windshield, the dome of heaven cracked, the lid taken off his world.

My friend David tells me that when he came out at nineteen, his parents took him to the family minister, who had known David all his life. The minister listened silently as his parents detailed their shame, their love, their confusion, and above all, their request that David be converted at whatever cost. David waited sullenly for the verdict, his dread tasting like tinfoil in his mouth. "I have three sons," the minister finally said. "My hope for each of them is that they turn out as well as David. So if you want David to change, I am not your man." I heard this story when I asked David, now a social worker in his late thirties, how his parents had become so active in gay rights. He dates it to this conversation, which he says began their conversion.

The formal demand that gays convert is loosening its grip on our culture. The triple engines of social regulation—law, medicine, and religion—have all begun to retire the demand. So where do I see its modern vestiges?

I see them in my own history. After my first term at Oxford, I started to see a psychiatrist. He looked like Orville Redenbacher from the popcorn commercials, with the white hair and the glasses, so I dubbed him Orville in my mind. If his home office was any indication, Orville was an avid gardener. Every surface was populated with flowers—hyacinths, cyclamen, and orchids, orchids everywhere, labial and purple or feathery and pert, arching off their supports. I hated those orchids on sight, as a too obvious metaphor for sexual knowledge, and, no doubt, for how they listed toward the light. Let us admit I was not well then.

I never asked Orville to convert me. But this was the cure I was secretly seeking. My depression and my homosexuality had formed such a terrible braid I could not imagine one going away without the other. When I said, *Take this away,* I could not have specified the referent.

I cannot remember all of Orville's attempts to pry these two conditions apart. I know time passed in that office, as the orchids unfisted into savage and delicate colors, grew papery and fell, and were replaced. I can see him now on the screen of my mind—speaking, listening, opening his hands toward me. But I cannot hear the words. I can only admire the locksmith patience with which he tried every combination to my padlocked mind.

The click, when it came, was simple. The orchid that session was spidery, yellow mottled with brown, smelling faintly of chocolate. I stared into its many throats as Orville asked me to describe a sexual fantasy. I tried to begin, schooling myself against the defenses I had identified in that ticking room—my tendencies to swerve into abstraction, intellectualization, beauty. But I could not. "I can't," I said. "It's perverted."

"It's not perverted," Orville said gently. "It's thwarted."

Of all that someone says, it's curious how one thing makes it through the haze. I try to recall this when teaching—*Try it a second way, and a third, you don't know what they're hearing.* Why did those words—"perverted" and "thwarted"—reach me? Did I like how they sounded against each other—the "vert" and the "wart"? Did I like that I needed to think about how they differed? I do not know. But I heard in them what I needed to hear. I heard my desire was not twisted, but blocked. I heard that I was sick and that I was gay and that these were not the same thing.

Orville did not lift my depression. But he showed me I was still in the grip of a conversion fantasy, which I needed to talk through to dispel. Even then, I felt lucky. I knew that only a few decades before, psychiatry would have fueled my conversion fantasy rather than helped me resist it.

In later sessions we talked about whence that fantasy, in the year 1992, arose. I knew most people no longer considered homosexuality a mental disorder. I wondered aloud why I did not experience it as normal human variation—a preference, chromosomally speaking, for the letter *Y* over the letter *X*. I came to see the demand to convert had become more diffuse, but in some ways harder to contest for that reason. It was the ambient fluid in which I swam. I could no more imagine life outside heterosexuality than a fish could imagine lolloping onto land.

Only after I came out broadly did this pressure ease. Once I was irrevocably gay, the fight for my soul was over—angels and demons alike looked for other quarry. I came to realize conversion demands were made most aggressively on sexual waverers—individuals whose sexuality seemed ambiguous or unformed.

When I started to look for contemporary conversion demands, then, I looked to the classic sexual waverers, that is, to children. My instinct was vindicated: I discovered a willingness to say point-blank that wavering children should be converted to heterosexuality. At least eight states currently have "no-promo-homo" statutes, prohibiting public educators from "promoting" homosexuality in schools. These laws can bar any mention of homosexuality, prohibit progay teachings, or even require antigay teachings.

In some states, no-promo-homo laws for children coexist with gay rights laws protecting adults. This legal tension reflects a broader cultural one. As psychology professor E. L. Pattullo states: "Surely decency demands that those who find themselves homosexual be treated with dignity and respect. But surely, too, reason suggests that one guard against doing anything which might mislead wavering children into perceiving society as indifferent to the sexual orientation they develop."

When I read this passage, I kept tripping over Pattullo's dual certainty that one should "surely" protect adults who were gay but just as "surely" protect children from becoming gay. It suggested the continuing vitality of a disease paradigm of homosexuality. For this is how we talk about people who have a disease—as in the claim that HIV-positive individuals should "surely" be protected from discrimination but just as "surely" should not spread their condition. This position makes sense for a disease. But didn't we retire the idea that homosexuality was a disease three decades ago?

Apparently not. Although the idea of homosexuality as a literal disease (a mental illness) has faded, the idea of homosexuality as a figurative disease (a disfavored contagious condition) has endured. Antigay psychologists have explicitly dubbed this the "contagion model of homosexuality," under which "homosexuality is taught by or caught by sexual interaction with homosexual practitioners."

The most infamous legal characterization of homosexuality as contagious comes from a justice of the Supreme Court. In 1978, five years after the *DSM* deletion, William Rehnquist gave credence to a public university's argument that it need not recognize a gay group's First Amendment right of association because the group would spread homosexuality. Rehnquist observed that in the university's view, the question was "akin to whether those suffering from measles have a constitutional right, in violation of quarantine regulations, to associate together and with others who do not presently have measles, in order to urge repeal of a state law providing that measle sufferers be quarantined." Gays were not citizens who could assemble with others to persuade them of their cause. They were lepers who would infect all they touched.

The metaphorical contagion model captures a fundamental fear about homosexuality—that gays will spread our condition to others—better than the literal mental illness model. Under the mental illness model, it is *heterosexuals* who transmit homosexuality through "bad parenting." Under the contagion model, in contrast, gays transmit homosexuality by infecting waverers. Casting homosexuality as such an act of aggression legitimates no-promo-homo measures by making them seem defensive.

This move obscures the aggression of the no-promo-homo statutes, much as a department renamed "Defense" obscures its war-making capacity. For if the children are honestly wavering, no-promo-homo laws are just as much attempts to convert them to heterosexuality. Moreover, to the extent such laws depend on a contagion model, they put the prestige of the state behind the figuration of homosexuality as a disease.

I want to pause to say something clearly: gays will not achieve full equality until the ultimate orientation of wavering children is a matter of state and social indifference. Those who seek equality for gays but support no-promo-homo measures should ask how consistent it is to treat gays as simultaneously equal and diseased.

The word "conversion" has mundane usages, as when applied to current or currency. When applied to human beings, however, "conversion" carries its weightier sense—a spiritual transformation of our core, something that happens on the road to Damascus. For me, the question of who will convert, who will be radically transformed, has always been the primal question of civil rights. Who will change? The gay son or the straight parents? The homosexual or the homophobe? Just thinking of such change can change us.

In grappling with these questions, early gay activists were wiser than many of us are today. Faced with a society that sought to convert them, they gave the plain-throated answer that gay was good. In recent years, I have seen a troubling trend toward defending homosexuality not on the ground it is "good" but on the ground it is "immutable." I see why this immutability argument is tempting, but I want, with others, to argue that it be taken up cautiously.

An early form of the immutability argument sought a biological source for homosexuality. In the 1990s, a slew of studies sought to locate homosexuality in the body—in the brain, the X chromosome, the dermal ridges of fingerprints. One famous study purported to show identical twins were more likely to share an orientation than other kinds of siblings. Many of these studies posited the existence of a gay gene.

These studies have all been challenged. Neuroanatomist Simon LeVay's brain study contended that gay men, like women, had smaller hypothalami than straight men. When I heard of this study, even the formulation of the hypothesis bothered me. The claim seemed too close to the historical stereotype that gay men were women trapped inside men's bodies—now it was women's brains that were so confined. As I began reading the study, I discovered that all of LeVay's "gay" cadavers had died of AIDS-related complications. Then I stopped reading. This was a disqualifying move for any number of reasons, including the possibility that HIV, not homosexuality, could have caused the smaller hypothalami.

Queer theorist Michael Warner has sent up the twins study conducted by J. Michael Bailey and Richard Pillard, respectively professors of psychology and psychiatry. The study argued for a genetic basis for homosexuality after finding that if an individual with an identical twin was gay, his twin was disproportionately likely also to be gay. One of the study's marquee claims was that this held true even for twins raised apart. Yet Warner observes that one pair of twins raised apart was not only gay but also shared a penchant for masturbating over pictures of construction workers.

Does this mean, Warner asks, that there is a gene for masturbating over construction workers?

Even if these studies had been perfectly executed, they would still be a leaky defense for homosexuality. These studies appear to assume biological traits are immutable, while cultural traits are mutable. Yet as literary critic Eve Sedgwick has pointed out, that conventional wisdom may be turning a cartwheel. As our scientific technology advances, genetic traits may become *more* susceptible to human manipulation than cultural ones. As envisioned in Jonathan Tolins's play *The Twilight of the Golds,* it is a short step from finding a gay gene to screening out fetuses that carry it. If scientists find a gay gene before gays have done the cultural work of securing the validity of homosexuality, gays will be more endangered than we are today.

Others have made subtler claims about immutability, observing that cultural attributes can also be immutable. Yet the more sophisticated the immutability defense becomes, the more convinced I become of its irreducible wrongness. The defense is flawed because it is an implied apology. It resists the conversion demand by saying "I cannot change," rather than by saying "I will not change." It suggests electroshock treatment for homosexuals is wrong because it does not work. But such treatment would be no less wrong if it did. Such a defense also leaves bisexuals, who can choose to express only cross-sex desire, without a defense for any expression of same-sex desire.

Of course, as a logical matter, immutability and validity defenses could coexist. As a practical matter, however, the two defenses tend to moot each other as rhetorical arguments. If an identity is immutable, people are less likely to ask whether it is valid, as no alternative exists. But the opposite is also true—if an identity is valid, people are much less likely to ask whether it is immutable. As literature professor Leo Bersani says, "the very question of 'how we got that way' would in many quarters not be asked if it were not assumed that we ended up the wrong way."

The gay critique of assimilation begins here. Conversion is the ultimate demand for assimilation—while passing and covering leave the underlying identity relatively intact, conversion destroys it. When someone asks for conversion, the difference between the two available refusals is immense. Which will we choose? Will we say we cannot change? Or will we, like the early gay activists, say we will not change, meeting the demand for conversion with a demand for equality?

I understand the seductions of immutability. When I speak of the books that hold me up, like Bill Rubenstein's book or Jonathan Katz's book, it is in part their unchanging quality that moves me. But what moves me more is their resistance to the cultures from which they arose. These books did not need to exist, and that is what makes their existence miraculous. They stand against a pull as strong as gravity. Against the call to go down, they hold us up.

# GAY PASSING

Samuel Taylor Coleridge's *Rime of the Ancient Mariner* depicts a sailor whose penance for shooting an albatross is to repeat the story of how he killed that bird of good omen. He instinctively knows who must hear his tale, and transfixes them with his "glittering eye." He is compelled to speak, and they are compelled to listen. So he tells and tells, hoping one day to tell the story well enough, or often enough, that he will no longer need to tell it.

We all have a story we must repeat until we get it right, a story whose conveniences must be corrected and whose simplifications must be seen through before we are done with it, or it with us. For gay people, that story is often the story of how we came out. There are times when I feel like the Mariner, wondering how many more times I will have to tell my tale. Sometimes the parallel seems so close I worry I will have to do so in rhyme. Each time I tell my story, I am released, yet this is also the story from which I yearn to be released. But who could release me? Release implies compulsion, and no one is forcing me to speak. Even those who ask when I came out generally expect—and want—no more than the one-line answer I often give—"The year after college."

Like the Mariner, my compulsion is internal. I experience my one-line answer as true, as it describes when I came out to my parents. Yet I also experience it as incomplete. Coming out is a process as endless as its audiences. If I were to give a true accounting, the kind that might free me to tell other tales, I would need to describe a series of audiences, a series of moments.

A cube enclosing a cube, the Louis Kahn library at Phillips Exeter is a mecca for architecture students. Its most striking feature is that each of the inner cube's vertical walls has a giant circle cut out of it. As a student, I would often pause on the Oriental rug on the bottom floor and look through the circles at four floors of books. I felt I was looking at an ant farm, privy to a cutaway perspective of the drones, unaware, at work.

One spring afternoon, when I was seventeen, I looked up and saw him. Matthew was lying on the curve of one of the circles, twenty feet above the floor on which I stood. I whipped my head around for some other watchful presence, but it was only he and I. I looked again. Matthew's face always looked a little melted. His Midwestern drawl could slow a conversation, and on the soccer field, the ball waited for him. He nestled on the lip of that circle as if to distill that languor. He looked down, saw me, and waved. As I waved back, I was the one in danger of falling.

I went to church that night. I was a believer then, in a cloudy, nondenominational way. I even worked at the church, though I was drawn to the job less by religious conviction than by a catlike instinct for the safe warm place in the school. On Tuesday evenings, the minister, whom we called Mr. Mac rather than by his longer Scottish surname, would give readings that were the still centers of my weeks.

By day, Mr. Mac was out of Dickens—tall, rubicund, balding. During his religion classes, he would hold his outsized hands over a student's shoulders as she struggled with an answer, as if to remind her they were on the same side. Even at service on Sundays, he was jovial—"Make a joyful noise unto the Lord," he would say after booming out a hymn—"Noise, not song, thank God." But in the evenings, he cast long shadows as he read James Agee's letters or a chapter of Paulo Freire. I never heard him crack a joke after sundown.

After service, he would speak to me from the same place in himself. I would snuff the candles, unplug the microphones, and lock the heavy doors. Then I would stop by his office to say good night. We would chat—briefly, for I had my curfew, but often memorably. More than anyone else at the time, Mr. Mac enlarged my sense of who I could be. He would lift his tortoiseshell glasses, squeeze the triangle of flesh above his nose, and speak with oracular concision. I questioned how he fed my messianic impulses—what end did it serve to tell me I was meant for some great work, that I was meant not for happiness but joy? But his aphorisms stayed with me.

That night, I told him I had seen a student balanced on one of the great circles in the library. I was not trying to indict Matthew, nor to protect him. I was trying to reassure myself that the scene, which had faded with its light, was memory rather than fantasy. Mr. Mac listened. Then he put his hands on my shoulders, epaulets of warmth and weight. He looked down at me, as if we were dancing.

"Your greatest gift," he said, "is your capacity to face yourself."

Those words rankled for years, beginning with my walk back to the dormitory. The words were comical, I thought, as I could not face myself even in the literal sense. I had a real unease around mirrors, and could not look into one except by approaching it obliquely—I would start a few feet back, then sidle up to it. It was as if I feared that if I looked at myself too quickly, I might see myself whole, that the halves I kept so separate might snap together. So I did not look. And hated my failure of courage.

In hindsight, I am gentler with myself. I see my desire not to see was a form of self-preservation. I was my own first audience, and I wasn't ready yet. But that I could see myself averting my eyes meant I was, however fitfully, preparing.

I feel the same tenderness for the early gay rights movement. The answer for when the movement "came out" is clear: the Stonewall Riots of 1969. The preceding decades are often described as a wasteland. During the gilded age of conversion therapy, many gays never told their tales, dying in closets that materialized into coffins. Others came out to one another in bars with blackened windows on the outskirts of town, or in the Communist-type cells of the early homophile organizations, or on the couches of their conversion therapists.

Homophobes knew gays could not bear to look at themselves. Writer Judy Grahn's account of a 1950s raid on the Rendezvous Bar calls up my own adolescent fear.

> Another night two policemen came up to the table where I sat
> with my friend from the service. They shined a flashlight into

our eyes and commanded us to stand up or else be arrested. Then they demanded that we say our real names, first and last, several times, as loud as we could. Sweat poured down my ribs as I obeyed. After they left, my friend and I sat with our heads lowered, too ashamed of our weakness to look around or even to look each other in the face. We had no internal defense from the self-loathing our helplessness inspired and no analysis that would help us perceive oppression as oppression and not as a personal taint of character.

Grahn's account shows how adroitly the police, like the conversion therapists, deployed the self-hatred of gays against them. Forcing the women to speak their real names shattered the convention of such bars, in which last names were never used and first names were usually fictitious. It compelled them to look into a mirror they were not ready to face.

Yet just as the years before I came out laid the groundwork for that revelation, the pre-Stonewall decades have been shown by a new generation of historians—George Chauncey, John D'Emilio, and Lillian Faderman—to have been more foundational than commonly thought. These historians have unearthed a gay world that existed alongside the straight one—a demimonde marked by shibboleths and winks, red cravats and hidden doors. This world sustained bars like the Rendezvous, as well as homophile groups like the Mattachine Society, founded in 1950, or the Daughters of Bilitis, founded in 1955.

This resistance has been difficult to appreciate because it was, by modern standards, so equivocal. The irony of early gay activism is that its most prominent names were pseudonyms. Edward Sagarin penned the first American tract for gay equality in 1951 as Donald Webster Cory. One of the five founders of Mattachine is

still identified by historians only as "R." The names of the homophile organizations were similarly shrouded. The Mattachine
Society took its name from a group of medieval mask-wearing
French bachelors. Its publication, *One,* referred to a Thomas Carlyle quotation—"A mystic bond of brotherhood makes all men
one." The Daughters of Bilitis took its name from *Songs of Bilitis,* a
collection of prose poems by Pierre Louys.

Such evasions have led the activism of this period to be described in patronizing tones. Yet just as I now refuse to view my
own closeted years with contempt, I resist any account deriding
these organizations. Pre-Stonewall activists were far more courageous, because they were far more alone, than the average member
of a contemporary American gay rights organization. For them, as
for me, silence had to pass through poetry before it crystallized
into prose.

At the end of my first term at Oxford, my father came to visit.
I had not told him I was gay, nor that I was in love with
Brian. I had only said I was having a quarter-life crisis, that I
didn't know what I wanted to be. But he heard the grief in my voice.

We met for dinner near his hotel. His eyes flickered over me as
he administered his parental CAT scan. Although he said nothing,
I could see he was shocked by my thin, unshaven self. He himself
was perfectly groomed in his button-down shirt and wool blazer.
Over dinner, we tried ordinary conversation, discussing my friends,
my studies, and my horror of English food. He laughed too hard at
my one attempt at humor: why is the English countryside so
beautiful?—they haven't found a way to boil it yet. Then he asked
me up to his room.

He did not begin immediately—the contraption by his bed distracted him. Like Kipling's mongoose, his motto is *Run and find out*. He examined it.

"What is this object?"

"That's a trousers press."

"They have them in hotels here?"

"Yes."

"They press trousers?"

"No, Papa, they send faxes."

"I see." He grinned. Then, more gently.

"It is not the courses, is it?"

"No." I was beyond lying—if he had asked the question point-blank, I might have been able to answer it. But I could not volunteer the words. He eased himself onto a high-backed chair and turned to me as I slumped on the luridly damasked comforter. He waited. He has this teacher's gift, the ability to find the edge of a student's capacity, and to wait there for him to leap.

I had always been able to leap for him. From the days when he would open his arms to me in the swimming pool to the days when he told me I could go to Exeter, or Harvard, or Oxford, I had trusted him, and leapt. If he could come to America at eighteen and become a professor, then I could do anything in my own country, the language that was my own. But where was I now? I could not sit still to read a paragraph, I could barely force myself to eat. I sat before him stripped of my carapace of accomplishment, the turtle unturtled.

"I'm sorry, Papa," I finally said. "I can't do anything. I've failed. I have nothing." Then I paused. Could I say it? I could not. Something dull spoke instead: "I am nothing."

I felt him before I heard him. It was not his usual brisk embrace, but as if, in the warm parentheses of his arms, he had made me part of him.

He said: "You are my son."

And I began to sob. Perhaps this is the worst any closet does to us—it prevents us from hearing the words "I love you." These were words my parents said to me, and I trusted the love, but not the "you." The real me was hidden, so the "you" they loved was some other, better son. But when my father claimed me—*This thing of darkness I acknowledge mine*—I began to suspect that no matter what I was, he would be next to me, the silent economist stroking my hair. My sobs dislodged something inside me, and I began to understand love is a narrative permission, that stories can be told within its bounds. But that night, the only sound I made was animal. And still he held me.

Three weeks later, I came home for Christmas. My mother met me at Logan Airport, a hummingbird of love and anxiety. I was still at the slow-moving end of the animal spectrum. She didn't make me talk. "Don't think so hard," she said in Japanese. "Life is not that simple." I loved her for this. It struck me that many parents would tell their children not to think because life wasn't that complicated.

The next evening, I spent hours staring out the window of my parents' apartment on the Charles River. While I saw my own reflection in the glass without flinching, I also noticed how spectral it seemed—I could see through myself. It had been snowing just enough to render my old world indistinct. The moon italicized the frozen S of the river as it scraped through its bridges. It read like an invitation.

I walked along the river. I found the spot where I had looked into Brian's eyes and lay down on the bank. My limbs outstretched, I myself was star-shaped, staring at stars. I thought of the coming-out stories I had heard. The best story was of a mother who hugged her son and said, "You've been so alone." That was better than "I love you." It was instant comprehension of a life. The worst story was of parents who disowned their eighteen-year-old son and drove him out into the snow in his pajamas and bare feet. As the boy's feet turned indigo, the front door opened, and he thought, of course, they didn't mean it. Then a suitcase full of his clothes launched out, and the door shut again, for good. I thought about what my own story would be. I knew it would be neither of these.

I trudged home to learn it. My parents were waiting for me—I had asked to talk to them before we went to bed. I felt a pang when I saw they were dressed up, as if for a parent-teacher conference. I sat on the immaculate ivory couch next to my mother, and tried to remember how I had meant to begin.

When I was nine, my mother told me about the invisible red thread. We were waiting for the train in Tokyo's sweltering Shibuya station. She bought me a Calpis soda from the vending machine— the sweet fermented milk that is, according to slogan, "the taste of first love." Noting the words amidst the blue polka dots on the can, my mother smiled and told me of love. She said some Japanese say we are tied to the one we love with invisible red thread—that it was already decided who my mate would be, and that if I could only grasp the thread, I could reel her in and claim her. I knew she was trying to keep me amused, so I went along, feeling the air around me for that elusive filament. Then something struck me. I asked her how they knew the thread was red if it was invisible. Her eyes widening, she put her hand on my neck and kept it there, despite the heat, and told me I might be missing the point.

In the midst of winter, Camus says, he discovered in himself an invincible summer. For the past months at Oxford, I had felt I could never get warm. I tried to make it back to that memory of how my mother had looked at me in the train station. The hotness of her hand.

"I know I have worried you," I said, eyes down. "I'm sorry, and I want to explain. It has to do with Brian." The words came more haltingly after that name. "When I was with him, I felt some things for the first time. I realized the person I will love—the person to whom I am tied—will not be a woman."

The silence arced and fell, and arced and fell, like a soundless telephone.

My father said slowly, quietly, "Are you saying that you are a gay?"

His grammar had at last been stressed beyond its usual perfection. But I was not about to quibble with the construction of words I did not have the courage to utter.

"Yes," I said.

I looked up. My mother's face as she looked at my father is one I will never be able truly to describe or forget. I can only say her eyes looked for translation, solace, meaning that he could not, for once in his life, provide. I thought: I, so confident of words, have now met the limits of language. I will find no words that will catch that gaze in their net.

"But if this is so," my mother said in Japanese, "we will never be able to go back to Japan." I realized then what I had feared about coming out to my parents. That someone—myself, my mother, my father—would die. Would curl up, turn face to the wall, and expire. When my mother spoke those words, I knew she was telling me of a death—a metaphorical death, a social death, but a death. That was the albatross I killed—her cross-shaped innocence, her idea of home.

She saw me flinch. She switched to English. "What you are

doing," she said, "is very courageous." It was as if one language could not contain her two voices.

We broke away awkwardly. I lay on my bed, breathing as if after a race. I experienced the moment as a shattering, an end to years of silence, lies, and equivocation. I felt cameras shifting, as if I were no longer the bit player in someone else's story, but finally the hero of my own. This moment is the cusp on which my life breaks, the talisman I touch to reassure myself I have not failed life's test.

For the movement, that moment occurred on June 27, 1969. When police raided the Stonewall Inn, gay patrons of the bar refused to go quietly. Barricading themselves inside, they hurled out beer bottles and slogans like "Gay power." Systematic resistance to the demand to pass rightfully began in a bar, as the bar itself was a symbolic closet, over which gays had finally wrested control.

Stonewall brought a new militancy to gay rights. The riots generated a fresh set of organizations, including the Gay Liberation Front, Radicalesbians, and the Third World Gay Revolution. These groups spoke prose. As journalists Dudley Clendinen and Adam Nagourney note, "There was no talk among these new activists of disguising their mission with ambiguous titles—no homophile, no Mattachine, no Bilitis." Stonewall also birthed new publications that, unlike the homophile periodicals *One* or the *Ladder,* sported the word "gay" in their titles—*Gay Times, Gay Flames, Gay Sunshine.*

The riots inaugurated the gay rights movement. As Cindy Patton describes it, "Stonewall divides a timeless time of oppression from the entry into the Time of History. *Before 1969:* we could only chafe and give up our fullest possibilities. *After 1969:* we could say who we are and in the unifying power of our speech, fight back." I used to find it bizarre that Stonewall has been elevated as the cusp on which gay history breaks. The riots did not last the week, and the mainstream press accorded them no significance. Then I came to see. We have fixed on this moment because we need, as a community, a moment that replicates the moment of coming out in our individual lives.

The story, however, cannot end there. Even after gays first come out of the closet, we often reenter it. Again, the issue is one of audience. Days after I came out to my parents, I went to see a mentor from college. John and I had not been personally close, but he had supported me intellectually and smoothed my way to Oxford. As he had ties with my professors there, I knew he knew I was in trouble. I owed him an explanation.

I did not think it would be hard, at least compared to coming out to my parents. Yet I had not counted on how much being back in the States would cast me back in the heterosexual role. Wretched as I had been at Oxford, I had also experienced the liberation of anonymity there. As I returned to my old haunts, I was tied back into place. I felt like Gulliver waking in the land of the Lilliputians, battened down by infinite and infinitesimal threads. Any one of them would have been easy to break, but collectively they immobilized me.

As soon as I walked into John's home, I felt a constraint. He was a jowly man who always looked freshly boiled. As if to soften his alarming mien, his manner was bonhomous, and that day was no exception. He asked after a college friend of mine, whom he kept referring to as my "girlfriend," and gaps in conversation were instantly filled with professional gossip. His living room was crowded with pictures of his children, and at one point he said, apropos of nothing, that having children was the achievement of his life. I became certain he knew I was gay and did not want to be told. That was the first time I experienced a person willing me not to come out to him by fashioning a field of resistance around himself. It is an effect that always enrages me, particularly when achieved through garrulity that feigns the communication it forecloses. As I tried to push through his gabble, he shook my hand and ushered me out.

Even when people were eager to know, or even when they knew, I had difficulty telling. Months into my friendship with Maureen, I still had not come out to her, even though she quickly intuited my secret and gave me every opportunity to divulge it. Her journal of the time has entries like "He didn't tell me again today," as if I were the letter that kept not arriving.

Many gay people have had this experience of the "open secret." I was gay—she knew I was gay—I knew she knew I was gay. Like mirrors held up to each other, we created an infinite regress of knowledge. But as the literary critic D. A. Miller says, there is a difference between knowledge and acknowledgment of knowledge. Because I would never acknowledge our collective knowledge, she could not do so either. So we carried on—each week more strained than the last. I berated myself, making resolutions to speak, telling myself she would think I did not trust her. While, of course, I did trust her, I felt I had lost the moment. But that had been—when?

Post-Stonewall gay history, too, has such moments of missed opportunity. There is a story—now lore in the gay legal community—about Justice Lewis Powell's gay clerk when *Bowers v. Hardwick* was decided. *Bowers* was the 1986 case in which the Supreme Court held that the constitutional right to privacy did not protect gays from prosecution for sexual intimacy in our homes. Until it was overruled in 2003, *Bowers* was a massive roadblock to gay rights—not just because it permitted the criminalization of private same-sex sexual intimacy, but also because it licensed other burdens on gays, such as denials of custody or employment.

The decision could easily have gone the other way. Not only was it decided by a five-four vote, but the deciding vote was cast by Powell, who was, at the eleventh hour, on the fence. As described by his biographer John Jeffries, Powell at that point discussed the case with Cabell Chinnis, his most liberal law clerk. Though Powell didn't know it, Chinnis was gay. In their discussion, Powell said he did not think he had ever known a homosexual. The astonished Chinnis agonized over whether to come out to his justice, but decided against it. He settled on an impassioned plea.

"The right to love the person of my choice," he said, "would be far more important to me than the right to vote in elections."

"That may be," Powell answered, "but that doesn't mean it's in the Constitution."

Powell then cast the deciding vote to uphold the sodomy statute.

After his story became known, Chinnis became a pariah in many gay circles. When I was in law school in the 1990s, I heard rumors that gays in Washington still refused him their homes. I found it hard to believe the animosity against him would be so intense. But according to journalists Joyce Murdoch and Deb Price, he was "labeled a self-hating homosexual, a latter-day J. Edgar Hoover, the devil's handmaiden."

Eve Sedgwick explains this anger by juxtaposing the story of the clerk against the Jewish Purim story. In the Jewish tale, King Ahasuerus plans the genocide of the Jewish people without realizing his own wife, Queen Esther, is hiding her Judaism from him. As the king moves on his plan, Esther comes out to him as Jewish, forcing him, in Sedgwick's words, to balance "the holocaustal with the intimate." Esther knows the king may resolve his internal conflict against her—she steels herself for death. Yet Esther's tiny, personal revelation moves the King to revoke his cataclysmic order. In the lineaments of her beloved face, he sees the humanity of the Jewish masses.

Is this not, Sedgwick asks, what many fantasized would have happened if Chinnis had come out to Powell? If Chinnis had put—now in Jeffries's words—"a familiar face to these incomprehensible urges," would they not have seemed "less bizarre and threatening"? Justice Powell later admitted he had "probably made a mistake in" *Bowers.* That confession honed the question—could Chinnis's revelation have tipped Powell's vote, tipping the Court away from its most antigay opinion?

Instances closer to hand than the Purim story attest to the transformative power of coming out. Faderman recounts that General Dwight Eisenhower asked WAC Sergeant Johnnie Phelps during World War II to find, expose, and discharge the lesbians in her battalion. She responded: "Yessir. If the General pleases I will be happy to do this investigation. . . . But, sir, it would be unfair of me not to tell you, my name is going to head the list." She then told the general he would "have to replace all the file clerks, the section heads, most of the commanders, and the motor pool." Eisenhower immediately withdrew the order.

The thwarted fantasy of transformation explains part of the rage against Chinnis. But it does not explain all of it. At first, I also deemed Chinnis a coward—he was out to the gay community, so what excuse did he have to reenter the closet? Over time, I came to see that if Chinnis was a coward, so was I. I, too, had engaged in selective passing after I had initially come out. Granted, the stakes of failing to come out to John or Maureen were lower, but so were the risks. Given my own history, I did not know what I would have done in Chinnis's place.

I think many gays revile Chinnis because they, like me, fear they might have done the same thing. By lambasting him, we persuade ourselves we are not like him. But we must be more forthright about how we are not forthright. Every gay person I know passes on occasion. It follows that until we can forgive the clerk for what he did, we will not be able to forgive ourselves for our own failures of courage. Only then can we assign responsibility where it belongs. While attacking Chinnis is easier than attacking the Court, this is a misdirection of progay energies. It is an internalization of homophobia, in which we criticize the gay person for passing rather than the antigay institution that commands him to do so.

What did it mean for Powell to say he knew no homosexuals? In a post-Kinsey age, he should have confronted the statistical impossibility of that claim. More to the point, Powell was famous for hiring gay law clerks, many of whom became his favorites. His failures of social and personal perception suggest he had a studious investment in ignorance, even as he visited vast harm on those he sought not to know.

The straight insistence on not seeing what's in plain sight would be comic if its consequences did not fall into another genre. A lesbian couple I know—Anne and Iris—recently went to an anniversary event at Oxford, a celebration that drew individuals of all generations. They were paired at dinner with an Australian couple in their seventies. Anne and Iris are in their mid-thirties. The older couple asked if they were graduates of Oxford. Iris took a breath and said Anne had gone to Oxford and that she and Anne were "together." The revelation passed without comment, as did other allusions over dinner to living and traveling together. At the end of the evening, the husband leaned over and told Anne how wonderful it had been to have dinner with her . . . *and her daughter.* Anne was horrified. Iris, who got to be the daughter, was less so.

These stories capture an era of gay rights. They underscore that the passing norm has been built not just on gay silence, but on an antigay insistence on such silence. Not until the formulation of the military's policy in 1993 was this bilateral social contract dubbed "Don't ask, don't tell." Yet the arrangement long predated the military policy, which did not spring from the head of Congress but grew organically out of an underlying culture. Unsurprisingly, then, the most serious shock to the passing norm did not originate in the cultural realm, but in the epidemiological one.

As a law student, I asked Bill Rubenstein how he had gotten involved in gay rights work. He responded that AIDS had hit America when he was in law school, in the mid-1980s, and had galvanized him politically: "We felt if we didn't do something, no one would." I filed that away, admiring his social conscience, but also wondering if he was being hyperbolic. Did people make lifelong career decisions based on one experience?

I now think of that conversation with Bill as an intergenerational one. Because gay rights has moved so fast, even a decade constitutes a generation. Although I don't recall feeling it from Bill, I sometimes feel a rage coming from gay men his age or older. I think it akin to that directed by Vietnam vets toward Gulf War vets—*We fight for years and people spit on us. You fight for weeks and people throw you a parade.* That difference in experience is in part made up by the AIDS epidemic. Bill lived in the center of the plague in a way that, a decade later, I could choose not to do. That was true when we had the conversation in 1994, and it remains true today. To my knowledge, no friend or even acquaintance of mine has died of AIDS, or aged ten years in a few months, or been ravaged by pneumonia or an intestinal parasite, or been covered with Kaposi's sarcoma lesions, or killed himself to hasten an inevitable end. This is what protease inhibitors and privilege mean now.

Nonetheless, AIDS has made its mordant claim on me. I have watched men's faces flinch and set as they tell me they are positive. I have had scares where I have read the virus in my every sweat or twinge. I have realized the bloodiness of blood in getting my own tests, and have watched the white stick for the red line that will mean my life has changed forever. I have felt the guilty grace of my negative results. And I have marveled at how all my gay male friends have wrestled with the fear of dying young.

AIDS galvanized the gay community. Passing is often associated with death, as in the racial context, where to pass as white has been to die a social death in one's community of origin. For gay men, AIDS transformed the figurative equivalence between "passing" and "passing away" into a literal one. Literal death was met with silence—in 1986, when AIDS had caused the deaths of more than sixteen thousand Americans, only a handful of obituaries identified the deaths as AIDS-related. Silence, in turn, has caused literal death, as in the lethal state censorship of AIDS education.

As AIDS closets became coffins in the 1980s and 90s, the felt costs of the gay closet, particularly for men, increased. While not identical, the AIDS closet and the gay closet interlock. AIDS has caused gay individuals to come out *as gay* to combat state and social indifference to the epidemic. The AIDS-inspired slogans "SILENCE=DEATH" and "We're here, we're queer, get used to it!" have come to testify more broadly to the gay experience. The AIDS closet has also undermined the gay closet because it is a less stable structure. The syndrome has left marks—perhaps most commonly the Kaposi's sarcoma lesion—that have outed its victims as AIDS sufferers and, associatively, as gay.

Radicalized by AIDS, many gays sought to revise the social contract of "Don't ask, don't tell." In the early 1990s, their activism took the form of outing—exposing people as gay against their will. Long viewed as taboo, outing finally found a pope in AIDS activist Michelangelo Signorile. The pulpit was the gay magazine *Out-Week*, which published a series of his articles outing public figures like tycoon Malcolm Forbes.

Public outing had a short career. For many gays, outing seemed uncomfortably close to the forced acknowledgment exacted by homophobes, like the police tactics used during bar raids. The mainstream press proved even more hostile. *OutWeek* closed its doors in 1991, allegedly because advertisers had withdrawn from the magazine. The norm moved back to one in which only active homophobia by a closeted homosexual could warrant outing—as Representative Barney Frank put it, "There is a right to privacy but not to hypocrisy." It's remarkable how little debate outing engenders today.

Like the gay community, passing has survived AIDS. When one converts, it is assumed one has converted to all audiences. With passing, there are as many closets as individuals in one's audience. This makes coming out a Sisyphean enterprise, at both the individual and collective levels. This is why, a dozen years after coming out to my parents, I still find myself passing in some contexts today. And it is why, thirty-seven years after Stonewall, passing is still a major issue for the gay community.

After Stonewall, the assimilation required of gays has shifted in emphasis from conversion to passing. From a gay rights perspective, that shift marks progress. It suggests some sectors of American society have accepted homosexuality to the point where they will accept silence in lieu of transformation. No matter how bad it is to live in the closet, it is preferable to electroshock treatment.

But because conversion and passing overlap, the shift from one to the other does not always represent an advance. Take the United States military's policy on homosexuality. The military used to be governed by 1981 regulations stating that homosexuality was "incompatible with military service." This was a formal conversion regime, under which gays technically had to convert to heterosexuality to serve. By the early 1990s, the exclusion of service members based on their homosexual status alone had come under fire. In 1993, Congress and the Department of Defense responded with the "Don't ask, don't tell" policy, which is still in effect. Under "Don't ask, don't tell," gays can no longer be excluded just for being gay, but can be excluded for coming out. The shift from the 1981 policy to the 1993 policy marks a shift from a conversion demand to a passing demand. Military and media voices touted this shift as palpable progress for gays.

But was it? The new policy hasn't changed life for gays, as closeted gays have always served in the military. It hasn't changed life for homophobes, who can still avoid confronting gays in their midst. Nor has it changed life for bisexual or questioning service members, who continue to lack role models who might make same-sex sexuality a viable way of life for them.

We could stop with the observation that "Don't ask, don't tell" is not much better for gays than its predecessor. Or we could go further, with law professor Janet Halley, and say the new policy is "much, much worse." While her contention may sound extreme, the numbers bear her out—in the years after the promulgation of "Don't ask, don't tell," the number of gays forced out of the military *increased*. I attribute this jump in discharges in part to the spin control accomplished by the new policy. Courts that would have struck down the old policy have accepted the new one because it is swaddled in a story of progress. Once upon a time, gays were asked to convert. Now, in more enlightened days, we are asked only to pass.

The military is banking on the fact that the passing demand sounds more reasonable than the conversion demand, without being so. We must call it on this bluff. Because conversion and passing are intricately intertwined, I believe they must rise or fall together. So long as there is a *right to be* a particular kind of person, I believe it logically and morally follows there is a *right to say what one is*. When the military says it is not against homosexuality but only against avowed homosexuality, I sense an inconsistency that calls the first part of the claim into question.

For this reason, the First Amendment should protect individuals for self-identifying as gay. The Supreme Court has not yet pronounced on this right, but the highest court to speak on this issue has rejected its existence. In 1984, a federal court of appeals confronted a case in which a guidance counselor, Marjorie Rowland, had been terminated by a public school for coming out as bisexual. Under controlling precedents, the court had to balance her interest in speaking on an issue of "public concern" against the school's interest in promoting efficient service. The court found Rowland's "coming out" speech failed to rise to the level of "public concern," as she was speaking "only in her personal interest." The court up-held Rowland's dismissal.

More recently, a lower court in a different jurisdiction dis-agreed with the *Rowland* court's contention that coming out was a private matter, sensibly observing that if so many individuals cared about a gay employee's revelation, her speech was of public con-cern. As courts reach different results, it becomes more likely the Supreme Court will step in to resolve the inconsistency. When it does, it should consider Justice William Brennan's comment on the *Rowland* decision. Dissenting from the Supreme Court's re-fusal to hear that case, the Court's great liberal said Rowland's coming-out speech should be protected because her speech was "no more than a natural consequence of her sexual orientation," insofar as it was "realistically impossible to separate her spoken statements from her status." The Supreme Court, and the country at large, should embrace this logic—that if there is a "right to be," there is a "right to say what one is."

Having now, like the Mariner, told my tale, I see I was foolish to think I could be free of it. Even the story I have told, more complete than any accounting I have ever given, is full of evasions and simplifications. Perhaps this is the Mariner's predicament—perhaps there are stories we can never get outside, even when we see we are caught inside them.

There is, nonetheless, satisfaction in having set it forth. If it does not free me to stop telling my story, perhaps it frees me to lis-ten better to the stories of others. When I came out, I was often called selfish, in a myriad of subtle and unsubtle ways—I was he-donistic, narcissistic, oversexed. Yet when I think of when I felt most selfish, I think of the time before I came out, when I was so afraid of myself, so unable to offer or receive intimacy. The great virtue of inhabiting a more authentic self is that one is simultaneously more alive and inert, and in both ways more available to others.

My gay students come out to me now, as I came out to Bill. Some of them are much further along than I was at their age. They tell me about coming out as teenagers, about taking minors in queer studies in college. I envy them—what it would be to come to law school with one's sexuality so fully theorized! But others quake, bringing me back to the moment I was sitting in their chair, and Bill in mine.

I try to do for them what Bill did for me. This includes telling them not to take my class. When I teach "Sexual Orientation and the Law," some students ask if I will change the name of the class on their transcript, so employers won't think they are gay. I refuse, saying this would be an implied apology on our part. I ask them if they want to be employed by someone who would discriminate against them on this basis. But I also tell them they can wait, and take the class when they are ready, and that I am here in the interim.

The real revelation, however, has been understanding the other closets my students inhabit. To be a teacher, at least of the subjects I teach, is to know the coming-out story is universal. It is not only gay students who have stories to tell, their hands tense in their laps. After telling me how she passes, a multiracial student reminds me that the primary historical association of the word "passing" has been with race, from the antebellum practice of slaves passing as white to the recent phenomenon of "cyber-race," or racial passing on the Internet. A Catholic student tells me he fears coming out as a believer, for he predicts his intelligence will go on a 25 percent discount in the law school. Based on such conversations, I tracked the word "closet" through a random news cycle to test my hunch the word had lost its gay specificity. I was not disappointed. The news is peopled with closet poets, closet Republicans, closet gamblers, closet artists, and closet fans of the Tampa Bay Devil Rays. We all have secret selves.

Such secrets want telling. Like so many Ancient Mariners, my students tell their stories of identity over and over, holding me with their glittering eyes. Even when these stories come hackneyed to my ear, I find pleasure in these incantations, which, through their very banality, secure these identities for the next generation. At other times, and unpredictably, a story elicits the old cloudless wonder. It recollects the verve and urgency of each of my own moments of coming out, that rush of feeling that says, Life changes now.

# GAY COVERING

I t is 1995, and my first boyfriend twitches in his sleep to wake me. In sleep, an electrical storm judders through Paul's body, sometimes waking me without waking him. At least in the initial months, I relish being startled awake like this: it enacts his startling presence in my life. From the beginning, lovemaking feels natural; I have a map of his body in my own. It is watching him asleep beside me that stills me to awe.

I met Paul at my favorite Italian restaurant, where he was working as a waiter. When I chatted him up, he handed me a card to fill out to be kept abreast of restaurant "Special Events." I received a letter a few days later informing me I had won the "Get to Know Your Waiter" event.

As I got to know my waiter, I learned he had been training at Juilliard to be a violinist. Close to graduation, he had developed an arm condition that prevented him from practicing for the hours a professional career required. So he had left music to do his undergraduate degree in English at Yale, and was halfway through at the age of twenty-three.

I first heard him play at a concert in his residential college. I have a stilted relationship to music. But listening to him, I knew this much: I had been speaking to him in his second language. To hear his talent was to feel his loss, the betrayal of his body.

Paul felt anything after music was a second-best life. And yet he gave that life the full force of his character. I once teased him about how finicky he was about his waiter's uniform as he ironed it before coming to bed. He replied that this was his life now, and that he still needed to be the best writer and waiter he could be. I fell in love with him then. We dated for my last two years of law school.

Perhaps none of us assumes romantic love to be a birthright. Yet the confidence it will come surely admits of degrees. Growing up, I assumed I was the word that rhymed with none other—like "silver" or "orange," glistering bright, but sonnet foiling, and always solitary traveling. Somewhere love happened, plausible as a catch of distant conversation. But not in the self's way.

So there is something seismic about holding Paul in my arms, of wondering what color his eyes, which in daylight shift through the shades of slate, settle into under his lids. No one has written adequately of what happens when enough of the body's naked surface is pressed against another human being's. It is a slow dismantling of the ego, a suspension of the instinct to distinguish *me* from *not me*. I shudder at my certainty that in other centuries I would have died without experiencing this indispensable warmth. I pull him closer, and he is lumpen, he is corporeal, he is that glorious inversion, reality come to soothe the imagination. Drifting off to sleep, I think it should end here, now.

It does not. We wake and dress, and Paul puts on a skirt to go to an ACT UP rally. Or we wake to a ringing phone, which I ask Paul not to answer because it might be my parents. Or we wake, and I make him breakfast because I feel guilty about not taking him to a party to which partners are invited. After I realize our fights almost always concern the outside world, I voice my wish we could live sequestered, have the food shipped in. He says I wish for a closet built for two.

This angers me. By this time, I have come out to my parents, my friends, my classmates, my professors. I am also just as activist as Paul in some ways, like making gay rights my work. Yet I know what he means. Paul is more radically queer than I. He grew up in San Francisco and came out at fifteen, and now experiences anything short of full-flaunting equality as self-hatred.

I puzzle over how much we fight about how to perform our gayness, even though we are both openly gay. Although I do not realize it then, we are having the debate of the gay moment—the debate between normals and queers over covering.

At millennium's turn, gay self-elaboration has entered its final phase. As sociologist Steven Seidman observes in his 2002 book, *Beyond the Closet,* many gays "can choose to live beyond the closet but . . . must still live and participate in a world where most institutions maintain heterosexual domination." The assimilation required of gays has begun to shift from conversion and passing toward covering. In some sectors of America, we can now be gay and out, so long as we do not "flaunt."

The gays I know no longer debate conversion and passing—we

categorically oppose conversion, and oppose passing while recognizing the importance of letting individuals come out on their own. We remain riven, however, by questions of covering—how much individuals should assimilate into the mainstream *after* coming out as gay. Should gays "act straight," or embrace gender atypicality? Should we be discreet about our sexuality, or "flaunt" it?

If conversion divides ex-gays from gays, and passing divides closeted gays from out gays, covering divides *normals* from *queers*. This last divide travels in many guises—as one between assimilationists and liberationists, or conservatives and sex radicals. Whatever we call it, it is the major fault line in the gay community today.

By *normals,* I mean openly gay individuals who embrace a politics of assimilation. Writer Andrew Sullivan can stand for this position. At least since his influential 1993 essay in the *New Republic,* Sullivan has urged gays to reject "the notion of sexuality as cultural subversion," because it "alienate[s] the vast majority of gay people who not only accept the natural origin of their sexual orientation, but wish to be integrated into society as it is." Because he believes gays have become "virtually normal" (the title of his 1995 book), Sullivan has argued for a strikingly modest politics: "Following legalization of same-sex marriage and a couple of other things . . . we should have a party and close down the gay rights movement for good."

By *queers,* I mean gays who emphasize their difference from the mainstream. Michael Warner, a professor of English at Rutgers, can stand for this position—his 1999 book, *The Trouble with Normal,* is the queer answer to Sullivan's *Virtually Normal.* Warner exhorts queers to resist the normalization of the gay rights movement: "People who are defined by a variant set of norms commit a kind of social suicide when they begin to measure the worth of their relations and their way of life by the yardstick of normalcy." For this reason, Warner believes queers should "insist that the dominant culture assimilate to queer culture, not the other way around." His sentiment is captured in the slogan "We're here, we're queer, get used to it," which not only gives difference a local habitation and a name ("We're here, we're queer") but also commands nonqueers rather than queers to accommodate that difference ("Get used to it").

While this rift dates back to Stonewall-era disputes between "suits" and "queers," it has become more pronounced in recent years. As social attitudes toward gays have softened, the historical line between "good" straights and "bad" gays has shifted in some quarters to distinguish between "good" straights and normals, on the one hand, and "bad" queers on the other. No longer an undifferentiated pathologized mass, gays feel increasing pressure to pledge an allegiance—to fade gratefully into the mainstream or to resist in the name of persisting difference. As African-Americans split between integration and separatism, or women split between equality and difference feminism, gays are splitting between normalcy and queerness.

So divisive has this schism proved that normals and queers sometimes seem to struggle against each other as hard as they struggle against homophobes. Normals rail against queers because they feel queers give all gays a bad name. Writer Bruce Bawer inveighs against the "men . . . in Speedos" and "bare-chested women" in gay pride parades, noting that these visible outliers "prop up misperceptions that undergird continued inequality." Queers attack normals because they feel sold out in the normal attempt to secure straight acceptance. Warner criticizes normals for "throw[ing] shame on those who stand farther down the ladder of respectability."

This debate fascinates me in part because I have been on both sides of it. I played the normal role relative to Paul—I didn't want to dress in gender-bending ways or engage in public displays of affection and didn't like it when he did. Yet I now find myself in the queer role relative to others—my gay rights work has led me to be described as "militant" (usually by those who would keep me out of "the military"). Like many gays, I have come to see myself as normal on some issues and queer on others.

This suggests gays can cover along many axes. I believe there are four. *Appearance* concerns how an individual physically presents herself to the world. *Affiliation* concerns her cultural identifications. *Activism* concerns how much she politicizes her identity. *Association* concerns her choice of fellow travelers—lovers, friends, colleagues. These are the dimensions along which gays decide just how gay we want to be.

Here my argument assumes a truly general form. Unlike conversion and passing, covering is a strategy of assimilation available to all groups, including but not limited to the classic civil rights groups of racial minorities, women, religious minorities, and people with disabilities. These four axes are the fundamental dimensions along which we *all* mute or flaunt our identities. In later discussion, I will not set these axes forth so formally, but in the hope of introducing them clearly, I do so here.

APPEARANCE

To think about gay appearance-based covering is to realize homosexuality may not be so invisible after all: people often assume gay men will be "feminine" and lesbians will be "masculine." In the nineteenth century, this link was sometimes attributed to "inversion"— the condition of being a woman trapped inside a man's body, or vice versa. The woman trapped in a man, it was thought, would express not only her desire for men but also her "feminine" affect. Foucault writes that the sexuality of the homosexual was "written immodestly on his face and body . . . a secret that always gave itself away."

Gays who counteract such stereotypes by "acting straight" are more likely to win straight acceptance. "I don't even think of you as gay" is a compliment reserved for gay men who outjock the jocks or lipstick lesbians who outfemme the femmes. As individuals and as a group, gays can be exquisitely self-conscious about self-presentation along this dimension. I recently came across a website that helps gays ascertain how "straight acting" we are—danger signs for men include burning candles, getting pedicures, or (my favorite) enjoying the receipt of flowers. And if we look at the gay plaintiffs presented to the courts and the world as the public face of gay rights, we see "straight-acting" men like navy midshipman Joseph Steffan or Scout leader James Dale. We see less of Perry Watkins—an African-American army service member with an equally exemplary record who performed as the drag queen Simone. In this, progay litigation and public relations are driven by the same imperative—present gays as identical to straights in all ways except orientation, as if conducting a controlled experiment. A 1993 *New York Times* profile describes Steffan as "the perfect symbol for this fight" in his embodiment of "the understated, well-scrubbed boy next door." To underscore that "perfect" means "straight-acting," the article clarifies that "no one will ever label Joe Steffan a screaming queen."

What are the harms of gender conformity? My answer is complex, as such conformity has brought me pleasure as well as pain. Growing up, women were not the mystery—I knew how they worked, or thought I did. Men were the mystery, obscure in their violences and their lusts and their ability to catch. Yet for many years I didn't try to conform to "straight-acting" norms. I didn't think I could—and perhaps achieved an integrity in that surrender.

Ironically, the impetus to "act straight" came from gays. (As Goffman observes, stigmatized groups often seek to "normify" their own with particular intensity.) After I came out at twenty-two, I realized how much the gay male community fetishized masculinity. "Be straight-acting," the ubiquitous gay male personals line read. "If I were into femmes, I'd date women." I thought, perhaps wrongly, that if I wanted to date in this world, I would have to acquire a "straight-acting" body.

So I hit the gym. What pleasure I found there! I realized there was no mystery to inhabiting a man's body—I just needed to pick up heavy objects and put them down again. This I could do. I let the truncated banister of the StairMaster guide me upward into manhood. Admittedly, my thoughts as I worked out were not the manliest. I dreamed of a gym spangled with lesbian poetry— Emily Dickinson's "I like to see it Lap the Miles" over the pool, Adrienne Rich's "the experience of repetition as Death" over the weight rack. But no one needed to know this.

Not every act of assimilation into "straight-acting" norms, however, felt like grace. When I began teaching, I worried about my self-presentation. Like many young professors, I was inundated with students. While I genuinely enjoyed working with most of them, I also struggled to establish boundaries. My primary concern had nothing to do with orientation—I knew the tenure decision would be made on my research, so I had to make time to do it. But a tiny voice also pressed me to avoid the stereotype of the pastoral gay man—that stock figure endowed with compassion and sensitivity unusual in a man. I wanted to be taken as seriously, and to be able to express my intellectual aggression as openly, as my straight male colleagues.

Like many covering demands, this voice was internal—no colleague ever imposed it on me. I came to distrust it. I have a nurturing quality or two, and value them in myself. To withhold them from my students to rebut a stereotype seemed self-defeating, even unethical. Nowadays, when I maintain boundaries, it is for different reasons.

## AFFILIATION

A few summers ago, I took a share on Fire Island. For years, gay men had asked why I hadn't joined the gay male community at the Pines. For years, I had demurred. My resistance came from my professorial parts—I was afraid my bookish self would be out of place there, and afraid of succumbing to cliché.

My curiosity got the better of me. My first time out, I liked how every leg of the journey got more gay. On the train from Penn Station to Babylon, the passengers were not noticeably gay. From Babylon to Sayville, the demographic grew solidly gay. By the time I reached the Sayville ferry station, everyone was gay, at which point the gay men were separated from the lesbians.

The downpour in which I arrived dampened my enthusiasm. The sheeting rain stippled every pixel of the harbor and threw up crowns on the famous boardwalks. I had no umbrella; I was alone; I couldn't find my house. A group of men came walking in the opposite direction, blooming with camaraderie and umbrellas. I stepped to one side of the boardwalk to let them pass, when one of them detached. To my shock, he proffered his own umbrella and uttered the words that have become my character note for the Pines.

"Honey," he said, "take this umbrella. Your hair has melted."

I was reminded then of a colleague, a nonobservant Jew, describing how it felt to go to Israel for the first time. He, too, had been asked by peers why he "hadn't been yet." He, too, had resisted into adulthood. Yet when the El Al plane touched down in Tel Aviv, and the passengers broke into the "Hatikvah," he wanted to kiss the earth.

A gay friend of mine recently took his mother to Fire Island, showing there is diversity in this matter of mothers. I tried to imagine her, a Midwestern septuagenarian, threading her way through those naked torsos shining with their business. I asked him what had possessed him. "I wanted her to understand I have a culture," he said, with a truculent tilt to his chin. I asked him to describe it. He said it was a culture in which he could imagine gay equality, in which his ordinary desires were not extraordinary, in which the closet opened onto a stage. He said it was a culture in which he could redeem time, experiencing the adolescence he had never had with friends from whom he was not estranged by an awful secret. He said it was a culture of sex and camp and whimsy that bound him to a community with a history and geography. I asked him if his mother had understood this, and he said he thought she had. He said that on the ferry ride home, she observed that gays must feel really suppressed in straight culture to need to flaunt so much when they were free of it. Then she asked if he shouldn't be exercising more.

The place is just a placeholder. A web of gay culture now extends over America: gay TV shows like *The L Word* and *Will and*

*Grace,* gay musicians like k.d. lang and Elton John, gay fashions like Carhartts and boxer briefs, gay divas like Garland and Garbo, gay authors like Barnes and Wilde, gay drugs like K and poppers, gay sports like figure skating and gymnastics. Historically, the practice of alluding to gay culture—known as "dropping hairpins"— was a means through which gays identified one another while passing to the rest of the world. Now such references also distinguish openly gay individuals: gays who immerse themselves in gay culture are seen as "in the life," those who eschew it as in the mainstream.

Some might question whether anyone is imposing a cultural covering demand on gays. Far from forcing gays to mute gay culture, America seems increasingly to ask us to flaunt it. A recent instance is the hit series *Queer Eye for the Straight Guy,* in which five gay men make over a straight man (and, by proxy, the viewer) in each of their areas of expertise: fashion, food and wine, interior design, grooming, culture. The success of *Queer Eye* suggests that gay men, at least, have assumed model-minority status—that, as my Korean-American dean Harold Koh says, "Gays are the new Asians." And just as Asian-Americans have pointed out that positive stereotypes are still stereotypes, gays have argued that *Queer Eye* puts gays in a box by implying we all know how to julienne a carrot. Yet as defenders of the show rightly say, "It's better than homophobia." When the show is placed in a history that begins with attempts to convert gays to heterosexuality, this fact is startling: gay men are now teaching straight men how to behave, rather than the other way around.

Yet *Queer Eye's* triumphs fall short of conquest. My friend's mother was right to read Fire Island as a symptom of the suppression of gay culture in everyday life. In fact, when I think about where I have experienced the cultural covering demand, I think of the journey back from the Pines. At some point on the train ride, I look up and realize the moment has passed—the moment when straight culture has reasserted itself. Men who were lolling in each other's arms are now separate, fingers that were interlaced are now disengaged, tattooed bodies have disappeared into their clothes, faces have tightened. It is a moment as imperceptible as the change of a season, or the moment one falls out of love.

The selective uptake of gay culture—gay fashion, yes; gay affection, no—shows that acceptance is driven by the desires of the straight cultural consumer rather than the dignity of the gay person. It is natural for consumers to be selective in their appropriation of minority cultures—they choose the parts that are meaningful to them, and that give them pleasure and self-definition. But in that respect these consumers are no different from members of those minority cultures. True pluralism would be receptive to traits valued by those who bear them, regardless of their mainstream appeal.

## ACTIVISM

It is 2001, ten years since I have come out to my parents, but somehow I am still sitting on the same ivory couch, which is somehow still immaculate, like a couch in a dream. I have come to Boston to tell my parents the *New York Times* is about to run a profile on my work that will mention I am gay. Given how long I have been out to them, this revelation should not be momentous. And yet it is.

After I came out to my parents, we settled into a form of "Don't ask, don't tell," in which I told them nothing of my personal life and they never asked. I met, dated, and broke up with Paul without their knowing of his existence. I now regret I didn't push harder—for my sake, for the sake of Paul and his successors, and for theirs. But I was chastened by my sense of how unacceptable homosexuality must seem to their Japanese eyes.

I began to learn about homosexuality in Japan in my late twenties. I read about a tradition of male-male sexuality that extended through the mid-nineteenth century. That tradition was similar to the Greek one—older men inducted younger ones into manhood, sexually and otherwise, while also having sexual relationships with women. In his widely sold 1687 book, *The Great Mirror of Male Love,* Ihara Saikaku addresses a bisexual male reader in asking a series of questions beginning, "Which is to be preferred?"—"Having lightning strike the room where you are enjoying a boy actor you bought, or being handed a razor by a courtesan you hardly know who asks you to die with her?"

This tradition of male-male sexuality withered when Japan's self-imposed isolation from the world ended in 1868. Saddled with the infamous "unequal treaties" that subordinated it to Western nations, Japan realized it would have to modernize to be treated as a peer. Modernization included the adoption of the Meiji Constitution, the embrace of industrialization, and the repudiation of "barbaric" cultural practices such as homosexuality. Japanese history was rewritten to cast homosexuality as an atavistic practice of the hinterlands. The purge has been effective. Although I spent every summer but one from birth through college graduation in Japan, I never met an openly gay Japanese, nor did I even hear one mentioned.

I am told gay rights is now budding in Japan. The first gay pride march occurred in 1994. In 1997, a Tokyo appellate court ruled in favor of a gay rights group on a freedom of association claim. The template is again a Western one—rather than citing native traditions of same-sex sexuality, progay courts and commentators have looked to the gay rights movement in America. Like a dutiful student who concurs with his teacher even when the teacher contradicts himself over time, Japan first agreed with the West that homosexuality was an abomination, and now is beginning to agree it is a benign variation.

So far as I can tell, the pace of change has been glacial. Or perhaps it is I who am frozen. To this day, the words "I am gay" feel unspeakable in Japanese. Drawing on that double consciousness in myself, I can glimpse homosexuality through my parents' eyes. For many years, this vantage chilled all speech.

So here we are again, sitting in perhaps the same positions as when I came out.

"We accept that you are gay," my mother says in Japanese. "But we don't understand why you have to be a *jandaaku*."

"A what?" I ask in English. I can tell the word is a borrowed one, but do not know from which language. Japanese takes from all tongues—*arubaito*, for part-time work, from the German; *pan*, for bread, from the Portuguese.

"The banner carrier."

"The who?" Our cross-talk is usually a form of pleasure between us.

"The woman who heard voices."

"A Joan of Arc?"

"Yes." From the French. "Millions of gay people live their lives without making it their cause. Why must you make it yours?"

I have wrestled with this question for years. In my self-lacerating moods, I think my activism is a form of protesting too much, a defense against my own self-loathing. Or an Oedipal rant, an attempt to speak more and more loudly until I am heard. Or an adolescent messianic impulse to have a cause. None of these answers feels correct. Yet the answer I want to give—that I have always had a commitment to social justice—also seems wrong.

Growing up, I was more interested in aesthetics than in politics. Even when I went to law school, I did so to protect myself, not others.

I was drawn to my work by doing what came naturally. My work seemed the consequence of being who I was, where I was, when I was. I went, in James Baldwin's essential phrase, the way my blood beat.

"It's what I do," I say, lamely. I think about making the argument for the "gay activist" gene.

"But why must you?" my mother asks. "Why can't you teach constitutional law, rather than the law of gays? You will become a lightning rod. People will hate you."

"It's a little late for that," I say. "I already get hate mail."

"You get hate mail?" I wonder why this detail has quickened my father into speech. I flash on him as an eighteen-year-old Japanese in 1950s America.

"It's one way to know I'm accomplishing something."

I say this lightly. I have tried to keep all my words light, skating across the surface of emotions I cannot feel enough to name. But this is a mistake. I sound too casual.

"What you do has consequences for us, too." My mother's voice is suddenly heavy with grief. "If you speak so loudly, our world becomes very small."

I plunge through the crust of my despair. I have for years had a recurring dream of a yellowing map of indistinct countries. A garnet stain spreads over them, following the long horizontal fibers of the paper. The stain has no visible source, so I expect it to exhaust itself. But it moves inexorably, sickeningly, over the whole. This dream began long before I came out, and probably has nothing to do with my orientation. But I have come to think of it as my "gay dream."

Listening to my mother, I wonder when it is most difficult to be gay—when one is in the closet? When one is lying awake worrying about dying young? Or is it this moment, when I feel my parents will never see my work as anything but a stain colonizing the habitable world?

ASSOCIATION

It is 1996, and Paul and I are breaking up. He crouches on the bed, hugging his knees. We are both close to graduation—I from law school, he from college. I am committed to spend a postgraduate year clerking in New Haven. Paul has agreed to stay here for another year, instead of returning to his beloved San Francisco. On one condition—that I slow down and spend more time with him. I tell him I cannot—I am about to start hunting for a teaching job while working a full-time job. I tell him this is the fight of my life, what I have been preparing for years to do. And that is the end.

Thousands of couples, straight and gay, have this conversation every day. What I experience—and regret—as specifically gay about our breakup was the lack of any flexibility on my part. I know I would not have been so rigid if Paul had been a woman. As it stood, it was all too easy to privilege my career over our relationship. The career was prestigious, a source of public esteem. The relationship was stigmatized, and mostly a secret. I had not introduced Paul to my friends in law school, or to my parents. He never figured in the verbal portraits I painted of my world or future. To excise him from a life into which he had never been grafted was a simple matter, however painful.

In denying our connection, I was heeding a culture that told me gay individuals are more palatable than gay couples. "I don't care what they do in their bedrooms," a classmate once said in col-

lege as we walked by two men kissing. "I just don't see why they
need to do it in public." Even then, I was able to give her the old gay
rejoinder, suggesting she only perceived it as flaunting against a
heterosexual baseline. Her displays of cross-sex affection with her
boyfriend were no less public, just more routine. And even then, I
found myself wondering why people unfazed by the statement "I
am gay" could take such offense when they saw a tangible expression of that fact.

My favorite answer comes from Foucault. In 1988, he said:
"People can tolerate two homosexuals they see leaving together,
but if the next day they're smiling, holding hands and tenderly embracing one another, they can't be forgiven. It is not the departure for pleasure that is intolerable, it is waking up happy." I love
this quotation for the counterintuitive truth it captures. Gays—
particularly gay men—are often portrayed as unstable, isolated,
and promiscuous. This portrayal implies that if gays were more re-
spectable, we would be more respected. If gays could love, we
would be more loved. Foucault challenges this conventional wisdom. He says people—here I would say "some people"—will not
love gays more if we love. If gays have clandestine relationships,
moralists can still figure our relations as abject. The "departure for
pleasure," after all, is a departure—people do not have to see where
the gay pair goes, and can imagine that offstage interaction to be as
fleeting or as unhappy as they wish. What is galling is to see a gay
couple demonstrate that their relationship works, that they are
happy.

Paul was good at waking up happy. He wasn't oblivious to the
looks of strangers, but could ignore them more easily than I. When
we took walks up Whitney Avenue, his hand would reach for mine
in an unconscious radiation of affection, making me feel small-
souled for wanting to reject it. And yet I usually did. I wince re-

membering one particular refusal. Paul and I had gone to the hospital to get a diagnosis for him that could have been serious. In the waiting room, his right leg was going like a jackhammer. He reached for my hand, and I brushed it away.

What does it matter? I would say to myself. He knows I care about him—in our apartments, in our private places, I show him. Yet I have come to see this differently. In saying I was gay, I showed I was willing to value myself over the world's opinion. In reaching for my hand, Paul was asking me to give him the same priority.

In 2004, Paul and his partner became one of the first couples to enter a same-sex marriage in San Francisco. Always practical, Paul asked his friends to send money to the Human Rights Campaign in lieu of sending gifts. I liked that he was one of the first men in the country to marry another man. I see it as his reward for extending his hand, against the odds.

Covering seems a more complex form of assimilation than conversion or passing. At the most basic level, it raises thornier issues of classification. I'm sometimes asked, for instance, whether I consider same-sex marriage to be an act of covering or flaunting. I think it is both. Along the axis of affiliation, marriage is an act of covering, as marriage has historically been associated with straight culture. This is why queers like Warner revile it and normals like Sullivan endorse it as an act of assimilation. Along the axes of appearance, activism, or association, however, marriage is an act of flaunting. This is why right-wing moralists object to it as a sign that gays are getting too strident in our claims for equality.

Covering is also morally complex. Many who accept that conversion and passing are severe harms do not feel the same way about covering. They often perceive the covering demand to be entirely appropriate. Do gays really need to dress in gender-bending ways, dance shirtless, handcuff themselves to government offices, or hold hands in public?

An easy response to those who are anti-passing but pro-covering is that their stance is hard to maintain, as passing and covering are often indistinguishable. The same behavior—such as not holding hands with someone of the same sex—can constitute passing or covering, depending on the literacy of the audience. As Goffman observes, "what will conceal a stigma from unknowing persons may also ease matters for those in the know." Just as conversion and passing grade into each other, so do passing and covering.

But I have a deeper, more visceral response that flows from my experience of these three demands. I experience the right to be gay, and the right to say I am gay, as critical prerogatives. Yet I also experience them as minimal ones. Being gay shifted for me from being a condition into being a life only when I began to overcome covering demands. This was where I came to possess my emotions, my culture, my politics, my lovers. This was where gay life assumed a tincture of joy.

When I say this, some hear me to say an "authentic" gay person must flaunt along all dimensions. This is not my view. I do not think Michael Warner is a more authentic homosexual than Andrew Sullivan. To the contrary, I believe authenticity will look and feel different for each of us. I have elaborated my own gay identity by covering in some ways and flaunting in others, and will doubtless change that balance over time. I am not against all covering, but only against coerced covering. For this reason, I am much more likely to contest a covering *demand* by a homophobe than a covering *performance* by a gay individual, just as I was more critical of Justice Powell's passing demand than of Chinnis's passing performance. And I am not against all coerced covering, but only coerced covering that has no justification. What is important to me is that I have the freedom to find or fashion my identity along all these dimensions without limitations based on bias.

My real commitment is to autonomy—giving individuals the freedom to elaborate their authentic selves—rather than to a rigid notion of what constitutes an authentic gay identity. I focus here on the demands of coerced assimilation because I think American history has shown it to be the greater threat to gay autonomy. Surveying gay rights litigation, it's uncommon to find gays suing for being forced to flaunt. I know of only one legal context in which such reverse-covering demands have been made—the immigration context, in which gay asylum seekers have to prove they are "gay enough" to establish a colorable fear of persecution. Given my commitment to autonomy, I of course resist that reverse-covering demand. But in general, gay plaintiffs sue to fight forced conformity, in the forms of conversion, passing, and covering. We see the final generation of such litigation in the case of Robin Shahar.

Robin Shahar, formerly Robin Brown, took her current name when she was married in July 1991 by Rabbi Sharon Kleinbaum. Because of this ceremony, Shahar lost her job as a staff attorney at Georgia's Department of Law. The problem was that Shahar had married—in the eyes of her religion, not the law—another woman, Francine Greenfield. (The couple took the name Shahar, which means "the dawn" in ancient Hebrew; I refer to Greenfield by her former name to avoid confusion.)

When I speak with Shahar, she tells me her relationship with the Department of Law began in 1990, during a summer internship she took while in law school. Her ultimate boss was Michael J. Bowers, the Georgia attorney general of *Bowers v. Hardwick* fame who had successfully defended Georgia's sodomy statute all the way to the Supreme Court. Shahar, however, was not particularly anxious. Out for five years by that time, she had a rule: "I would not lie if someone asked me about my boyfriend or what I did over the weekend. But I wouldn't initiate." The effect of this rule was that most of her coworkers knew she was gay. Shahar's strategy of not passing but covering worked. In the fall, Bowers offered her a full-time position as a staff attorney after she completed law school.

When she received her offer, Shahar was preparing for her Jewish marriage to Greenfield. While no United States jurisdiction at the time recognized the legality of same-sex marriages, the Reconstructionist Movement accepted the validity of same-sex marriages performed within the faith. The movement views such marriages not only as commitments between two individuals, but also as commitments those individuals make to their congregation and to all Jewish people. Because the movement deems these marriages sacred, it considers them indissoluble without the intervention of a rabbi.

In November 1990, Shahar filled out a department personnel form with this in mind. One question inquired: "Do any of your relatives work for the State of Georgia?" As Shahar recalls, "I remember thinking long and hard about what I wanted to write. I thought, this is a conflict-of-interest question, and Fran works for the state of Georgia. But I also knew she wasn't my spouse in straight society's view. In the end, I went back to my rule: do not lie." Shahar wrote that Greenfield, her "future spouse," worked for the state. The department received and filed this form without comment.

Listening to Shahar, I reflect I would never have answered the question as she did. I would have experienced a simple "no" as both honest and politic. Indeed, I have a twinge of exasperation at Shahar for her high-mindedness. It is a dirty secret among lawyers that plaintiffs are often troublemakers—pious and unbending Cordelias. But then I reflect that Paul would have analyzed and answered the question as Shahar did. Like Shahar, he would have reasoned from his own visceral principles of equality. I realize through Paul that Shahar is acting on my behalf, moving gay rights forward for the rest of us who duck our heads when confronted with our second-class citizenship.

In May 1991, Shahar graduated from Emory Law School. Ranked near the top of her class, she had earned a distinguished scholarship and a position on the law review. That month, Shahar discussed her upcoming employment with Deputy Attorney General Robert Coleman. Shahar requested a late starting date because of her marriage, without specifying it would be to a woman. Coleman congratulated her.

Coleman began to tell coworkers Shahar was getting married. In Shahar's view, Coleman was obsessed with the news because he thought it meant Shahar had converted to being straight. If Coleman was rejoicing over a prodigal daughter returning to the heterosexual fold, he was soon disappointed. He learned through a colleague Shahar was marrying a woman.

This news caused a maelstrom. The five senior aides held several meetings, and confirmed through Shahar's personnel file that she considered Greenfield her "future spouse." After they briefed Bowers, the attorney general decided to withdraw Shahar's job offer. Bowers delegated the termination of Shahar to a subordinate, who read a script in the presence of a witness. The deputy told Shahar that Bowers had canceled the employment agreement, and told Shahar to direct any comments to Bowers in writing. Reading from the script, the deputy concluded, "Thanks again for coming in, and have a nice day."

Shahar sat through this performance in disbelief. "It put me in a state of shock. I thought if I could just sit down and explain to Bowers what this was about, he would understand." She was told Bowers would not meet with her. She tried to absorb her jobless state: "It was unbelievable. It was a couple weeks before the ceremony. I had graduated law school, I had a job that I was looking forward to, I had a commitment ceremony that was a weekend long to the woman I had been with for five years. This was like a grenade being thrown in it."

The wedding took place on a campground in South Carolina, where one hundred people gathered for what Shahar describes as "a weekend out of time." The rabbi made only a passing reference to the Bowers incident: "There are people who would like us not to do this. But we have created what we wanted to create." For Shahar, that statement captured the ceremony: "We had a vision of what we wanted to create and we succeeded. Not just that we were in a Jewish setting, but that we had gotten our families of origin to where they were supportive. This was not in isolation, this was being surrounded by our community."

Before the couple left for their honeymoon in Greece, they met with an attorney from the ACLU. This was Bill Rubenstein, in the days before he became an academic. While he agreed to take the case, Shahar remained uncertain about filing suit. As a lawyer, she knew being a plaintiff in a major civil rights suit was a Herculean undertaking. The couple decided to think it over on their trip. When they returned, both their mothers were waiting at the airport imploring them not to file. But the couple had decided to do so.

When terminated, Shahar was told to direct comments to Bowers in writing. In October 1991, she did so in the form of a lawsuit claiming he had violated her right to exercise her religion, her right to intimate and expressive association, her right to equal protection on the basis of sexual orientation, and her right to due process. Shahar lost all her claims in federal district court, but then won a victory from a three-judge appellate court. At this point, a majority of the judges on the Eleventh Circuit (one of the thirteen circuits into which the federal judiciary is divided) made the unusual move of calling for a rehearing of the case before all judges on the circuit. This twelve-member body issued an en banc opinion that annulled Shahar's prior victory.

I focus on Shahar's claim, made under the Equal Protection Clause, that Bowers discriminated against her on the basis of her orientation. Bowers's response to this claim reflects a shift toward the covering demand. As the trial court (where facts are established) observed, Bowers contended "he would never exclude a homosexual from employment solely on the basis of his or her sexual orientation." Bowers here said Shahar did not need to convert to work for him. Bowers also stated that "when he extended plaintiff an offer of employment, he had constructive knowledge of plaintiff's sexual orientation." Bowers here alleged he was not requiring Shahar to pass. Bowers's disavowal of the conversion and passing demands shows how far gay rights had moved—in prior decades, government offices had routinely terminated individuals for homosexuality alone.

Bowers rested his termination of Shahar solely on her failure to cover. Bowers noted that the couple had flaunted their homosexuality by engaging in a commitment ceremony, by changing their names, by living together, and by holding insurance jointly. He viewed this conduct as "activist." Indeed, in a letter written to the dean of Emory Law School, Bowers hypothesized Shahar had set him up by obtaining a job with the department to pursue her activism. In court, Bowers asserted that employing a flaunter like Shahar would hurt the department's credibility, making it harder for it to deny same-sex marriage licenses or to enforce sodomy statutes.

Purely as a matter of legal strategy, Bowers was wise to focus on Shahar's conduct. In the 1996 case of *Romer v. Evans*, the Supreme Court struck down an antigay amendment to the Colorado state constitution. The Court's opinion suggested that punishing gays because of their status alone was disfavored, if not impermissible. In isolating Shahar's flaunting conduct as the reason for terminating her in 1991, Bowers was cannily intuiting the trend of the case law.

The year after *Romer*, the en banc court rewarded Bowers by adopting his argument. In discussing Bowers's interests, it accepted his contention that his office would lose credibility if it employed Shahar. The court cited a precedent that upheld a sheriff's termination of an employee who belonged to the Ku Klux Klan. In discussing Shahar's interests, the court noted that Bowers was punishing her not for her gay status, but rather for her behavior. It observed that *Romer* was not applicable as precedent because "*Romer* is about people's condition; this case is about a person's conduct." Balancing Bowers's interests against Shahar's, the court found his interests were greater.

Yet Bowers's claim that retaining Shahar would compromise the department's ability to deny same-sex marriage licenses is hard to credit. At no point did Shahar seek to marry Greenfield legally, nor did she agitate for the legalization of same-sex marriage. The Georgia citizenry could not fairly have assumed that Shahar's private religious ceremony would entitle same-sex couples to a public civil license.

Bowers's statement that Shahar's wedding would lessen her ability to enforce sodomy statutes seems superficially stronger. The problem here was that his objection was too broad to justify firing *only* Shahar. Georgia's sodomy statute (which has since been struck down) punished "any sexual act involving the sex organs of one person and the mouth or anus of another." Because the statute prohibited cross-sex as well as same-sex acts, any heterosexual in the department who had ever had oral sex was as compromised as Shahar.

Just as the court overestimated Bowers's interests, it underestimated Shahar's. The court stated it would protect only Shahar's status, not her conduct. The question the court seemed to pose was whether Shahar could be gay without getting married. Of course, the answer is yes. But this is the wrong question. It cannot be that individuals committed to equality for gays would ask only whether the conduct in question was necessary to being gay. Gays can survive without many things, including equality. A better question is whether the same conduct is acceptable for straights but not for gays. In Shahar's case, this double standard clearly existed. When she told Coleman she was getting married, he congratulated her. When he discovered she was getting married to a woman, he lobbied to fire her. In fact, it was wrong to say Shahar was terminated for her conduct rather than her status, as it was her status that cast the same conduct—a religious marriage—in a completely different light. Shahar was not fired for marrying, or for marrying a woman, but for marrying a woman *as a woman.*

The en banc decision was handed down on May 30, 1997. "I was speechless," Shahar says, and is, as she recollects the moment, speechless. "The court compared me to a KKK recruiter. I was beside myself." She had her lawyers press for review by the United States Supreme Court. "I felt I couldn't have my name associated with a case that drew these conclusions." The Supreme Court denied review.

When Bowers heard of the decision, he had resigned his position as attorney general to run for governor of Georgia. Although he was the runaway favorite for the Republican nomination, Bowers said he "felt funny about the whole thing." Voters soon learned why—Bowers confessed to a fifteen-year adulterous relationship with a former department employee. As adultery has long been a crime in Georgia, Bowers was breaking a sex law even as he enforced another one against Michael Hardwick all the way to the Supreme Court. Moreover, he fired Shahar because he said *she* could not enforce sex laws while breaking them. "Mr. Bowers penalized me for being honest," Shahar said in an interview with ABC News, "while he rewarded himself for lying."

After the press trumpeted forth his hypocrisy, Bowers lost the Republican nomination to a candidate with no political experience. Bowers, who now works as a lawyer in private practice, claims he has retired from public life.

Today, Shahar works as an attorney for the city of Atlanta. In that capacity, she has drafted and defended a domestic partnership ordinance for same-sex couples. She and Greenfield recently celebrated their fourteenth anniversary. Even at this distance, the decision weighs on her. I have some understanding of this burden, as I have a friend who was a gays-in-the-military plaintiff. To this day, he cannot bring himself to read the opinion that upheld his separation. As a lawyer in the jurisdiction in which her case was decided, Shahar has not had the luxury of ignoring her decision. She recently had to reread the case as a precedent for a matter her office was handling. "It's still awful," she says, "to see my name on that opinion."

As I explored the law's treatment of gay covering, I expected to have difficulty finding cases like Shahar's. Everyone knows the flaunting homosexual will generally get less sympathy than the discreet one. But I did not think courts, which must defend the logic and dignity of their distinctions, would say so.

I was wrong. I found case after case in which courts predicated an entitlement on whether a gay or lesbian individual covered. Individuals whose homosexuality, even if avowed, was "discreet" or "private" kept their jobs or children. Those whose homosexuality was "notorious" or "flagrant" were not so fortunate. Far from being an outlier, Shahar's case epitomized the rising generation of gay rights cases.

The case law relating to parenting rights shows the critical difference covering can make. Here I focus on a particular form of parenting dispute in which two individuals of different sexes marry and procreate, one of them later comes out as gay, and the two individuals vie for rights over the offspring. The rules governing custody or visitation are diverse, as they are enacted state by state. A survey of state practices, however, reveals convergence around the same general rule—gays who cover retain their children, gays who fail to do so risk losing them.

Historically, homosexuality automatically disqualified an individual from getting custody or visitation rights in many states. This was a conversion regime, in which one technically had to be straight to parent. Over time, most states have moved toward rules granting gays custody and visitation rights, so long as they cover. In 1994, the Indiana Court of Appeals awarded custody to a lesbian mother after applying a common standard:

> Had the evidence revealed that Mother flagrantly engaged in untoward sexual behavior in the boys' presence, the trial court may have been justified in finding her to be unfit and, accordingly, awarded custody to Stepmother. However, without evidence of behavior having an adverse effect upon the children, we find the trial court had no basis upon which to condition Mother's custody of her sons.

As the court's references to the "flagrant" or the "untoward" suggest, courts have not hesitated to punish parents they view to be flaunters. In affirming the denial of custody to a lesbian mother in 1975, a California appellate court observed: "Appellant does not merely say she is homosexual. She also lives with the woman with whom she has engaged in homosexual conduct, and she intends to bring up her daughters in that environment." In reaching a similar result in 1988, the Connecticut Supreme Court noted that the trial court had been concerned not "with her sexual orientation per se but with its effect upon the children, who had observed in the home inappropriate displays of physical affection between their mother and M while M had resided with them."

I believe, of course, that parents should not expose their children to most forms of sexual behavior. So I tried to find out whether courts that objected to "inappropriate sexual behavior" were referring to sexual acts that would have been problematic even if they had occurred between individuals of different sexes, or whether they were referring to hugging, kissing, or other acts that would be expected of heterosexual couples. Although courts are sometimes too vague for anyone to tell what sort of behavior they had in mind, it is generally clear that what counts as sexually appropriate behavior for straights is out of bounds for gays. While courts require gays simply to *cover* to the courts, they often require gays to *pass* to their children. A Missouri court of appeals granted custody in 1998 to a lesbian mother after finding that "the children were unaware of Mother's sexual preference, and Mother never engaged in any sexual or affectionate behavior in the presence of the children." Applying the same standard to deny custody to a lesbian mother in 1990, a Louisiana appellate court cited "open, indiscreet displays of affection beyond mere friendship . . . where the child is of an age where gender identity is being formed." If acceptable sexuality for same-sex couples is limited to the appearance of friendship, then the expectations for parents are clearly not orientation-neutral.

Notice as well *why* such covering is required—parental flaunting is dangerous because it could convert a child whose "gender identity is being formed." All three demands for assimilation are simultaneously in play—because children must not be *converted,* parents must *pass* to their children and *cover* to the courts. The shifts from conversion to passing to covering I have described are never categorical ones in which one demand supplants another. They are shifts in emphasis.

Courts can demand covering even more baldly through visitation restrictions. In 1974, a New Jersey court noted various ways in which a divorced gay father flaunted his homosexuality, observing that he was the director of the National Gay Task Force and took the children to the "Firehouse," which the court described as "a meeting hall for homosexuals." Based on these findings, the court held that during the visitation periods, the father could "1) not cohabit or sleep with any individual other than a lawful spouse,

2) not take the children or allow them to be taken to 'The Fire-house,' . . . 3) not involve the children in any homosexual related activities or publicity," and "4) not be in the presence of his lover."

More recently—in 1982—a Missouri court of appeals barred a gay father from taking his children to any church that "supports the practice of homosexuality to the extent that it recognizes a 'holy union' between homosexuals as the equivalent of marriage." An Indiana appellate court, citing this case with approval in 1998, prohibited a gay father from having any "non-blood related persons in the house overnight when the children are present."

These cases enrage me. Courts are using the vulnerability all parents experience through their children to force gays to surrender the basic rights of citizenship, such as the rights of political advocacy or association. In doing so, they chill the expression even of gays who are not in court. A lesbian I know was a stalwart activist for years. When she had a son, however, she muted her activism. As an attorney, she knew the case law made her child a hostage of the state. Sex columnist Dan Savage similarly writes about how he and his male partner encourage their adopted son DJ to play with male-identified toys in which they had no interest as children. Given the credence the law attaches to the fear that gay parents will convert their children, I cannot say this is irrational. Again, Savage is experiencing a vulnerability to straight norms through his child that he has long since overcome on his own behalf.

Shahar's case is anything but an aberration. Courts that prohibit conversion or passing demands still permit covering demands. Such courts will not protect gays who fail to cover from losing their jobs or children. The covering demand is the final symptom of gay inequality, and it is the challenge that faces the gay rights movement of the future.

A s I sat in the Supreme Court listening to oral arguments in *Lawrence v. Texas* on March 26, 2003, I was struck by how many openly gay individuals packed the courtroom. I should not have been surprised, as it was one of the most important gay rights cases in the history of the Court. In *Lawrence,* the Court was considering constitutional challenges to a Texas sodomy statute. In granting review, the Court had instructed the lawyers to address the question of whether it should overrule *Bowers v. Hardwick.* But I was still agog that every gay rights person I could think of was there—the attorneys from Lambda Legal and the ACLU, law professors from around the country, Representative Barney Frank and his entourage. A few rows behind me, I saw some students who had worked with me on the friend-of-the-court brief a Yale Law School team had filed in this case. They looked a little rumpled: they had camped out on the Supreme Court steps overnight to secure their seats. As one of them, a gay man, wrote me, it would be "a good story to tell the grandkids." I liked that he was planning to have grandkids, and thought the outcome of this case might make it easier for him to do so.

First-time visitors to the Court are often struck by how close the lawyers stand to the justices. This proximity heightens the drama of oral arguments, as the exchanges are quiet and intense, with no quarter for grandstanding. Deep into the argument, Chief Justice Rehnquist asked Paul Smith, the counsel for the gay appellant, whether ruling in his favor would permit gays to be kindergarten teachers. Smith said he would need to know why the state would object to gay kindergarten teachers. Justice Antonin Scalia clarified that the state would have an interest in preventing children from being steered into homosexuality. As he made that no-promo-homo argument, a ripple of disbelieving mirth swept over the courtroom. A bailiff raced to the front of my section and sought to quash the laughter with his downturned hands. I thought of the Sir Thomas Wyatt line "Since in a net I seek to hold the wind." That was the moment I became convinced we would win.

One way of tracking the gay rights movement is to listen to the laughter attending it. In his firsthand account of the 1969 Stonewall Riots, Edmund White says that when one of the gays in the bar cried out, "Gay is good," other gays laughed. Still in the grip of the conversion demand, gays could not take their own claim to equality seriously. In 1986, the *Bowers* Court enraged the gay community when it characterized the argument that the right to privacy protected same-sex sodomy as, "at best, facetious." While we gays had stopped laughing at ourselves, the Court still deemed our civil rights claims a joke. Now, in 2003, as a justice on the Court made a no-promo-homo contention about wavering children, gays in the audience were laughing at him. Who is laughing, and with what emotion, has changed very much, very quickly.

Our history of gay assimilation is now complete—we have moved from conversion, through passing, toward covering. As we shift into the covering demand, gays are nearing full equality. Yet with that movement, gays have become more ambivalent about assimilation. While most gays strenuously resist conversion and passing, many gays have embraced covering. They do not view covering—even when coerced—as a harm to personhood.

But we should not become complacent about coerced assimilation now. Why, after all, is covering required of gays? Consider the punishment of displays of same-sex affection: the kissing gay couple criticized by my college friend; Shahar fired for a same-sex wedding; parents deprived of children for affectionate same-sex behavior. What were these individuals flaunting that needed to be penalized so severely? Straights engage in this activity all the time, so the activity is not intrinsically indiscreet. I am left with no answer but that they were flaunting their belief in their own equality. They were flaunting the belief that they, and not the state or society, should determine what kinds of human bonds are worthy of expression in the public sphere.

So the demand to cover is anything but trivial. It is the symbolic heartland of inequality—what reassures one group of its superiority to another. When straights ask gays to cover, they are asking us to be small in the world, to forgo prerogatives that straights have, and therefore to forgo equality. If courts make critical entitlements—such as employment or custody—dependent on gay covering, they are legitimating second-class citizenship for gays.

For this reason, I have more intellectual respect for people who say they oppose gay equality and want gays to convert than for people who say they support gay equality but want gays to cover. It is consistent to abhor homosexuality and to demand all three forms of assimilation. It is not consistent to support gay equality but to push gays into second-class citizenship through the covering demand.

Gays should not rest now, but move forward by looking back. From the beginning, the gay rights movement has grasped the dark side of assimilation, and has understood that we should not buy an equality conditioned on such assimilation at the price of our souls. This is why gays have much to say to other groups about the dangers of assimilation. Decades of battling conversion, passing, and covering have distilled our call of resistance. It is now time to sound that call more broadly.

two

# RACIAL COVERING

No one here can tell why the bells ring in the village temple. The chimes roll in widening circles through the August heat—through the walls of the low-eaved house of my grandparents, through the stiff paper of our handheld fans. I sit with my grandparents at the *kotatsu*—a low table fitted over a square cavity. In the winters, a heater hums in the cavity, and a table quilt traps the heat. Then, my grandparents huddle here for warmth. In the summers, we settle here because, in this chairless house, it is the only place we can sit with legs extended. Even at thirteen, I cannot kneel for long with my legs folded beneath me. Happily, in their seventies, my grandparents have a new appreciation for dangling their feet.

They confront heat with dignity. The paddle-shaped fans scattered throughout the house are blue, splotched with white. As fast as it pulses, my grandmother's fan cannot disturb hair pulled taut as a tatami mat. My grandfather wields his fan more equably. We have cups of hot tea in front of us, which will make us feel cooler if we can bear to drink them. My grandparents drink.

Each chime passes through the house as if it is the last. My grandmother eats silver mints from a stoppered glass bottle. I have tried to acquire a taste for these but have not—they taste as metallic as they look.

Her tongue is made of quicksilver. She speaks of how our neighbor has belied his name of "All Riches," of how his long-lashed daughters grow portly and unmarriageable, coming home like switched cows in the hungering nightfall. She speaks of how her friend's Akita died in the summer floods because the dog knew only one way home and followed it into the floodwaters. Hearing the bells continue, she speaks of how my father spent hours of his youth scaling the roof of the temple. At the slip of his knee, a fish green tile rattled the monks at their brooms.

Someone must be counting the chimes, and carefully. Yet it seems they will never end. My mind begins to swing like the monkey my grandmother says I am, from toll to toll, to the counterfeit last one. The lulls between the chimes begin to ring.

Later that afternoon, my grandmother gives me a calligraphy lesson. I fold a sheet of rice paper into quadrants, a beginner's trick that crafts a trellis on which the characters can hang. I pour water into a trough and rub a new inkstone against its slick downward slope. The edge of the stone squeaks against the trough before surrendering to its surface, what is hard being taken by what is harder. The water darkens to jet. I dip the horsehair brush, and the ink rises into it.

The moment before the brush descends is a long moment. In the centuries of peace that followed the unification of Japan in the seventeenth century, the samurai traded their swords for calligraphy brushes. Now, as then, the character on the page is thought to reveal that of the calligrapher.

My grandmother's script represents her well. When she writes me in Japanese cursive, I find her all but incomprehensible. From what I can make of these cards and the etiquette they follow, these are conventional words of weather, of cherry blossoms. So I have never asked her to untangle that thread. Her characters are artifacts I can see without seeing through—I cherish my ignorance of them as I cherish my ignorance of constellations.

My grandmother tells me to think of rain as I form the character for "rain"; she tells me to envision the dashes I must make under a line as raindrops leaking through a roof. I get the stroke order right. I am full of information about these characters—how the bottom of the character for "fish" splays out like a fish's tail, how the character for "flight" is difficult to balance. Yet these ideas do not survive their executions. My brush clumps with too much ink, then the hairs separate because they are too dry. The creases that should have guided my characters now rebuke them.

Does my grandmother sigh as she rubs a red stone in a smaller trough? This ink is cinnabar, the color of Shinto gates, the color of the emperor's rescripts. With a smaller brush, she begins each stroke where I began it, to show the path I missed. How can she produce, time after time, these thinning strokes that end in nubs or swishes of fire? She circles particular mistakes. As I watch her brush, it seems to travel over my entire summer—circling the honorifics I have misused, the bows I have failed to make.

I have come to my grandparents' house in the country after two months in a Tokyo junior high school. My parents have been heroic in their quest to preserve the Japaneseness of their two children. In America, a sheaf of mustard yellow paper arrives each month from a correspondence school. It is homework in Japanese, which will teach us the characters we will need to read a newspaper. As a child, I hate these pages for showcasing my inadequacy—my very name is rickety. But resistance to Japanese makes the faces of my parents close like doors.

The capstone of their plan was to bring my older sister and me back to Japan each summer so we could attend school in June and July. We began at a private school called the Family School, whose mission was to assimilate returnee children like ourselves into Japanese society. The place carried an aura of wrongfulness. Japanese children are not meant to leave Japan, as it is believed only children raised in Japan can become true Japanese.

Many of these students were half Caucasian, what the Japanese call *konketsuji,* or "children of confused blood." Over lunch, we debated whether it was better to be *haafu*—half Japanese—or pure. The *haafu* would say it was easier to be pure Japanese, because we could pass. People didn't rake us with their eyes in the subway, children didn't run after us yelling *"Haroo."* We pure Japanese would retort we were expected to be more Japanese than we actually were. The Japanese proverb says "the protruding nail gets hammered," and all Japanese society seemed entitled to do the hammering. A pure girl described a taxi ride. Her driver kept asking her questions, and grew increasingly exasperated by her broken Japanese. Suddenly, he pulled the cab over and slammed open the partition between them. The words came in a mist of spittle—

he asked if she wasn't ashamed to be so ignorant. It was when his face softened and he asked if she was retarded that she fled the cab in tears.

When I was in fifth grade, my parents decided the Family School was inadequate. How could we learn to be Japanese from returnee children? They enrolled us in a normal Tokyo public school. I do not know how they convinced the superintendent to let two nonresident children flit into his school for two months of every year. Perhaps the urgency of the case spoke for itself. Where else would I have learned to inhabit a Japanese body—to rise, to straighten, and to bow; to do morning calisthenics on the count of eight; to sit ramrod straight in my high-collared uniform; to pass the handkerchief, tooth, and fingernail tests? Where else would I have read textbooks mandated by the Ministry of Education— a curriculum whose uniformity makes the most conservative American defenders of the Western canon sound recklessly pluralistic? From whom but my Japanese peers would I have learned the "Japlish" lyrics to the latest hit song by the Pink Ladies and to mispronounce these and all other English phrases, so as not to be pummeled for being arrogant? Where else would I have heard a teacher try to thwart suicides around college examinations by describing how students soiled themselves in midair as they jumped off buildings?

Perhaps my allergy to assimilation began at Higashiyama School, in Matsumoto-sensei's fifth-grade classroom. The class had a darling. She could have been the heroine of a *shojo manga*, the ubiquitous comics for preteen girls, with her chestnut eyes set off by double eyelids, and skin so vellum-thin blue deltas shone at her wrists. When she stood to answer a question, the other girls would croon *"Kawaiiiiii,"* elongating the word for "adorable." The class also had a pariah, a stoop-shouldered mumbler. He would elicit the cry *"Kuraiiii,"* an extension of the word for "gloomy." Matsumoto-sensei smiled benignly at these rituals. It was good to come to consensus.

The Japan scholar Edwin Reischauer once compared the Japanese to a school of fish, darting one way together, then, if startled, darting the other, but always in seamless synchronicity. Over the years, I would conjure other similes for my classmates, who seemed at times like army ants with their single hive mind, or, when bobbing through their calisthenics, like the chuntering pistons of a well-tempered engine. Yet only Reischauer's fish capture their occasional beauty. I have seen these fish in the Boston aquarium, have seen them undulate together as if each fish were a single scale on one larger fish. This is the closest thing to magic fish do, the triangles of their steel heads drawn to an unseen magnet. I have looked to see if there was a single fish out of place in that silent churn, and have realized that if I cannot find that fish, it may be because I am it.

My parents emphasized that the grades on my Japanese report cards were unimportant—this was an education not in social studies or chemistry but in becoming Japanese. I would have wished it to be the opposite. Subjects could be learned from books. Becoming Japanese required an ability to read my social situation. And this I could not do. I clumped indoors with my outdoor shoes, or called a student in the grade above me by her first name. I passed Japanese language but flunked Japanese race.

It is an exacting subject. The Japanese believe they are a race apart, proclaiming their blood more pure than that of other peoples. Over the years, I would repeatedly watch Japanese racism dawn on white Americans. Initially, the American would be charmed, as Japanese would praise his halting Japanese as much as his exoticism. He would tell me he felt an affinity for the culture, that he might be Japanese inside. I would give a noncommittal nod. In a month, or a year, or five years, he would realize he would never be accepted as Japanese. It might come to him when he went to a hospital for the first time, and watched the doctor recoil from his "butter-stinking" torso. Or it might come when he realized only an exceptional Japanese woman would date him seriously, that her family would probably oppose a marriage, and that his children, if he had them, would face discrimination as "children of confused blood." Or it might come, paradoxically, when he had perfected his Japanese. While many Japanese laud foreigners who speak broken Japanese, many find it *kimochiwarui*—nauseating— when foreigners become fluent.

By virtue of my two native parents, I had a chance to assimilate no American of non-Japanese descent possessed. As my sister demonstrated, it was a real chance. Living now in Tokyo, she has gone so native that Japanese compliment her *English*. I used to marvel at how she passed until one day in college I watched her answer the telephone with Japanese manner and mannerism and realized she was no longer passing. She was Japanese.

Today, when Japanese encounter me here, they often ask if I am half Caucasian. My sister never fields this question. This may be due to physical variation between us. But it seems more likely I do not code as Japanese because of a set of behaviors—how I hold my body, how I move through space, how I speak. Japanese who interact with me are assaulted by my difference from them. They make sense of that difference by implanting it in my body.

In Japan, I realized racial identity has a behavioral component. I am not alluding to the postmodern idea that race is entirely a social construct. I am invoking the more modest notion that perceptions of an individual's race do not rest on biology alone. Both my sister and I have the blood and skin of the Japanese majority. Yet while these biological traits were necessary to our status as "true Japanese," they were not sufficient. Our race was also defined by our behaviors.

It would be some time before I would apply that insight to my identity as an Asian-American. I was, of course, aware of the demand to assimilate to American norms. I had spent two days in my Boston nursery school before my mother received a call from my teacher, who complained I was teaching the other children Japanese and asked my mother to stop me before I confused them beyond recall. At dinner, my parents gently impressed on me that while I should be proud to be Japanese, I should also keep it private. That was the first iteration of what would become a mantra in the home: "Be one hundred percent American in America, and one hundred percent Japanese in Japan."

That mantra shaped their lives. My parents fashioned a racial sanctum within their Boston apartment, keeping their Japanese magazines and newspapers in their bedroom. It was on their king-sized bed, beneath a massive maroon and amber scroll I could not read, that I tested my Japanese on newspapers whose vertical print smudged so easily under my laboring index finger. It was here, too, that I leafed through the back issues of *Bungei Shunju* magazine, whose stylized covers depicted *tanabata* bamboo hung with the colorful wishes of children, or snowmen whose features were made of dried seaweed rather than carrots and coal. The public spaces of the apartment, where guests might roam, were filled with other books—books in English—so clearly meant for show I never thought to read them. I once took down *David Copperfield* from an endless row of navy hardcovers embossed with gold. It was

abridged. The shelf looked gap-toothed without it, so I quickly slid
it back into place.

But even my parents did not keep the injunction to be purely
American in America. Every window of their apartment was fitted
with sliding rice paper screens. As a child, I thought this was because my father was a scholar, that even the light had to be read
through paper. When I was older, I heard a friend of mine say her
Greek mother papered over the windows of her house because she
was "tired of looking at America." I thought my parents had arrived at the more elegant solution.

Nonetheless, as a young child, I took the injunction at face
value. I was abetted by the lily-whiteness of my school, which
meant I was usually the only Asian child in my classes. Surrounded
at all times by whites, I could half forget my difference. Recently, a
Caucasian friend of mine who is a Japanese literature professor
said the object he most abhors while in Japan is a mirror. In the absence of reflection, he can pretend he is Japanese—surrounded by
Japanese, speaking Japanese, what else could he be? Listening to
him, I saw my own childhood aversion to mirrors in a new light.

Only when I went to boarding school did I encounter Asian-
Americans in any numbers. In one of my first calls home, I mentioned to my father there were many Asians here, that they even
had a group. My father asked if I was planning to join it, and I said
I didn't know. "What can they teach you that you do not already
know?" he asked. This sounded familiar—in Japan, he had pulled
me from the Family School because only pure Japanese could
teach me to be Japanese. Here, I heard him saying only pure Americans could teach me to be American. And pure, in this case, meant
white. I did student government instead.

In hindsight, I see my father and I misunderstood the purposes of the Asian-American group, one of which was to resist the notion that American meant white. Yet I still appreciate what my father wished for me. He wanted me to be at the center of any experience—Japanese, American, or otherwise. I will always be grateful to him for teaching me to be bold, to be unafraid of the center.

I suspect other minority students were getting similar advice from their parents. Exeter is a bastion of privilege, self-consciously schooling its students for influence. Many of the racial minorities there had a predilection for assimilating to white norms. Some behaviors were common across groups. Avoiding ethnic organizations was one. Exercising class privilege was another. As if in adherence to the Brazilian proverb "Money whitens," a cadre of minority students outprepped the preps, dressing out of catalogs that featured no racial minorities. And each group followed strategies of its own—Asian-Americans got eyelid surgery, African-Americans straightened their hair, Latinos planed the accents off their names.

The stereotype that plagued me the most was the portrait of the Asian-American as the perpetual foreigner. I came to hate the question "Where are you from, *really*?" that followed my assertion that I had grown up in Boston. I washed away this tincture of foreignness with language. I wish to be careful here, as my pleasure in language feels largely independent of any other identity. Yet my racial identity did spur my will to command English. I could see my parents struggling with a language in which neither of them would ever swim. And my own failure at Japanese gave me direct experience of illiteracy. I collected English words like amulets.

At Exeter, I noticed this mastery whitened me. I liked mathematics too, those rectangles thinning to fit a curve in calculus, "like gold to airy thinness beat." But to excel at mathematics was to collude in a vision of my Asian mind as an abacus, when I experienced it as a blood-warm runnel of ink. And it was in English classes that the teacher's eyes would widen as I talked about a book in a headlong access of speech.

In college, I dated a woman who felt the same way. Janet was Korean-American, a premed English major. We met in a poetry writing seminar. I was drawn to her for many reasons, but one was that I sensed her relationship to language was similar to my own. Her parents were also immigrants—she spoke to them in English, they responded in Korean. We recognized our common desire to write ourselves out of the inscrutability of Asian-American experience—and to do so in the most traditional ways. We disdained classes marked as ethnic, like Asian-American literature. We flew into the heart of the canon: I specialized in Shakespeare, she in Milton.

Our evenings were filled with the happiness of people learning to read, to write. We read to each other from opposite ends of a couch, like a two-headed disputatious literary creature. Much of our pleasure had nothing to do with race. But race was an explicit part of our connection. We confessed our mutual love of the literal color blindness imposed by writing. Our ink was as black, our page as white, as anyone's.

I smile now to see I had the debates with Janet about Asian-American assimilation I would later have with Paul about gay assimilation. In one moment, Janet would rail against a mutual acquaintance, an Asian-American woman, who had gotten eyelid surgery—the "Asian nose job," as she put it. She thought it was self-hating, an attempt to "act white." I wasted my words reminding her that double eyelids were cherished in Japan, and that eyelid surgeries were done there too. She insisted that the spread of the surgery worldwide only proved that white standards of beauty had colonized the world. It was likewise futile to point out she often criticized me for *failing* to assimilate. Whenever I got my hair cut too short, it was Janet who would needle me for looking "fresh off the boat." When I suggested a tension between these two positions, she quoted Whitman. *I am large, I contain multitudes.*

Only in America, my mother would say, shaking her head with bemusement, could a Japanese date a Korean so naturally, quoting American poetry all the while. What had the two countries shared but centuries of racial enmity? When I went to visit Janet's family in Connecticut, my mother told me to get them an "American" gift. I wasn't about to proffer a portrait of the emperor, but I knew what she meant. She wanted me to meet them on the common ground of our assimilation into Asian America.

Yet if dating Janet represented assimilation in one sense, it was also its rejection. To date another Asian was to be raced apart. We would often be the only Asians in a social group, and some would presume we were together from our race alone. Even today, strangers at social functions sometimes assume me to be married to a female Asian colleague. True assimilation would have meant avoiding romantic association with Asians in the way I avoided Asian groups.

Did I yearn to convert to whiteness? As a child, if it had been a matter of pushing a button, there were times when I would have pushed it as idly and insistently as a man waiting for an elevator. Yet the desire to be white never forced me down on my prayer bones as the desire to be straight did. I used to ascribe this difference to the fixity of race until I saw that fixity had not kept peers from aspiring to whiteness. Asian-American friends have described the turmoil they caused in their families when they came home as young children demanding to know when they would be-

come white. And of course I have the indelible image of Arad trying to bleach his skin as a child.

I believe I accepted my race with relative equanimity because of the racial pride my parents gave me. In this regard, their strategy of shuttling their children between the United States and Japan worked brilliantly. They permitted me to access Japanese culture as an affirmative birthright, in moments that shone like mints. Throughout my youth, they also kept steadily visible that my minority status in America was an accident of geography. In Japan, I was part of the majority.

It is a sad truth that one of the most potent psychic antidotes to racism is racism. Every racist belief I encountered in one country had its mirror image in the other, like the Escher in which doves fly into crows. I drew sustenance from that symmetry. After watching an American quiz show in which a white champion dominated the field, my mother turned to me. "Some Americans," she said with wonderment, "actually know quite a lot." I understood then why she assumed I would turn up at the top of any academic class— I was only competing with Americans.

Of course, Americans also expected me to excel academically. During my college years, magazines blared out headlines about "those amazing Asians." Yet the affirmation I got from American culture for being a "model minority" still felt like a patronizing pat. I got more sustenance from Japanese nativism, which toppled the white judge from the dais. I felt like the giant son of Earth in Greek mythology who could draw strength from his mother, so that whenever he was thrown down in combat, he would spring up again, entirely replenished. As alien as Japan felt to me, it was still the earth that renewed me when I touched it.

started to think rigorously about racial assimilation only when I was deep into my work on gay assimilation. I began to read in Asian-American politics, and recognized covering behaviors in much of what I found. In his memoir, *The Accidental Asian*, Chinese-American Eric Liu follows the statement "Here are some of the ways you could say I am 'white' " with the following catalog:

*I listen to National Public Radio.*
*I wear khaki Dockers.*
*I own brown suede bucks.*
*I eat gourmet greens.*
*I have few close friends "of color."*
*I married a white woman.*
*I am a child of the suburbs.*
*I furnish my condo à la Crate & Barrel.*
*I vacation in charming bed-and-breakfasts.*
*I have never once been the victim of blatant discrimination.*
*I am a member of several exclusive institutions.*
*I have been in the inner sanctums of political power.*
*I have been there as something other than an attendant.*
*I have the ambition to return.*
*I am a producer of the culture.*
*I expect my voice to be heard.*
*I speak flawless, unaccented English.*
*I subscribe to* Foreign Affairs.
*I do not mind when editorialists write in the first person plural.*
*I do not mind how white television casts are.*
*I am not too ethnic.*

*I am wary of minority militants.*
*I consider myself neither in exile nor in opposition.*
*I am considered "a credit to my race."*

Liu stresses his "yellow skin and yellow ancestors"—he has not passed or converted. Yet he believes these covering behaviors have transformed him. Observing that "some are born white, others achieve whiteness, still others have whiteness thrust upon them," he says he has become "white, by acclamation." That metamorphosis is also internal. Liu says that insofar as he has moved "away from the periphery and toward the center of American life," he has "become white inside."

My first reaction to this list is a jolt of Linnaean pleasure. Liu's list includes all four of my covering axes: *appearance* ("I wear khaki Dockers," "I own brown suede bucks"); *affiliation* ("I listen to National Public Radio," "I furnish my condo à la Crate & Barrel," "I speak flawless, unaccented English"); *activism* ("I do not mind how white television casts are," "I am not too ethnic," "I am wary of minority militants"); and *association* ("I have few close friends 'of color,' " "I married a white woman").

But then I become puzzled. I could, with minor revisions, sign my name to this list. This suggests I have covered my own Asian-American identity as much as I have covered my gay one. Yet these two forms of covering feel different. I regret covering my gay identity—refusing Paul's extended hand or abstaining from gay activism. Contemplating my racial covering behaviors incites no such self-recrimination. It strikes me that I, like Liu, am an "accidental Asian"—someone who only "happens to be" Asian.

I believe this country is in the grip of white supremacy as it is in the grip of heteronormativity. So why is it I am so comfortable covering my Asian identity? Is it because Asians are more accepted than gays? Is it because I have always had a place to elaborate my racial self? Is it because racial covering does not feel like a response based on fear?

Like many of my colleagues, I sometimes teach seminars to puzzle through problems. A student once posted a mock course description titled "Law and Me," spoofing the golden thread of narcissism that ravels through our pedagogy. As a student, though, I always welcomed engagements in which the professor was willing to risk transformation. So I teach a seminar to explore the relationship between assimilation and discrimination across race, sex, orientation, and religion.

I give my twelve students Liu's list. Julie, an Asian-American woman, says she is struck by the grammar of the sentences. She points out that each sentence begins with the word "I," that each takes Liu as its subject and not as its object, and that each is declarative and unhedged by qualifiers. This sense of agency, she continues, extends to content—"I am a member of several exclusive institutions," "I expect my voice to be heard." But then she notes this power comes at a price. She says these statements can be paired like contracts—"If you let me into 'the inner sanctums of political power,' I will not be 'too ethnic.' " "If you let me be a 'producer of the culture,' I will 'not mind how white television casts are.' " This, she says, is the deal—if you want to be central, assimilate to the white norm.

I ask the class what they think of this bargain. Jean, also an Asian-American woman, takes Liu to task for being a "banana," an Asian who is yellow on the outside but white on the inside. She thinks Liu is in denial, as she cannot imagine any self-respecting minority could remain untroubled by the whiteness of television. This comment engenders a murmur of disagreement. She retorts that we need not speculate about whether denial is occurring, as

Liu says on the list that he has never been a victim of blatant discrimination, but says elsewhere in the book that he grew up being called "chink." She says it bothers her that he thinks any form of English could be "unaccented," and that she thinks of him as an Uncle Tom.

I look at Jean more closely. She has taken a class with me before, in which she said almost nothing, and turned in a perfect exam. What startles me is the passion in her voice. In this class, she will begin a paper, which will later be published. The paper argues that Asian-Americans occupy a kind of closet, in which attributes associated with our culture must be muted in the public sphere. Actors who have made it into the mainstream—such as Keanu Reeves or Dean Cain—closet their racial difference in their very bodies, downplaying their Asian ancestry. Other prominent Asian-Americans, like Liu, cabin their ethnicity in the private spaces of their homes. I read her paper as a primer on Asian covering, and I am startled at how closely it describes my own experience.

Like Robin Shahar, Jean kindles my conscience. I still find many items on Liu's list—the gourmet greens, the suede shoes, the expectation my voice will be heard—unproblematic. Others look more suspect when I revisit them. I realize I accept the whiteness of television casts in part because I dread how Asians will be portrayed if we are included. I also know the absence of Asians from these public portrayals means that Asians—like gays—will be less likely to see ourselves as the protagonists of our lives. I see my students have intuited my long and thoughtless history of not associating with other Asian-Americans—gay students seek me out far more than Asian ones do. I see that my pleasure when I am deemed a "credit to my race" always reinscribes the primacy of an actual or imagined white audience.

Later in the seminar, we read Paul Barrett's *The Good Black*. It breaks our hearts. Barrett, who is white, is a journalist for *The Wall Street Journal*. His subject is his African-American law school roommate, Lawrence Mungin. The book describes how Mungin sought all his life to be the "good black," or the black who covered his race. Growing up in poverty in Queens, Mungin was told by his biracial mother: "You are a human being first, . . . an American second, a black third." She favored Martin Luther King Jr. over Malcolm X, punished Mungin for talking "street talk," and told him to "get past" his race. Mungin strove to do so—blazing through high school, Harvard College, and Harvard Law School with a relentless covering strategy. He laughed along with racially laden comments, avoided African-American groups and the "soul tables" in the dining halls, and never spoke of his experiences with racism. When he arrived at law school, a delegation of the Black Law Students' Association visited Mungin to ask why he hadn't joined and why he was rooming with a white law student. Mungin answered that he was there to get a credential, not to become an activist.

After graduating from Harvard Law School, Mungin worked at three law firms before landing at Katten Muchin & Zavis. At Katten Muchin, Mungin continued to cover along all four axes. With respect to appearance, Barrett's book makes repeated reference to Mungin's sartorial style—he is described as the best-dressed man at the firm. While this might make Mungin seem a fop, Barrett shows that Mungin's attire directly affected perceptions of his race in the middle-class white circles in which he lived and worked. When wearing a suit, Mungin received friendly nods from his neighbors in the suburbs of Alexandria, Virginia. When dressed for the gym, he saw the same neighbors tense up and clutch their purses. Mungin also engaged in affiliation-based covering, stressing his double Harvard pedigree because it sent "another reassuring signal to whites," and speaking with a precision that led him to be described as "very articulate." He avoided anything that might smack of activism, responding to perceived racial slights with exceeding mildness. He also eschewed contact with other African-Americans in the firm and in the broader legal community. As Mungin stated his own credo: "I wanted to show that I was like white people: 'Don't be afraid. I'm one of the *good* blacks.' "

Mungin's relentless covering strategy, however, did not succeed. Isolated in the branch office in which he had chosen to work, Mungin gradually realized he had no chance of making partner. Believing his predicament to be a product of race discrimination, he sued under Title VII of the Civil Rights Act of 1964, a federal law that prohibits race-based employment discrimination. A mostly black jury awarded him $2.5 million, which a mostly white appellate panel reversed as unreasonable.

The tragedy of Mungin's story is not that he lost his lawsuit. After reading Barrett's book and the public documents in the case, I do not think Katten Muchin discriminated against him on the basis of race, by imposing covering demands or otherwise. The tragedy is that Katten Muchin had no occasion to make such covering demands, as Mungin came to the firm covering so assiduously, negating every possible stereotype about African-Americans in his behavior. That negation, of course, was no simple escape from his racial identity. In so carefully reversing every term of the racial stereotype, Mungin was defined by it as surely as a photograph is defined by its negative.

Yet it was only after Mungin left Katten Muchin that he was able to see the costs of this strategy:

> I was going to have to be more publicly honest about the lie I was living. It wasn't that I was around people who were open minded, who thought blacks are terrific. It's that I was bending

over backward all the time to avoid making white people un
comfortable. Like my neighbors [in Alexandria]: Now I'm just
tired of making them feel comfortable, I don't even talk to them.
If they say hello, I'll say hello, but I don't even bother anymore
making them feel comfortable late at night. It's too much work.

Sometimes covering comes in the mindless ways we hold ourselves
or exchange pleasantries on a bus. At other times, covering is the
exhausting burden that Mungin ultimately felt it to be. In either
case, however, covering is work.

As I read *The Good Black,* I keep thinking back to Julie's notion
of the contract. The book is about a social contract, in which racial
minorities are told we will be rewarded for assimilating to white
norms. In my view, Mungin sued not for the breach of his employment contract, but for the breach of this broader social contract.
For this reason, I believe he should have lost his legal case, but that
his challenge to the social contract deserves our sympathy and attention.

I have received the benefit of the social contract of racial covering. Like Liu, I have covered my race and moved to the center of
American society. And like Liu, I understand this to be an advance
over categorical exclusion: "Times have changed, and I suppose
you could call it progress that a Chinaman, too, may now aspire to
whiteness." Yet it is worth asking when we will live in a society
where Americans will feel central without feeling white.

To measure how far we are from that society, I began to
look at racial minorities who breached the social contract of
assimilation—individuals who flaunted their racial identities
rather than covering them. As in the orientation context, I found
the consequences to be grim—an African-American woman was
prohibited from wearing cornrows, a Latino was struck from a

jury for acknowledging his *capacity* to speak Spanish, a Filipina nurse was barred from speaking Tagalog at work. I felt the old outrage, and looked to the law.

B ecause the federal Constitution and Title VII of the Civil Rights Act of 1964 both protect race much more robustly than orientation, I expected individuals to fare better against race-based covering demands. This proved overly optimistic. The courts have made the same distinction between *being* and *doing* in race cases that they have made in the orientation cases, protecting the immutable but not the mutable aspects of racial identity. A racial minority fired for her ancestry or skin color will win her suit in a hot second. But a racial minority fired for refusing to cover a cultural aspect of her racial identity will generally lose.

*Rogers v. American Airlines*—decided in 1981 and never overruled—demonstrates this dynamic. Rogers was an African-American woman who worked for American Airlines as an airport operations agent. This job fell under a grooming policy that prevented employees from wearing an all-braided hairstyle. On its face, the policy was race neutral and gender neutral, prohibiting individuals of all races and sexes from wearing all-braided hairstyles. Yet the policy disproportionately burdened African-American women, with whom cornrows are strongly associated. Rogers, who wore cornrows, challenged the policy under Title VII as race and gender discrimination. The district court opinion, which is the final disposition of this case, ruled for the airline on both claims. I focus on her race discrimination claim.

Under Title VII, a plaintiff can prevail if an employer enacts a policy that disproportionately burdens racial minorities and lacks a business justification. The *Rogers* court refused to acknowledge that the no-cornrows policy disproportionately burdened African-Americans. It pointed out that Rogers had not maintained "that an all-braided hair style is worn exclusively or even predominantly by black people." It further noted that the defendants had "alleged without contravention" that Rogers adopted her all-braided hairstyle only after it "had been popularized by a white actress in the film '10.' " We might call this the "Bo Derek" defense. This defense, of course, turns back on itself, because Bo Derek's cornrows were themselves an appropriation of an African-American style.

As if admitting its analysis fell short, the court provided a separate ground for its ruling. It found the cornrow style was not an immutable aspect of race. The court posited that an "Afro/bush" style might be protected under Title VII "because banning a natural hairstyle would implicate the policies underlying the prohibition of discrimination on the basis of immutable characteristics." The court then maintained that "an all-braided hairstyle is a different matter," insofar as "[i]t is not the product of natural hair growth but of artifice." The court observed that "[a]n all-braided hairstyle is an 'easily changed characteristic,' and, even if socio-culturally associated with a particular race or nationality, is not an impermissible basis for distinctions."

Just as the *Shahar* court distinguished between Shahar's status as a gay person and her same-sex conduct, the *Rogers* court distinguished between Rogers's status as a racial minority and her race-related conduct. The court made clear that if Rogers had been discriminated against on the basis of immutable aspects of her racial identity, like her skin color or a "natural" Afro, she could have prevailed. It made equally clear that Rogers would not receive protection for the mutable aspects of her racial identity, such as cornrows. She was not protected from the demand to cover—to minimize the race-salient traits that distinguished her from the white mainstream.

I can't resist noting that "natural hairstyle" sounds like a contradiction, as the "natural" and the "styled" are generally understood as opposites. To remain purely "natural," the Afro would have had to remain uncut and untended—surely not the style the airline would tolerate or the court would protect. This odd moment in the court's opinion underscores its commitment to the axiom that only immutable traits should be protected. Seized with the desire to protect Afros, the court reclassified that hairstyle as "natural" or "immutable," showing we can gauge the depth of our commitments by how much absurdity we will risk in defending them.

This analysis may not seem shocking for the reason the court gave—hair may seem such a trivial thing. But if hair is trivial, we might ask why American made it grounds for termination. In reading the *Rogers* case, one can hear American Airlines and the court asking Rogers: "Why is this so important to you?" To which Rogers would respond: "Why is this so important to *you*?" It is worth lingering with both questions.

So far as the opinion shows, Rogers gave only a short answer to why wearing cornrows was important to her—she contended that the cornrow style "has been and continues to be part of the cultural and historical essence of Black American women." That answer has been elaborated in an essay on the *Rogers* case written by law professor Paulette Caldwell, herself an African-American woman. Caldwell describes the different reactions she elicits depending on how she wears her hair. When her hair is long and straightened, she is complimented for her "competence, unusual insights, and mastery of subject matter." When she wears an Afro, she is told she looks like a "teenager." When she wears cornrows, she receives questions about the case in which an African-American woman was prohibited from wearing cornrows—namely *Rogers*. Caldwell concludes from these experiences that her hair is a site of racial self-expression, and that "good" hair for African-Americans is "white" hair because "the public equates progress for black women with the imitation of white women." She notes that virtually all novels and autobiographical works by black women writers treat discrimination on the basis of hair, citing instances from Maya Angelou, Gwendolyn Brooks, Alice Walker, and Toni Morrison.

Caldwell's essay shows that a hairstyle can be transformed from a neutral grooming preference into a site of racial contest. Rogers may have been initially indifferent to her hairstyle, as the court suggests through the Bo Derek comment. But that does not weaken her right to resist the airline's demand that she cover it. I have no desire to put a pink triangle button on my bulletin board at work. But it would be perfectly logical for me to fight for such a pin if my dean asked me to take it down. The button would then be freighted with social meanings it did not have before.

To think about what those social meanings might be, we can now ask why it was so important to American that Rogers not wear cornrows, even to the point of suggesting she literally cover them with a hairpiece. As litigation does not provide incentives for employers to be forthright, I looked to grooming manuals written for corporate employees. Republished in 1988, John T. Molloy's perennially popular *New Dress for Success* contains some frank styling advice for racial minorities: "Blacks selling to whites should not wear Afro hair styles." Molloy also tells African-Americans to "wear conservative pinstripe suits, preferably with vests, accompanied by all the establishment symbols, including the Ivy League tie." Similarly, he tells Hispanics to "avoid pencil-line mustaches" and "any hair tonic that tends to give a greasy or shiny look to the hair." He advises them to eschew "any articles of clothing that have Hispanic associations, and anything that is very sharp or precise."

Molloy explains why racial minorities should engage in such appearance-based covering:

> It is an undeniable fact that the typical upper-middle class American looks white, Anglo-Saxon and Protestant. He is of medium build, fair complexion, with almost no pronounced physical characteristics. He is the model of success; that is, if you run a test, most people of all socioeconomic racial and ethnic backgrounds will identify him as such. Like it or not, his appearance will normally elicit a positive response from someone viewing him. Anyone not possessing his characteristics will elicit a negative response to some degree, regardless of whether that response is conscious or subconscious.

Success, it seems, is white and bland. Molloy describes the continuing vitality of white supremacy in American culture, a supremacy that requires racial minorities to bend behavior toward Anglo-conformity. Indeed, Molloy says racial minorities must go "somewhat overboard" to compensate for immutable differences from the white mainstream. After conducting research on African-American corporate grooming, Molloy reports that "blacks had not only to dress more conservatively, but also more expensively than their white counterparts if they wanted to have an equal impact."

Molloy's statement—that racial covering soothes fears of racial difference—is historically well supported. If we travel back to more racist times, we see racial minorities escaping discrimination through covering. Law professor Ariela Gross describes how "acting white" could save a black from a life of slavery in the antebellum South. In so-called race-determination trials, individuals who would have been classified as black under a "one-drop-of-black-blood" rule were often deemed white by judges and juries so long as they behaved in ways associated with whiteness: "Doing the things a white man or woman did became the law's working definition of what it meant to be white." Some of the conduct the courts found salient has a chilling contemporary resonance—individuals were deemed white for their association with and acceptance by whites, for the gentility of their demeanor, and for the straightness of their hair. For these individuals seeking to escape slavery, no less than for Mungin or Rogers, covering was rewarded.

We cannot assume American wanted Rogers to cover in the name of white supremacy. We would need to ask American for the reason behind its covering demand, and to evaluate the credibility of its answer. What's frustrating about the *Rogers* opinion, and what's flawed about the Title VII jurisprudence generally, is that it does not force American to answer that question. Instead, the court only looked at Rogers's capacity to conform. Once the court determined she could assimilate, it assumed she should do so, without regard to the legitimacy of the demand for assimilation.

A reader attentive to dates could fairly ask if I am making too much of a case decided in 1981 and a grooming manual written in 1988. Today, it may seem racial covering demands are no longer made. Black style, Asian cuisine, and Latin music are all staples of American culture. If the application essays to Yale Law School are any indication, applicants feel pressure to flaunt rather than to cover their ethnic diversity. Such pressure to "reverse cover" may be problematic in its own right. But pressure to "act white" may seem a thing of the past.

As in the gay context, however, we should not confuse selective appropriation of minority cultures with general acceptance. The fact that cases like *Rogers* are still on the books means employers can still make such demands for racial assimilation with impunity. And they do: the Molloy book came to my attention because an employee sued his employer in 2003 for assigning the manual to him. Social science data also show that racial minorities perceived to be flaunters continue to encounter discrimination. Economics professors Marianne Bertrand and Sendhil Mullainathan conducted a study in 2002 in which they sent out résumés that were identical except for the names at the top. Half the names were distinctly "white-sounding" names like Emily Walsh or Greg Baker, while the other half were distinctly "African-American-sounding" names like Lakisha Washington or Jamal Jones. The "white" résumés received 50 percent more callbacks from employers than the "African-American" ones. It may be that employers were discriminating against all supposed African-Americans rather than only African-Americans who flaunted. But this just means passing and covering blur into each other here as well.

This bias toward assimilation also surfaces in Title VII claims based on language. An increasing number of employers have English-only rules that require employees to speak English in the workplace. These policies have been challenged as discrimination on the basis of national origin. Predictably, monolinguals sometimes win their cases, while bilinguals almost invariably lose. As one court put it, "To a person who speaks only one tongue ... language might well be an immutable characteristic like skin color, sex or place of birth. However, the language a person who is multilingual elects to speak at a particular time is by definition a matter of choice." Because bilingual employees can choose to speak English, they must.

When I teach these language cases, my students generally feel the stakes are higher on both sides than in the grooming cases.

Language is widely recognized as an important aspect of ethnic identity. As sociolinguist Joshua Fishman observes, "since language is the prime symbol system to begin with and since it is commonly relied upon . . . to enact, celebrate and 'call forth' all ethnic activity, the likelihood that it will be recognized and singled out as symbolic of ethnicity is great indeed." From the employer's perspective, however, the reasons to force employees to speak English—such as promoting better service to customers or workplace harmony—also seem plausible.

Again, I am not saying employees should always win these cases. The ultimate determination should balance the interests of the individual against the interests of the employer. Frequently, however, the courts scrutinize only the employee, asking whether the burdened trait is mutable. An affirmative answer often formally or practically ends the inquiry. But stopping there transforms the descriptive claim that the employee *can* assimilate into the normative claim that she *must*, without any exploration of why the employer is demanding assimilation.

When the employer's reasons are examined, they often fall short. In 1988, a federal appellate court considered a challenge to an English-only workplace rule enacted by a state court in Los Angeles. The defendants justified the provision by observing that the employees' use of Spanish threatened to transform the workplace into a Tower of Babel. Yet when the court examined the facts, it found the employees' capacity to speak Spanish was essential in serving non-English-speaking clients. Far from being a liability, the employees' bilingualism was an asset—an unsurprising revelation given that bilingualism is not a lack of knowledge (such as the inability to speak English) but a surfeit of knowledge. English-only statutes punish individuals not for knowing too little, but for knowing too much.

Dissenting from the court's decision denying a rehearing of that case, federal judge Alex Kozinski supported the English-only rule by observing that the United States has been able to avoid the controversies that language difference has evoked in countries such as Canada because, as "[a] nation of immigrants, we have been willing to embrace English as our public language, preserving native tongues and dialects for private and family occasions." This vision goes far beyond requiring that people be able to speak English. It forbids people to speak any language *but* English in the public sphere, requiring us to closet our difference in the ethnic enclave or the family.

When not justified by a reason that stands up to close contextual scrutiny, that ethic unnecessarily pushes national origin minorities into second-class citizenship. It prevents our lives and our culture from making a mark on the common semantic stock. When that cost is considered, Canada starts to look less like a cautionary landscape and more like a utopian one. Where the United States has embraced the metaphor of the melting pot of assimilation, Canada has espoused the countermetaphor of the mosaic of persisting diversity. It may be time to mix those metaphors.

First performed in 1908, Israel Zangwill's *The Melting Pot* follows the fortunes of David Quixano, a Russian Jewish immigrant who lives in penury as a musician and composer in New York with his uncle and his grandmother. The three generations play out the usual pattern of assimilation. The grandmother speaks little English, and weeps over how her son and grandson must break the Sabbath to earn their livings. Fluent in English, David's uncle Mendel navigates American culture more adroitly, but still turns on David when David declares his love for a gentile, Vera

Revendal. A "*pogrom* orphan" whose parents were killed by an anti-Semitic mob, David is a poster child for assimilation. He aspires to compose an "American symphony," inspired by the idea that "America is God's Crucible, the great Melting-Pot where all the races of Europe are melting and re-forming."

This vision leads Vera, also an immigrant from Russia, to overcome her anti-Semitism, and the couple gets engaged. Then David's own commitment to relinquishing old "blood hatreds and rivalries" is tested when he learns the massacre of his parents in Russia was superintended by Vera's father. Traumatized, David breaks off the engagement. The couple, however, is reunited at the first performance of his American symphony. Sitting on a roof garden, they look at a sunset, which David likens to "the fires of God round His Crucible." The play ends with David's paean to the "great Melting-Pot" that will absorb "Celt and Latin, Slav and Teuton, Greek and Syrian, black and yellow" so that "the great Alchemist" can "melt[ ] and fuse[ ] them with his purging flame."

*The Melting Pot* is overwrought—it is no accident the title has had a longer run than the play. Yet when I first read it in college, my sympathy for its ideals checked my critical faculties. My reaction was akin to that of Theodore Roosevelt, who allegedly called out, "That's a great play," from his box when it was performed in Washington, D.C., and to whom the published version is dedicated. I shared Roosevelt's vision of a nation peopled by citizens who would cut their ethnic ties—an "America for Americans" in which the hyphenation of identity was a "moral treason." This, after all, was the ideal I had absorbed at home—Roosevelt, too, spoke of the "one hundred percent American." Even now, I am moved by the American ethic of inclusion, which contrasts so sharply with the Japanese ethic of exclusion. I question only the price of admission.

*The Melting Pot* captures a great sociological truth about assimilation—that older generations cannot assimilate and that younger generations cannot help *but* assimilate. I can read the three generations of Zangwill's play against my own family history—my grandparents, who died Japanese; my parents, who toggle between the two countries; and I, who am now inexorably American. And yet one of the reasons I cannot embrace Zangwill's play is that the fit is not entirely true.

I think of my name, which is more Japanese than my father's American name. When my father came to the States, no one could pronounce his first name. So he asked a friend to rechristen him. He has used his "American" name for his entire professional career. If Zangwill's narrative of the melting pot were truly my own, my parents should have given me an American name—the Mendels of his generation should have ceded to the Davids of mine. Yet they did not.

Even as a child, I found this curious, especially given that there were names that worked in both languages—Ken and Dan and Eugene for boys, Naomi and Amy and Kay for girls—that odd concatenation of Jewish and Irish lexicons. If my parents had truly wanted me to be "one hundred percent American in America, one hundred percent Japanese in Japan," they could have chosen one of these names.

For many years, I felt my name misrepresented me. The character for *Ken* is that for "health," the character for *ji* means "leadership." Neither noun seemed to describe the quiet child I was. Yet now I see my parents encoded a wish in my name—a wish that I could live in an America that would not force me to surrender my ethnicity. They must have intuited that people with white-sounding names fare better than individuals with ethnic ones. But they flaunted a little, on my behalf.

# SEX-BASED COVERING

The portraits that range the walls of this Yale Law School classroom are, with one exception, of men. They figure honored graduates—judges, professors, and deans. As the seats ripple from the lectern in scalloped tiers that widen as they rise, these portraits hover like a row of backbenchers, whose flushes will never fade, whose hands will never fall. We who reason under their gaze are scraps of unrecorded history.

The seventy people sitting in this classroom tonight are, with few exceptions, women. We are law students, faculty, and staff who have come to a town-hall meeting to discuss the charge that the law school disadvantages women.

In 2001, when this meeting takes place, women have made national headlines for comprising more than half the nation's entering law-school class. The day the story broke, one of my female students worried aloud the profession would lose prestige if it came to be associated with women.

I think she, at least, should be reassured by these portraits, which testify that men still dominate law's upper echelons. According to the American Bar Association, women in 2001 made up only 15 percent of federal judges, 15 percent of law firm partners, 10 percent of law school deans, and 5 percent of managing partners of large law firms. While some believe this is just a "pipeline" problem, others are less sanguine. Confirming that differential treatment persists, law professor Deborah Rhode shows that men in legal practice still earn about $20,000 a year more than comparably qualified women and are at least twice as likely to make partner. A 2000 *ABA Journal* poll showed female lawyers to be less optimistic about professional opportunities than they were in 1983.

The meeting begins. Having started my work on covering, I sift what I hear through my framework. Many comments confirm that women, too, face covering demands. Female students describe pressure to mute attributes stereotypically associated with women, such as compassion, when speaking in class. Others assert peers and professors discredit work with a feminist bent. A mother says a female faculty mentor sent her to a clerkship interview with the parting advice "Don't front the kid to the judge."

But I also discern a contrapuntal theme—pressures that sound like the opposite of covering demands. A woman describes how a student received an anonymous letter telling her not to be so outspoken in class. Others report that professors are more likely to give housekeeping or hand-holding responsibilities to female teaching assistants. Such actions pressure women to be more like stereotypical women than stereotypical men. They are reverse-covering demands.

For the first time, I find myself entirely outside the covering experience I am considering. I recall an English professor asking whether the empathetic and analytic faculties are distinct: "Can we weep for the heroine while we admire the zoom shot?" I can choose to listen uncritically, to weep with these heroines. But I resolve not to suspend my disbelief. I look for zoom shots.

I wonder if the experience of being forced to quash emotional responses in class is specific to women. I, too, felt pressure to tone down such responses, and assumed it was part of becoming a lawyer. I remember being appalled when the "You talk too much" note was brought to my attention. But I wonder now how representative it is, given that it took only one person to send it. I teach many aggressive and brilliant women, who go off to high-powered clerkships, corporate jobs, and tenure-track positions every year. None of my students is in the room tonight. Does this mean disaffected law students find gender an acceptable place to put their angst? In short, I hear myself asking the questions a straight or white person might ask of my gay or Asian-American experience. I realize I am more likely here to be the source of the covering demand than its target. It is not a comfortable feeling.

And of course, if I reflect for even a moment, I know women are subjected to gender-specific covering demands. I modeled my own refusal to cover my gay activism on a mentor's work on sex discrimination. She told me that when she was untenured, she was repeatedly warned off writing on gender issues. But she saw no point in being an academic if she didn't write from her passions. So she lived like a graduate student, saving to go into a public interest job in the event she didn't get tenure. She made her reputation writing on abortion, domestic violence, and housework. As a student, I admired her stringent adherence to principle—I took her class on sex discrimination in a local movie theater because she refused to cross picket lines during a strike at the university. To this day, when I read those cases, I smell popcorn.

So after the town-hall meeting, I take my critical self to the library to read up on gender dynamics in legal education. I'm most struck by the book *Becoming Gentlemen* by Lani Guinier, Michelle Fine, and Jane Balin—professors, respectively, of law, psychology, and sociology. In a study conducted in 1990–91, these researchers found that although women and men entered the University of Pennsylvania Law School with identical credentials, men were two to three times more likely to rise to the top 10 percent of their class. The book explains this discrepancy by arguing that long after traditionally male institutions admit women, they retain cultures favoring men.

In unpacking that culture, the book describes the covering and reverse-covering demands articulated at the Yale meeting. On the one hand, it recounts how women at Penn experienced pressure to desexualize themselves, to eschew stereotypically feminine traits, and to avoid feminist activism. In the words of one professor, women were told: "To be a good lawyer, behave like a gentleman." On the other hand, women were pressed in the opposite direction. Women who spoke out in class were subjected to hissing, public humiliation, and gossip. Women who did not conform to stereotypically feminine behavior were called "man-hating lesbians" or "feminazi dykes."

The literature on sex equality is shot through with accounts of this predicament, variously described as a "double bind," a "Catch-22," or a "tightrope." In many workplaces, women are pressured to be "masculine" enough to be respected as workers, but also to be "feminine" enough to be respected as women. (I put the adjectives "masculine" and "feminine" in quotation marks when otherwise unmodified because I use them to describe perceptions rather than realities about traits held by men and women.) The sheer mass of evidence further persuades me that demands for conformity made of women are not generic, but target them as women. I also become convinced these contradictory demands mean the story of contemporary sex discrimination is more complex than a simple narrative of forced conformity to the dominant group.

To see how distinctive this Catch-22 is to women, consider the absence of a gay equivalent. If gays were in the same position as women, straights would constantly ask me not only to cover but to reverse cover. If I dressed conservatively, I would be asked to wear edgier attire. If I "acted straight," I would be urged to be more flamboyant. But I do not think gays occupy this position. With significant exceptions of the "queer eye for the straight guy" variety, straights generally ask me only to cover. In my experience, the reverse-covering demand is more likely to be made by gays themselves.

Racial minorities are more like gays than women in this regard. If I, as an Asian-American, "dress white" and speak "perfect unaccented English," I will find safe harbor. Whites make occasional reverse-covering demands—"Speak Japanese so we can hear what it sounds like," or, "No, tell us where you're *really* from." But again, I have fielded reverse-covering demands more often from other Asian-Americans, who tell me to get as politicized about Asian-American issues as I am about gay issues.

When gays or racial minorities are caught in the crossfire of covering and reverse-covering demands, it is often because we are caught between two communities. The majority community (straights or whites) makes the covering demand, and the minority community (gays or racial minorities) makes the reverse-covering demand. Recent literature on African-American "oppositional culture" illustrates this dynamic. In response to white demands that African-Americans "act white," some African-Americans have developed a culture of "acting black." An African-American could easily be caught in a Catch-22, but not one generated by whites alone. More generally, negative epithets for racial minorities who cover—such as "oreo," "banana," "coconut," or "apple"—seem to come from minority groups rather than from whites.

What makes women distinctive is that the dominant group—men—regularly imposes both covering and reverse-covering demands on them. Women are uniquely situated in this way because their subordination has more generally taken a unique form. Unlike gays and racial minorities, women have been cherished by their oppressors. Men have long valued the "feminine" traits women are supposed to hold, such as warmth, empathy, and nurture.

The mind-set through which men limit women in the name of loving them is known as "separate spheres"—an ideology under which men inhabit the public sphere of work, culture, and politics, while women inhabit the private sphere of hearth and home. The two spheres ostensibly track the different characters of men and women—men are thought to be suited for the public sphere because of their "masculine" attributes, women for the private sphere because of their "feminine" ones. This ideology permits men to cherish and to confine women at the same time—women are revered, but only in the home. In *Democracy in America,* Alexis de Tocqueville describes this arrangement with the approval typical of his period: "I have no hesitation in saying that although the American woman never leaves her domestic sphere and is in some respects very dependent within it, nowhere does she enjoy a higher station."

For centuries, separate-spheres thinking barred women from the workplace. In 1872, the Supreme Court upheld an Illinois statute prohibiting women from practicing law. Concurring in that judgment, Justice Joseph Bradley observed women were unfit to be lawyers because of their "natural and proper timidity and delicacy." He concluded: "The paramount destiny and mission of woman are to fulfill the noble and benign offices of wife and mother. This is the law of the Creator."

Notice how Bradley does not exclude women by devaluing them. Instead, he underscores how much he admires women—their attributes of "timidity and delicacy" are "natural and proper" and the offices of wife and mother are "noble and benign." "I really like women," Justice Bradley seems to say. "And I really like wives, and mothers. It's because I like women and wives and mothers so much that I don't want women to be lawyers." It's hard to imagine a justice denying the rights of any other group with such affirming language. I would be more reconciled to my exclusion from the military if the courts would admit my "natural and proper" sodomitical tendencies better suit me for the "noble and benign" office of law professor.

A century later, the Court changed its thinking. In the 1973 opinion that began the Court's sex-equality revolution, a plurality of the Court observed that the tradition of cherishing women so long as they remained in the home put them "not on a pedestal, but in a cage." That recognition gradually swept away the most obvious barriers to women's equality in the public sphere. Today, few places exist where the state or employers can post a "No Women Allowed" sign.

Nonetheless, separate-spheres ideology has contemporary

traces. Men often require women who enter traditionally male workplaces to display the attributes of both spheres. If women are not "masculine" enough to be respected as workers, they will be asked to cover. If they are not "feminine" enough to be respected as women, they will be asked to reverse cover. Separate-spheres ideology has modern life in the Catch-22.

A cottage industry of advice manuals has sprung up to address this generation of sex discrimination. Grooming manuals for professional women—blazoned with titles like *New Women's Dress for Success*—promise to help women satisfy both demands. They instruct women to avoid pastels or floral prints lest they be perceived as too "feminine," but also to wear makeup lest they be perceived as too "masculine." They recommend shoulder pads, but not "shoulder pads on steroids"; earrings, but not earrings that dangle; and hair that is neither too long nor too short.

Work-style manuals similarly tutor women in the art of acceptable androgyny. Consultant Gail Evans's bestseller *Play Like a Man, Win Like a Woman* begins with the premise that to work in corporate America is to play a game whose rules have been written by men. She encourages women to assimilate by following rules of "masculine" behavior, such as "Speak out," "Speak up," "Don't expect to make friends," and "Be an imposter." At the same time, Evans stresses "things men can do at work that women can't," such as sexualizing their work demeanor, behaving rudely, or looking unkempt.

A generation ago, such manuals emphasized covering. Recent manuals like Evans's, however, increasingly underscore reverse covering. In her book *Same Game, Different Rules,* executive coach Jean Hollands describes a program she runs for "Bully Broads"— "aggressive and driven women who are completely misunderstood by their friends and colleagues." She cautions that working women "need to be aware of the typical response to the very behaviors we learned from men." "Women," she observes, "are expected to be fair, nurturing, and caring. When we don't appear so, the shock is huge and the punishment is often fatal to a career." Hollands's book is a reverse-covering primer, which urges women to listen, to cry, and to express their vulnerability. Her twenty-five rules include "Lead with vulnerability," "Soft sell is the best sell," and "You are not Joan of Arc."

Nowhere does this double bind cinch more tightly than in the work-family conflict. Women are insistently asked to cover their status as potential or actual mothers. At its extreme, work can press women to forgo having children altogether. As writer Sylvia Ann Hewlett has recently argued, "cloning the male competitive model" leads many high-achieving women to experience childlessness as a "creeping non-choice," given that the years between twenty-five and thirty-five are key to both career building and childbearing. For her, "one pair of figures from corporate America says it all: 49 percent of women executives earning $100,000 or more a year are childless, while only 19 percent of 40-year-old male executives in an equivalent earnings bracket do not have children."

Women who do have children run up against what law professor Joan Williams calls the "Maternal Wall." Williams adduces the testimony of Barbara Billauer, president of the Women's Trial Board, that "every single woman [lawyer] that I have spoken to without exception, partner or associate, has experienced rampant hostility and prejudice upon her return [from maternity leave]. There is a sentiment that pregnancy and motherhood [have] softened her, that she is not going to work as hard." Williams also quotes a Boston lawyer who puts it more pungently: "Since I came back from maternity leave, I get the work of a paralegal. I want to say, look, I had a baby, not a lobotomy."

Many women respond to this hostility by muting their status as mothers. Sue Shellenbarger, author of the *Wall Street Journal*'s "Work and Family" column, regularly features working mothers who cover—the woman who limits her maternity leave to six weeks to make her pregnancy "invisible," the woman who plans "her children's birthday parties on her office telephone while talking in hushed, serious tones," or the woman who jams her preschoolers' naked Barbies out of sight before picking up a client in her car. Sociologist Arlie Hochschild similarly describes how women cover by downplaying their child-care responsibilities, by building up stores of goodwill before having a child, or by not displaying photographs of their children at work.

A critic might fairly observe that most workers, male or female, must surrender their children when they enter the workplace. Yet the degree to which they must do so is not sex-neutral. Hochschild's study of a major corporation describes how top male executives routinely displayed photographs of their children behind their desk. Women managers did not, favoring diplomas and awards instead. As one female manager put it: "Women on a career track make a conscious effort to tell the men they work with, 'I am not a mother and a wife. I'm a colleague.' "

Working mothers also face the reverse-covering demand. Sociologist Cynthia Epstein describes law firms where working mothers are made to feel guilty for covering too well: "Comments made by various lawyers often reflected the belief that a woman's first priority should be her children." Hochschild discusses how men pinned a "mother identity" on professional women by constantly asking women but not men about their children, or by making more pointed comments: "It takes a lot more than paying the *mortgage* to make a house a home."

These cross-cutting demands lead to a classic double bind. In her study of women lawyers, Rhode points out that "working mothers . . . are often criticized for being insufficiently committed, either as parents or as professionals. Those who seem willing to sacrifice family needs to workplace demands appear lacking as mothers. Those who want extended leaves or reduced schedules appear lacking as lawyers." Rhode concludes that "these mixed messages leave many women with the uncomfortable sense that whatever they are doing, they should be doing something else."

In exploring the Catch-22, I never found a woman who, like Eric Liu, made a list of her conforming behaviors. But I could easily imagine two such lists, arranged along the conventional axes of appearance, affiliation, activism, and association.

Here are some of the ways in which a woman could say she acts "masculine":

*I avoid pastels.*
*I avoid floral designs.*
*I do not wear my hair too long.*
*I do not cry.*
*I am aggressive.*
*I am ambitious.*
*I am analytical.*
*I am assertive.*
*I am athletic.*
*I am competitive.*
*I am individualistic.*
*I am self-reliant.*
*I work in a traditionally male-dominated field.*

*I am childless.*

*If I have children, I made my pregnancy "invisible."*

*I built up stores of goodwill in anticipation of my pregnancy.*

*I never admit it when I leave work to take care of my children.*

*I do not have photographs of my children at the office.*

*I do not self-identify as a feminist.*

*I do not make women's issues part of my work.*

*I am told I am exceptional, not like a typical woman.*

*I dissociate myself from other women.*

Here are some of the ways in which a woman—and in many cases it could be the same woman—could say she acts "feminine":

*I wear earrings.*

*I wear makeup.*

*I do not wear my hair too short.*

*I am never unkempt.*

*I am affectionate.*

*I am cheerful.*

*I am compassionate.*

*I am gentle.*

*I am loyal.*

*I am sensitive.*

*I am soft-spoken.*

*I am sympathetic.*

*I am tender.*

*I am understanding.*

*I am warm.*

*I am yielding.*

*I listen.*

*I do not yell at work.*

*I express vulnerability.*

*I perform "nurture" functions at work, like counseling and
    mentoring.*

*I perform "housekeeping" functions at work, like arranging office
    events.*

*I work in a "pink-collar" ghetto.*

Of course, many women behaving in these ways are not covering or reverse covering, but just being themselves. But women are
often forced to adopt behaviors from both lists simply because
they are women. I think of how prosecutor Marcia Clark started
wearing pink during the O. J. Simpson trial, allegedly in response
to jury consultants who thought she looked too "severe." To do her
job well, she had to exhibit "masculine" attributes. That display
caused her to violate expectations about how women are supposed
to behave. The allegations that she was too severe were reverse-
covering demands pushing her toward "feminine" behavior. Presumably unwilling to act more "feminine" in her prosecutorial
style, she did so with her attire. It need hardly be said that a male
prosecutor would not have had to "tone down" his "masculine" attributes in this way. As law professor Susan Estrich observes: "This
woman is in the business of prosecuting murderers, and the notion that she has to do it wearing pink is a stunning indictment of
how far we've come in terms of equal rights."

Given its pervasiveness in our culture, I was not surprised to
find the Catch-22 surfacing in the Supreme Court case law.
In 1982, when seven of the 662 partners at Price Waterhouse were
women, Ann Hopkins was the sole woman among eighty-eight
nominees for partnership. Of the nominees, Hopkins possessed

the best record for generating new business, including a $25 million contract with the State Department. Nonetheless, the firm passed her over for partnership. When the partners refused to nominate her the next year, Hopkins sued under Title VII, alleging sex discrimination.

Price Waterhouse systematically asked Hopkins to cover and to reverse cover. The firm expected all partnership candidates to act "masculine"—to be aggressive, forceful, and so on. Hopkins had no trouble with these demands. The partners in her office praised her as "an outstanding professional" who had a "strong character, independence, and integrity." At trial, one State Department official described her as "strong and forthright, very productive, energetic and creative," while another praised her "decisiveness, broadmindedness, and intellectual clarity."

Some partners, however, thought Hopkins's aggression graded into abrasiveness. They imposed reverse-covering demands. One partner advised her to "walk more femininely, talk more femininely, dress more femininely, wear make-up and jewelry [and] have [her] hair styled." Another suggested Hopkins take "a course at charm school." Others described Hopkins as "macho," or as "overcompensat[ing] for being a woman." Still others complained of her use of profanity, although one partner admitted that her swearing made a particularly negative impression "just because it's a lady using foul language." Previous female candidates for partner had been criticized for being too much "like one of the boys," for being "women's libber[s]," or for behaving like "Ma Barker."

The contrast between the two demands should not obscure what they share—both relate to behavioral aspects of Hopkins's identity. When Hopkins first perceived her career was endangered, she desperately hoped the problem was something "other than sex, that I could start to work on, especially given that changing sex was not an option." This comment reflects her naivete about how sex can be "worked on" without having a sex change. Only one partner at Price Waterhouse said he would never vote for a woman, and others scrambled to distance themselves from him. Yet many partners unwilling to exclude *all* women were willing to exclude a certain *kind* of woman. This was the woman who did not perform her gender in the middle band. As the trial judge observed: "Candidates were viewed favorably if partners believed they maintained their femin[in]ity while becoming effective professional managers."

An expert witness for Hopkins—psychologist Susan Fiske—offered a crucial characterization of this predicament as a "double bind." Fiske first explained stereotyping, testifying that "the overall stereotype for feminine behavior is to be socially concerned and understanding, soft and tender, and the overall stereotype for a man, all other things being equal, is that [he] will be competitive, ambitious, aggressive, independent, and active." Fiske maintained that because stereotypically male traits are valued in many work environments, women in such environments are placed in a "double bind"—a "conflict between the assertiveness and aggressiveness required to get the job done and the image required to fit the female stereotype."

Fiske's concept played a major role in the Supreme Court's analysis. In 1989, six justices ruled in Hopkins's favor, leading Hopkins to be the first person admitted to a partnership under a court order. No one opinion commanded a majority of the Supreme Court's nine justices, but four justices wrote a plurality opinion that, although not binding precedent, has been followed in subsequent cases. This opinion first articulated a "Catch-22" theory of liability: "An employer who objects to aggressiveness in women but whose positions require this trait places women in an intolerable and impermissible catch 22: out of a job if they behave aggressively and out of a job if they do not. Title VII lifts women out of this bind."

The plurality's Catch-22 theory is urbane and naïve. It is urbane in recognizing women's unique subjection to both covering and reverse-covering demands. It is naïve in assuming women cannot extricate themselves from such binds. As the plethora of how-to manuals show, professional women can and do. Yet that naivete may have been deliberate—the plurality may have characterized women as trapped in a Catch-22 to place limits on its new theory of liability. Like immutability, the Catch-22 is another "I can't help it" argument. In the plurality's view, it is because women cannot extricate themselves from the Catch-22 that Title VII chivalrously "lifts women out of this bind." This formulation implies that if women *were* able to meet the employer's demands, no matter how stereotypical, they would have to do so.

Subsequent cases illustrate the limitations of the Catch-22 theory. In *Dillon v. Frank,* the Sixth Circuit considered the case of a male postal worker harassed because his coworkers thought he was gay. Dillon claimed that just as Hopkins was punished for not being "feminine" enough to fit stereotypes of women, he was punished for not being "masculine" enough to fit stereotypes of men. In rejecting Dillon's argument, the court observed that the *Hopkins* plurality had stressed the Catch-22 in her case: "A desirable trait (aggressiveness) was believed to be peculiar to males. If Hopkins lacked it, she would not be promoted; if she displayed it, it would not be acceptable. In our case, Dillon's supposed activities or characteristics simply had no relevance to the workplace, and did not place him in a 'Catch-22.' " Dillon was not protected under *Hopkins*'s Catch-22 theory because his workplace asked him only to be more "masculine."

The Catch-22 theory focuses on whether individuals *can* meet the two demands rather than on whether they *should have to* accede to either. This focus obscures the real problem with the covering and reverse-covering demands. The problem is not that both cannot be met, but that neither (absent a justification) should be made at all. If an employer asks an employee to conform to gender expectations, it should have to back that demand with a reason other than the preservation of sex roles. Here the court mentions that Dillon's "feminine" affect "simply had no relevance to the workplace." It's odd to hear those words accompanying a ruling *against* Dillon.

Fortunately, the *Hopkins* plurality offers a second, more expansive theory of liability—a prohibition on sex stereotyping. The plurality notes that "we are beyond the day when an employer could evaluate employees by assuming or insisting that they matched the stereotype associated with their group." This sex-stereotyping theory prohibits employers from requiring women to behave in "feminine" ways, even if those employers are not also asking women to behave in "masculine" ways. Under this sex-stereotyping theory, women would be protected not just from Catch-22s, but also from reverse-covering demands. This theory would also protect men from being required to behave in "masculine" ways. If the *Dillon* court had applied this sex-stereotyping theory, the "feminine" man in that case would have prevailed. In a more recent case, an appellate court relied on the sex-stereotyping strand of *Hopkins* to give a "feminine" man relief.

Even the sex-stereotyping theory, however, is not a silver bullet.

In 2004, an appellate court upheld the termination of a female bartender who was fired by a Nevada casino for refusing to wear makeup. Throughout the 1980s and 1990s, Harrah's Casino encouraged its female beverage servers to wear makeup without requiring them to do so. Darlene Jespersen, who began working at Harrah's in the 1980s, tried wearing makeup for a short period of time, but found it "made her feel sick, degraded, exposed, and violated." She stated that it "forced her to be feminine" and made her feel "dolled up" like a "sexual object." She also believed it diminished her effectiveness as a bartender. The job required her to deal with unruly or intoxicated patrons, and she felt the makeup diminished her "credibility as an individual and as a person." Even without makeup, she garnered consistently positive reviews for her entire term of employment. Her supervisors observed that she was "highly effective" and "very positive," and customers praised her service and attitude.

In 2000, Harrah's implemented a "Personal Best" program, which required beverage service employees to attend sessions with "Personal Best image facilitators" focusing on their physical appearance. The facilitators groomed the employees and took two Personal Best photographs of them. These photographs became an "appearance measurement" benchmark against which the daily appearance of the employees was judged. Under the Personal Best program, female beverage servers were required to have their hair "teased, curled, or styled" and to wear stockings and colored nail polish. Jespersen went through this training and conformed to the required grooming standards.

Later that year, Harrah's amended its Personal Best standards to require that female beverage servers wear makeup, including foundation, blush, mascara, and lipstick. When Jespersen balked,

Harrah's fired her. Jespersen sued, alleging sex discrimination under Title VII. The district court rejected her claim, and the court of appeals affirmed by a two-to-one vote.

As the dissenting judge in the appellate decision observes, Jespersen's case presents a "classic case of *Price Waterhouse* discrimination," given that she was fired for "failure to conform to sex stereotypes." (Male beverage servers were, of course, prohibited from wearing makeup.) The majority disagrees, asserting that *Price Waterhouse* did not reach grooming or appearance discrimination. This is false. The *Price Waterhouse* decision addressed demands made by partners that Hopkins "dress more femininely" and "wear make-up and jewelry." But it is easy to see the *Jespersen* court's intuition. Like the *Rogers* court, the *Jespersen* court seeks to exempt "trivial" behaviors such as grooming or appearance from the ambit of civil rights law. For Jespersen and Harrah's, however, grooming was obviously not trivial—Jespersen felt demeaned by the makeup and Harrah's made it a condition of her employment.

Although its protections are imperfectly applied, the sex-stereotyping theory shields women from at least some reverse-covering demands. In contrast, it does not protect women against any covering demands. A familiar picture favoring assimilation emerges. After *Hopkins,* women will be protected if they are asked both to cover and to reverse cover (if courts adopt the Catch-22 theory), and they will be protected if they are asked to reverse cover (if courts adopt the sex-stereotyping theory). Women who are asked only to cover will remain vulnerable. As law professor Catharine MacKinnon observes: "Ann Hopkins was made partner . . . for meeting the male standard, a victory against holding her to a 'femininity' standard. The victory lies in the recognition of women's merits when they meet the male standard. The limits lie in the failure to recognize that the standard is the male one."

Law professor Mary Anne Case supports MacKinnon's claim with cases, noting that "feminine" women have often been left unprotected by Title VII. In 1987, the Seventh Circuit upheld the dismissal of Marsha Wislocki-Goin, a teacher at a juvenile detention center, for her overly "feminine" appearance and affect. It was uncontested that Wislocki-Goin "performed her teaching duties in a thoughtful, capable, and professional manner." Yet in 1983, Wislocki-Goin was terminated for "wearing her hair down and wearing excessive makeup," as well as for engaging in other stereotypically feminine behavior. She brought a Title VII claim alleging discrimination on the basis of sex. The court, however, held for the employer.

Although the Wislocki-Goin case predates *Hopkins,* the *Hopkins* plurality does not require a different outcome. Cases subsequent to *Hopkins* bear this out: I could find no federal Title VII case after *Hopkins* in which a "feminine" woman prevailed against an affect-based covering demand on sex-stereotyping grounds. This finding suggests what women have in common with gays and racial minorities: a profound legal vulnerability to the demand that they cover the behaviors stereotypically associated with their groups.

One covering demand overwhelms the others. Thinking back to the Yale Law School town hall meeting, I do not believe women will "naturally" rise into the portraits on the walls a generation from now. I do not think my female students will be stymied by the covering demand that they be more "masculine" in their appearance or affect. Nor do I think they will be hobbled by pressure to downplay their activism or their association with other women. Rather, my pessimism arises from the assumption that these women are disproportionately likely to be the primary caretakers of their children.

As Joan Williams and union adviser Nancy Segal note, "over eighty percent of women become mothers," and "ninety-five percent of mothers aged twenty-five to forty-four work fewer than fifty hours a week year-round." This suggests most of my women students will not be working the hours it takes to make it into one of those portraits. Indeed, as my students are painfully aware, the now-ubiquitous term "mommy track" was coined in a *New York Times* article about lawyers. A related article describes the "frightening possibility" that law firms will develop into institutions "top-heavy with men and childless women, supported by a pink-collar ghetto of mommy lawyers."

A doctor friend of mine says she believed sex discrimination was a thing of the past until she became pregnant. In medical school, she had a professor who became visibly pregnant over the course of the semester without ever making reference to it. "She would talk about obstetrics without ever mentioning her own enormous belly," my friend recollects. "I thought it was completely bizarre at the time, but now I understand." Now, as a doctor and mother, she feels the bite of the second shift. "I love my husband, but he can make decisions to privilege work over our son in a way I can't," she says. "I don't experience that as a choice. Then I go into work and a colleague who brings his infant son to a meeting is praised for being a good dad. This makes me crazy—if I did that, it would be career suicide. Women do more child-care at home, then have to hide it more at work. Men can do less, and can hide it less."

Mothers are the queers of the workplace. It is hard to grasp this point, as mothers seem like paragons of normalcy. But separate-spheres ideology means an identity that is normal in one sphere will often be queer in the other. For this reason, one of my students deliberately hid the fact that she had a husband and child from her professors until she secured a clerkship. When I learned of this, I flashed on how I kept Paul away from my law school professors and classmates. And I feel a rush of admiration when a junior colleague speaks out against the scheduling of workshops after business hours because of its exclusionary effect on mothers like her. I identify with the courage it takes to "flaunt" such an identity in the extreme vulnerability of pretenured life.

What will laws prohibiting sex discrimination do about disadvantage based on pregnancy or motherhood? The Supreme Court delivered a shocking answer to this question in the 1974 case of *Geduldig v. Aiello*. The Court held that discrimination on the basis of pregnancy was not sex discrimination under the Constitution because not all women got pregnant, or in the Court's words, because the group of "nonpregnant persons . . . includes members of both sexes."

When I teach this case, my students laugh nervously. Is the Supreme Court really saying pregnancy discrimination is not sex discrimination? I not only answer in the affirmative, but suggest the Court is making a familiar move, protecting the unchosen but not the chosen aspects of an identity. Just as courts protect skin color but not language, here the Court is protecting chromosomes but not pregnancy. What makes the logic in the pregnancy case harder to swallow is that while all individuals can learn a language, only women can get pregnant. I ask my students why the *Geduldig* Court chooses in 1974 to cast pregnancy as unprotected conduct, rather than casting the *capacity to get pregnant* as a protected biological status. They soon realize the case was decided the year after *Roe v. Wade*. As law professor Dan Danielsen has noted, once *Roe* protected a woman's right to choose, it was a short step to defining that choice as outside the ambit of the Court's equality protections. *Geduldig* has never been overruled, which means the state can still discriminate on the basis of pregnancy with relative impunity.

By passing the Pregnancy Discrimination Act of 1978, Congress prohibited employers from discriminating on the basis of pregnancy. When women face employment discrimination as mothers, however, their lawyers must make subtler arguments, as the statute does not explicitly protect the status of being a mother. Courts have gone both ways on those arguments, sometimes holding that discrimination against mothers is sex discrimination, and sometimes not. Cases brought by the subset of women who are mothers, like cases brought by the subset of gays or racial minorities who "flaunt," will represent the next wave of civil rights litigation for women.

# three

# THE END OF CIVIL RIGHTS

A fter hearing my argument to this point, a lawyer friend accuses me of playing doctor without the penicillin. "It's true the law doesn't shield people from assimilation in the areas you've mentioned," he says. "But it does better in the cases of religion and disability, where it requires that difference be accommodated. If you're concerned about coerced conformity, accommodation is your most powerful weapon."

He's right to some degree. Like all outsider groups, religious minorities and people with disabilities are asked to cover. Unlike other groups, they have a formal legal right to accommodation. Accommodation means that absent a reason for demanding conformity, the state or employer must bend toward the individual, rather than vice versa. In theory, accommodation is the antidote to coerced covering.

In practice, however, this antidote is in short supply. Far from embracing the accommodation principle, the courts have limited it, even in the areas of religion and disability. This limitation fascinates me, as it suggests some nonlegal force is pressing the courts toward favoring assimilation across different areas of doctrine. I wonder what that force is, and whether it spells the end of civil rights.

A colleague of mine is an Episcopalian priest as well as a tenured law professor. Some of our colleagues worry he is spread too thin over the two vocations. Yet he "flaunts" his religious identity, proclaiming his faith and teaching at the intersection of theology and law. When I ask him why, he says it is for his students. "In the academy, being a believer means your intellectual credibility takes a savage hit," he says. "I'm open about my faith to show my religious and intellectual identities are compatible."

My surge of identification with him reminds me that despite our frequent political differences, religionists and gays share a special bond. In fact or in the imagination of others, we can engage in all three forms of assimilation. When Mormons led the charge against same-sex marriage in Hawaii in the 1990s, I was struck by how I could retell the history of Mormonism as I have retold the history of gays—as a movement from coerced conversion, through passing, toward covering. In the nineteenth century, Mormons were forced to convert their religion by repudiating the practice of polygamy. Those who refused—self-described Mormon fundamentalists cast off by the Mormon church—went underground, practicing plural marriage in a form of "Don't ask, don't tell."

More recently, authorities have turned a blind eye to polygamists who cover, reserving prosecutions for flaunters like Tom Green. Chargeable polygamy is now apparently defined as marrying more than one person and going on *Jerry Springer.*

In the new millennium, many religious minorities are entering their covering phase. For many American Jews, the question has shifted from whether they should convert or pass to whether they are "Too Jewish?"—the title of a museum exhibit that traveled the nation in 1997. Riv-Ellen Prell describes women who straighten their noses or hair to achieve a "Queen Elizabeth exterior" while retaining a "Jewish heart." Abraham Korman recounts how Jewish men in corporate settings must "give up many of the symbolic behaviors that tie them to their Jewish heritage," with the yarmulke having "particular significance as a symbol to be avoided." Academics like Phyllis Chesler describe how Jews are sanctioned for writing on Jewish topics. And journalism professor Samuel Freedman notes in his book *Jew vs. Jew* that American Jews are increasingly breaking apart based on whether their primary associations are with gentiles or other Jews.

In exploring Jewish covering, I take pleasure in how the concepts I have been wrestling with have all been captured in the vernacular. (I'm sure this holds across cultures, but my fondness for Yiddish heightens my sensitivities here.) The idea of closeting ethnic identity in the home—Jean's "Asian-American closet"—resonates with the injunction to "be a Jew in your own tent and a *mensch* when you go out." The idea of covering to avoid mainstream criticism is captured in the command to *sha shtil*—to keep quiet—out of fear of *shande far di goyim,* experiencing shame before the gentiles. The dual nature of "flaunting" is reflected in *chutzpah,* which means both "unmitigated gall" and "a willingness to demand what is due." Like queers who seek to transform a politics of shame into a politics of full flaunting equality, law professor Alan Dershowitz argues that the Jewish byword must change from *shande*—"fear of embarrassment in front of our hosts"—to *chutzpah*—"assertive insistence on first-class status among our peers."

In the United States today, Muslims are the most visible targets of the religious covering demand. Soon after the terrorist attacks on the World Trade Center, I found an article about Muslims in New York City that read like a covering ethnography. The piece reports that Muslim private schools are telling children to conceal "any religious emblems," and that "some Muslim leaders are discussing plans for women to change the way they dress, perhaps exchanging headscarves for hats and turtleneck pullovers." It depicts a woman who, "a day after the attack, arrived at a New York City Health Department office demanding bureaucrats change her son's surname from 'Mohammed' to 'Smith.' " The article also observes that "neighborhoods in New York where you were more likely to see Egyptian, Jordanian, or Syrian flags . . . are now covered in American flags, their Middle Eastern flags discreetly hidden for the time being." Finally, it notes that "some Middle Easterners have confessed that they would be happy now to be mistaken for either Hispanics or African Americans." Other sources reveal similar post-9/11 covering strategies among American Muslims, such as not speaking Arabic in public, not attending mosques that preach against Israel, and not giving to Islamic charities for fear of government investigation.

I could multiply examples, describing Native Americans told to cut their hair, Seventh-day Adventists told to break their Sabbath, or Jehovah's Witnesses told to pledge allegiance to the flag. But it should be intuitive that in our secular culture, all religious minorities will be pressed to tone down expressions of their faith.

My student Tom waited until his second year of law school to tell me he was going blind. Having excelled in two of my classes in his first year, he was working as my research assistant on the covering project. After he read my description of how the visually impaired cover, he told me he adopted many of the strategies himself.

Startled, I asked how well he saw. He replied that it was like sitting behind a dirty sunlit windshield. Across a desk, a person looked like a television interviewee digitally rubbed out for anonymity. He said he felt his impairment most in social interactions, as people would think him unfriendly when he glared at them or failed to gauge their facial responses.

During his third year, Tom applied for clerkships. As I wrote him a lavish reference, I had a vision of him interviewing with federal judges through a bright dusty pane. I e-mailed him asking if he wanted me to include anything in my letter that might otherwise go unaddressed. He couldn't think of anything besides his addiction to MTV. So I let it go.

Tom got many blue-chip interviews, but no offer. I wondered if his impairment had hurt him. It had not affected our interactions, but I had not been dependent on my initial impression. I could see Tom coming across as reserved or shy. When he reapplied the next year, I posed the question more bluntly—could I mention his sight? He considered it. "I don't want them to hire me because they feel sorry for me," he said. "But I'll leave it to you." I included the information, and a federal judge immediately hired him.

Tom's failure to reveal his impairment to judges was a form of passing, his failure to emphasize it to me a form of covering. My experience with him underscored again my ambivalence toward assimilation. I admired him for refusing victimhood, and for proving himself to me on neutral ground before divulging his condition. At the same time, I was glad he trusted me to negotiate on his behalf. While he downplayed his condition, he was likely to be misunderstood.

People with visual impairments widely report covering strategies. In her memoir, *Sight Unseen*, Georgina Kleege describes dressing meticulously, forgoing a cane, and memorizing passages she was expected to read aloud. Steven Kuusisto writes about hiding his telescopic glasses, pretending he was clumsy, and walking quickly. The most famous instance of a blind person who covered while not passing is Helen Keller, who insisted as a youth on being photographed from angles that hid her protruding eye. She later had her eyes replaced with glass, leading unsuspecting journalists to comment on the beauty of her blue eyes.

Covering is rife among individuals disabled in other ways, such as those with motor-function limitations. Jenny Morris notes how some people in wheelchairs use able-bodied people as "fronts," relating how she takes her daughter shopping with her for this purpose. Others describe pressure to laugh along with jokes about how much room they take up or whether they have a license to drive a dangerous vehicle. Irving Zola writes about refusing a wheelchair for years to appear normal, and the shock at how much relief he got when he finally used one. When I read his account, it struck me that disability is a particularly stark instance of how counterproductive conformity can be. Zola paid for the appearance of normalcy not just with psychic repression but physical pain.

What distinguishes religious minorities and people with disabilities is not their susceptibility to covering demands, but the protection the law ostensibly gives them against such demands. In laws protecting both groups, we see an assimilation model of civil rights formally ceding to an accommodation model.

The assimilation model protects *being* a member of a group, but not *doing* things associated with the group. Under this model, courts protect skin color but not language, chromosomes but not pregnancy, and same-sex desire but not same-sex marriage. In the context of religion, Americans have historically been more skeptical of this distinction between *being* and *doing*, viewing belief to be inseparable from practice. The Constitution's protection of the "free exercise" of religion distills that social understanding. As Justice O'Connor put it in a 1990 opinion, "because the First Amendment does not distinguish between religious belief and religious conduct, conduct motivated by sincere religious belief, like the belief itself, must be at least presumptively protected by the Free Exercise Clause."

Through the early 1970s, the Court sometimes interpreted the First Amendment to require the accommodation of religious practice. The 1972 case of *Wisconsin v. Yoder* concerned Amish families who refused to send their children to school after age thirteen. They were prosecuted under a Wisconsin law compelling school attendance until age sixteen. The Amish sought a free-exercise accommodation, arguing that their faith required them to preserve their children from the worldly influences of high school. Wisconsin responded with the familiar distinction between *being* and *doing*, contending that while it could not burden religious belief, it could regulate religious conduct. The Court, however, found that "in this context belief and action cannot be neatly confined in logic-tight compartments." It asked Wisconsin to provide a compelling reason to justify the burden on the Amish. Finding no such reason, the Court required the accommodation.

Accommodation is also a key concept in disability law, as the Americans with Disabilities Act of 1990 requires employers to offer "reasonable accommodation" to employees with disabilities. Employers can refuse only if the accommodation would impose "significant difficulty or expense." In a case litigated under the precursor to the ADA, an individual with nocturnal epilepsy, dyslexia, and cerebral palsy challenged a requirement that he be able to drive a school bus to be hired as a preschool teacher of the handicapped. Because the court found that he could have been accommodated, it awarded him damages for loss of earnings and mental anguish.

No surprise, then, that progressive lawyers like my friend think of the accommodation principle as legal penicillin. They have sought to extend that principle from religion and disability to race, sex, and sexual orientation. As law professor Linda Krieger puts it, the ADA's passage raised the hope that "the theoretical breakthrough represented by reasonable accommodation theory would eventually play a role in solving other equality problems, which the more broadly accepted equal treatment principle had proven inadequate to redress."

Unfortunately, the optimism of these lawyers and scholars has been unfounded. Far from extending the accommodation principle, courts have limited it in the contexts of religion and disability. In 1986, the Court upheld an air force uniform regulation that prohibited a Jewish rabbi from wearing a yarmulke. Because courts must defer to the military, it was unclear whether that analysis would apply in civilian contexts. In 1990, however, the Court upheld a denial of unemployment benefits to two members of a Native American church because they had smoked peyote, even though they had done so for sacramental purposes.

The duty to accommodate was harder to read out of the ADA, given the plain wording of the statute. But the Act requires the "reasonable accommodation" only of individuals who qualify as "disabled." So the Court ingeniously applied its ethic of assimilation to the definition of disability, holding in the 1999 case of *Sutton v. United Air Lines* that individuals would qualify as disabled only if their condition was immutable.

That interpretation might seem innocuous, given the common presumption that most people would want to correct their disabilities. But some people with disabilities—like deaf individuals who reject cochlear implants—choose not to correct them. The Court's interpretation also permits employers to discriminate against people even when they *are* willing to correct their condition. In *Sutton,* United Airlines required pilots to have perfect uncorrected vision, rejecting Karen Sutton because she had only perfect corrected vision. If Sutton had triggered the accommodation requirement, United would have had to defend its rule. It may have been able to do so—an anxious flyer myself, I can easily conjure the scene in which the pilot hunts for her dropped contact lens as the plane plummets toward an Alp. But Sutton might have suggested effective safeguards less burdensome on the visually impaired, such as requiring pilots to carry a backup pair of glasses. We don't know how that conversation would have gone, as the Court preempted it. Once it found Sutton's condition was mutable, it decided she was not disabled, and hence not entitled to accommodation.

G iven that the law protecting religion and disability was crafted to require accommodation, I was initially perplexed by the court's continued preference for assimilation in these areas. I soon realized the source of that preference lay outside the cases. "The life of the law," Oliver Wendell Holmes once said, "has not been logic: it has been experience." What Holmes meant is that doctrinal formulations are less important to the law's development than the cultural experience in which those laws are embedded.

The Court has bunkered into an assimilationist posture to weather the explosion of identity in the United States. Already the most diverse industrialized democracy on earth, we are in the midst of a pluralism supernova. That explosion has raised the fear that we are seeing, in historian Arthur Schlesinger's terms, "the disuniting of America." Schlesinger argues from a liberal perspective that multiculturalism should not be permitted to destroy our common identity as Americans, and that we should recommit ourselves to values of "assimilation and integration." His prescription, made most recently in 1998, is part of what sociologist Rogers Brubaker calls the "return of assimilation." Looking at the United States, France, and Germany, Brubaker maintains that the "differentialist turn" of prior decades—which encompassed open immigration, the autonomy of indigenous peoples, difference feminism, and the affirmation of alternative sexualities—may have exhausted itself. We are seeing a renaissance of the melting pot ideal.

The Supreme Court has explicitly cited identity proliferation to justify limiting its protections. The early cases in which religious minorities were accommodated—such as those protecting Seventh-day Adventists in 1963 and the Amish in 1972—represented an age of innocence. By the 1980s, the Court realized the complexity of granting such accommodations. In the yarmulke case, some justices reasoned that if the Court accommodated the Jewish rabbi's yarmulke, it would soon be confronting the Sikh's turban, the yogi's saffron robes, or the Rastafarian's dreadlocks. In the 1990 peyote case, the Court observed that in "a cosmopolitan nation made up of people of almost every conceivable religious preference," accommodating religious drug use would "open the prospect of constitutionally required religious exemptions from civic obligations of almost every conceivable kind."

The Court is raising the bugbear of common law adjudication— the slippery slope. The commitment to treating like cases alike means that if the Court protects one group behavior, it must protect all analogous group behaviors. The Court has solved this problem by moving toward protecting *no* behaviors, safeguarding only the immutable aspects of identity. "Immutability" is the word scrawled on the wall the judiciary has built across the slippery slope.

While weighty, this slippery slope concern cannot justify depriving groups of protection against covering demands. To see this, we must think about the "end" of civil rights law in a different sense, looking back to its purpose rather than forward to its demise. Civil rights law has always sought to remedy subordination—the subordination of racial minorities by whites, of women by men, of gays by straights, of religious minorities by religious or secular majorities, of people with disabilities by the able-bodied. Covering demands are the modern form of that subordination: racial minorities must "act white" because of white supremacy, women must hide parenting responsibilities at work because of patriarchy, gays must hide displays of same-sex affection because of heteronormativity, religious minorities must downplay their faith because of religious intolerance, and the disabled must mute their disabilities because of a culture that fetishizes the able-bodied. If civil rights law fails to protect these groups against coerced conformity, it will have stopped short of its end.

We should not slide to the bottom of the slippery slope, where outsider groups would always win their cases. But we should require what I will call a *reason-forcing conversation*, making the state or the employer justify burdens placed on a protected group. The state or employer can demand conformity so long as it backs the demand with a reason rather than a bias. Far from fostering a culture of complaint, this paradigm encourages a culture of greater rationality. Rationality should replace immutability as the wall across the slippery slope.

To speak concretely about how rationality might help us balance the interests of the individual against those of the state or employer, consider the internationally contested issue of whether Muslim women should have to remove their veils or head scarves. (This is a covering demand that requires uncovering.) In a 2003 case, a Florida state judge rejected a woman's request to have her face covered by a veil in the photograph on her driver's license. I believe this case was correctly decided. The judge did not assume Sultaana Freeman's ability to remove her veil meant she had to do so. Instead, the judge acknowledged the sincerity of Freeman's belief and considered the burden the photograph would place on her. The judge then forced the state to produce a compelling reason to justify that burden. The state maintained it had a security interest in having individuals be fully visible on their primary form of state identification. The judge accepted this reason.

My agreement with the judge in this case, however, does not commit me to giving the state carte blanche on the head scarf issue. In the fall of 2003, a student in Oklahoma was suspended for wearing a head scarf in a public school. The school's stated ratio-nale was that the scarf violated its dress code. In my view, this rea-son, which presumably relates to uniformity or neatness, is not sufficient to require the student to mute her religious affiliation. Permitting the preservation of a common culture to stand as a justification for coerced covering would make the reason-forcing conversation pointless, as demands for assimilation can always draw on that justification. I was heartened that in 2004, the school district and the Justice Department (which intervened on the girl's behalf) reached a six-year settlement agreement. The district changed its dress code to allow exceptions for religious reasons, and the student, Nashala Hearn, is back in school with her head scarf.

This leaves a thornier question unanswered—would the preser-vation of a *secular* culture (as opposed to a more generic common culture) be sufficient to force Muslim women to lift their veils? France and some German states have categorically prohibited head scarves in public schools. The 1994 instruction from the French education minister frames the issue as a prohibition on flaunting, banning "ostentatious display of religious allegiance." Proponents of the ban underscore its importance to the separation of church and state, an ideal that has its American embodiment in the Estab-lishment Clause of the U.S. Constitution.

The case for permitting secularism to trump religious obser-vance might rest on the distinction between coerced assimilation to a secular norm and coerced assimilation to a state religion. Muslim women are not being asked to submit to Christian norms, but rather to the relatively neutral norms of public secular life. A parallel could be drawn to the "melting pot" ideal, under which racial minorities are in theory not being asked to assimilate to a white identity, but to a neutral "American" identity. Assimilation to an identity to which all have contributed is less pernicious than assimilation to a dominant group's norms.

Even under that formulation, however, the individual religionist has a grievance. The Muslim woman is still required to remove her veil. Moreover, a ban on "ostentatious displays" will have a greater impact on religions that require adherents to wear visible paraphernalia. It will also disfavor less familiar religions, as the ordinary practice of those religions will be more likely to be seen as ostentatious, in the same way that a gay couple holding hands will be seen as more ostentatious than a straight couple engaging in the same action. Because even a ban that seems neutral will in practice fall harder on certain religions, I come down against it.

A useful lesson of the religious apparel cases is that no one argues that the covering demand is trivial. Opponents of the law see the demand as a profound injury, with radical Muslims going so far as to hold French journalists hostage in an unsuccessful attempt to have the law repealed. Proponents of the French prohibition on head scarves also feel a great deal is at stake, arguing that if this accommodation is made, others—such as single-sex education for Muslim women—will follow. Religious appearance-based covering is much less likely to be cast as trivial than racial or sex-based analogues. It is a useful thought experiment to consider whether some racial minorities and women might not think of their own grooming practices as constitutive of their personhood in a quasi-religious way. It might seem ludicrous to say Wislocki-Goin's refusal to remove her makeup was as deeply rooted as a Muslim woman's refusal to remove her veil. But only a reason-forcing conversation, in which the interests of the individual are weighed against the interests of the state or employer, will provide adequately nuanced answers to that question.

Those who see slips in every slope will point out that such

reason-forcing conversations will tax the courts by involving them in endless disputes about identity. Here I find myself thinking of a rebuttal Justice Brennan made to the Court in the death penalty context. In 1987, the Court declined to consider statistical studies showing racial disparities in the administration of the death penalty, saying the use of such studies would lead to challenges to all dimensions of criminal sentencing. Brennan dryly observed that this slippery slope argument seemed "to suggest a fear of too much justice." That phrase revealed the perversity of making the magnitude of a social injustice a reason for letting it stand. In the context of antidiscrimination law, the "too many reason-forcing conversations" concern is a "too much justice" argument.

I know the sky will not fall if the accommodation model of antidiscrimination law is adopted, because the heavens still hang (however wanly) over England. Based in part on our Civil Rights Act of 1964, the British Race Relations Act requires employers to justify employment practices that disproportionately burden a racial group. Under the 1976 version of the act, a plaintiff could prove he was burdened only if he could not comply with the employment practice. This "cannot comply" language could have functioned as an immutability requirement, but the House of Lords interpreted it differently. In a 1983 case, the court found that Sikhs (whom it construed to be a racial group) could not comply with an employer's no-turban requirement. As Lord Fraser stated, "can comply" did not mean the person could conform "physically," but rather that he could conform "consistently with the customs and cultural conditions of the racial group." Finding the plaintiff could not comply in this sense, the court struck down the no-turban requirement. (Note the contrast with the cornrows case in the United States, in which Renee Rogers's physical capacity to conform resulted in a reflexive ruling for American

Airlines.) In 2003, amendments to the Race Relations Act dispensed with the "cannot comply" language altogether, inviting even broader protections for race-related cultural attributes.

The House of Lords similarly construed the Sex Discrimination Act of 1975. In 1978, women challenged an employer's age limit of twenty-eight for promotions to executive-officer grade, arguing that women were less likely to meet this requirement because of work interruptions due to child-care responsibilities. The employer stated the age limit was permissible because women could choose to forgo having or caring for children. The court rejected this argument, finding that "it should not be said that a person 'can' do something merely because it is theoretically possible for him to do so: it is necessary to see whether he can do so in practice."

These cases correctly look beyond the physical body to the body politic, focusing not on people's capacity to assimilate, but on the legitimacy of the social demands made on them. They impel courts to look at difference in life as it is lived. American antidiscrimination law, in contrast, too often conflates equality with studious nonperception of difference. As the rhetorics of "color blindness" or "Don't ask, don't tell" indicate, the law's dominant reaction to difference has been to instruct the mainstream to ignore it and the outsider group to mute it.

Of course, the concepts of justice and blindness have long been intertwined. Since classical times, Justice has been blindfolded to show her imperviousness to fear or favor. Until a few centuries ago, however, the iconography included a caution about blindness. It took the form of an ostrich with its head buried at Justice's feet.

B ut now I must temper passion with realism. I believe we should adopt a group-based accommodation model to protect traditional civil rights groups from covering demands. I believe with equal conviction, however, that courts are unlikely to adopt this course. The explosive pluralism of contemporary American society will inexorably push this country away from group-based identity politics—there will be too many groups to keep track of, much less to protect. Indeed, I expect English jurisprudence to look more like American jurisprudence fifty years from now than vice versa. Americans are already sick to death of identity politics; the courts are merely following suit.

We must find a way to protect difference that does not balkanize the country into separate fiefdoms of competing identity groups. We need a new paradigm of civil rights.

# THE NEW CIVIL RIGHTS

To describe the new civil rights, I return to the source of my argument. What most excited me about gay civil rights was its universal resonance. Unlike other civil rights groups, gays must articulate invisible selves without the initial support of our immediate communities. That makes the gay project of self-elaboration emblematic of the search for authenticity all of us engage in as human beings. It is work each of us must do for ourselves, and it is the most important work we can do.

In looking for a vocabulary for this quest for authenticity, I found psychoanalysts more helpful than lawyers. The object-relations theorist D. W. Winnicott makes a distinction between a True Self and a False Self that usefully tracks the distinction between the uncovered and covered selves. The True Self is the self that gives an individual the feeling of being real, which is "more than existing; it is finding a way to exist as oneself, and to relate to objects as oneself, and to have a self into which to retreat for relaxation." The True Self is associated with human spontaneity and authenticity: "Only the True Self can be creative and only the True Self can feel real." The False Self, in contrast, gives an individual a sense of being unreal, a sense of futility. It mediates the relationship between the True Self and the world.

What I love about Winnicott is that he does not demonize the False Self. To the contrary, Winnicott believes the False Self protects the True Self: "The False Self has one positive and very important function: to hide the True Self, which it does by compliance with environmental demands." Like a king castling behind a rook in chess, the more valuable but less powerful piece retreats behind the less valuable but more powerful one. Because the relationship between the True Self and the False Self is symbiotic, Winnicott believes both selves will exist even in the healthy individual.

Nonetheless, Winnicott defines health according to the degree of ascendancy the True Self gains over the False one. At the negative extreme, the False Self completely obscures the True Self, perhaps even from the individual herself. In a less extreme case, the False Self permits the True Self "a secret life." The individual approaches health only when the False Self has "as its main concern a search for conditions which will make it possible for the True Self to come into its own." Finally, in the healthy individual, the False Self is reduced to a "polite and mannered social attitude," a tool available to the fully realized True Self.

This paradigm captures my coming-out experience. My gay self, the True Self, was hidden behind an ostensibly straight False Self. Yet it would be wrong to cast the closeted self as purely inimical to the gay one. In my adolescence, this False Self protected the True Self until its survival was assured. Only at this point did the False Self switch from being a help to being a hindrance. And even after I came out, the False Self never disappeared. It was reduced to the minimum necessary to regulate relations between the True Self and the world.

I could slot other civil rights identities into Winnicott's paradigm. The importance of the paradigm, however, lies in its self-conscious universality. Winnicott posits that each of us has a True Self that must be expressed for us to have the feeling of being switched on, of being alive. And if the True Self embodies the importance of authenticity, the False Self embodies our ambivalence about assimilation, which is both necessary to survival and obstructive of life. The goal is not to eliminate assimilation altogether, but to reduce it to the necessary minimum. This is what the reason-forcing conversation seeks to do.

When I describe the uncovered self in Winnicott's terms, many people respond immediately with stories that attest to the concept's universality. Most of these have little to do with conventional civil rights categories. They often pertain to choices about people's careers or personal lives, like the woman who left a career in law to write plays, or the man who left his fiancée at the altar to pursue his first childhood love. I nonetheless hear the same themes threading through these stories as I do through the traditional civil rights cases. These individuals cannot articulate what authenticity is, but know an existence lived outside its imperative would be a substitute for life.

Parents often respond to the concept of the True Self by speaking of their children. Based on extensive clinical research, psychologist Carol Gilligan argues that children have an authentic voice they lose as they mature, with girls retaining it longer than boys.

(The breaking of this emotional voice mirrors the breaking of the physical voice, as the voices of boys break earlier and more dramatically than those of girls.) Gilligan's work is replete with instances of parents awed by the directness and realness of their children. These parents suggest that one of the most agonizing dilemmas of parenting is how much they should require their children to cover in the world.

This psychological discourse about authentic selves sounds distant from current civil rights discourse. We must close that gap. The new civil rights must harness this universal impulse toward authenticity. That impulse should press us toward thinking of civil rights less in terms of groups than in terms of our common humanity.

Two recent cases show that the Supreme Court is sympathetic to that shift. In the 2003 case of *Lawrence v. Texas*—whose oral argument I described earlier—the Supreme Court struck down a Texas statute that criminalized same-sex sodomy. Many assumed the Court would use this case to decide whether to give gays the judicial protections currently accorded to racial minorities and women. But while the Court struck down the statute (and overruled *Bowers v. Hardwick* in the process), it did not do so based on the equality rights of gays. Rather, it held that the statute violated the fundamental right of all persons—straight, gay, or otherwise—to control our intimate sexual relations.

Similarly, in the 2004 case of *Tennessee v. Lane,* the Supreme Court considered the question of whether two paraplegic individuals could sue Tennessee for failing to make its courthouses wheelchair accessible. (One plaintiff was forced to crawl up the courthouse steps to answer criminal charges against him; the other, a certified court reporter, alleged she had lost job opportunities because some county courthouses were inaccessible.) Again, the Court ruled in favor of the minority group without framing its ruling in group-based equality rhetoric. Rather, it held that all persons—disabled or otherwise—have a "right of access to the courts," which had been denied in this case.

In an era when the Supreme Court has closed many civil rights doors, it has left this one wide open. It is much more sympathetic to "liberty" claims about freedoms we all hold than to "equality" claims asserted by a subset of the population. It is easy to see why. Equality claims—such as group-based accommodation claims—inevitably involve the Court in picking favorites among groups. In an increasingly pluralistic society, the Court understandably wishes to steer clear of that enterprise. Liberty claims, on the other hand, emphasize what all Americans (or more precisely, all persons within the jurisdiction of the United States) have in common. The claim that we all have a right to sexual intimacy, or that we all have a right to access the courts, will hold no matter how many new groups proliferate in this country.

The Supreme Court's shift toward a more universal register can also be seen in its nascent acceptance of human rights. I worked on a friend-of-the-court brief in the *Lawrence* case produced by a team centered at Yale Law School. With the former President of Ireland and U.N. High Commissioner Mary Robinson as our client, we argued that decisions by international tribunals and courts in other Western democracies had recognized the fundamentality of the right to adult consensual sexual intimacy. We knew this argument would be resisted by some justices on the Court, who do not take kindly to arguments that decisions outside the United States should guide their jurisprudence. But to our surprise, the majority opinion cited our brief for the proposition that *Bowers* violated "values we share with a wider civilization."

At the end of their lives, both Martin Luther King Jr. and Malcolm X argued for this transition from civil rights to human rights. Both believed that civil rights unduly focused on what distinguished individuals from one another, rather than emphasizing what they had in common. As Stewart Burns, one of the editors of the King papers at Stanford, observes, King "grasped that 'civil rights' carried too much baggage of the dominant tradition of American individualism and not enough counterweight from a tradition of communitarian impulses, collective striving, and common good." Similarly, Malcolm X exhorted Americans to "expand the civil-rights struggle to the level of human rights," so that the "jurisdiction of Uncle Sam" would not prevent us from allying with our "brothers" of other nations.

The universal rights of persons will probably be the way the Court will protect difference in the future. I predict that if the Court ever recognizes language rights, it will protect them as a liberty to which we are all entitled, rather than as an equality right attached to a particular national-origin group. And if the Court recognizes rights to grooming, such as the right to wear cornrows or not to wear makeup, I believe it will do so under something more akin to the German Constitution's right to personality rather than as a right attached to groups like racial minorities or women.

One of the great benefits of analyzing civil rights in terms of universal liberty rather than in terms of group-based equality is that it avoids making assumptions about group cultures. I've touched on the problem that the covering concept might assume too quickly that individuals behaving in "mainstream" ways are hiding some true identity, when in fact they might just be "being themselves." A female colleague of mine gave me a powerful version of this critique: "Here is what I dislike about your project. When I do something stereotypically masculine—like fixing my bike—your project makes it more likely people will think I'm putting on a gender performance rather than accepting the most straightforward explanation for what I'm doing. I don't fix my bike because I'm trying to downplay the fact that I'm a woman. I fix it because it's broken."

She gave another example: "When I was in graduate school, there was an African-American man who studied German Romantic poetry. Under your model, I could easily see someone saying he was 'covering' his African-American identity by studying something so esoteric and highbrow. But it was clear to me he was studying Romantic poetry because he was seized by it. And if someone had assumed he was studying it to 'act white,' they would have diminished him as a human being."

The coup de grâce: "Your commitment is to help people 'be themselves'—to resist demands to conform that take away their ability to be the individuals they are. But the covering idea could perpetuate the stereotypes you want to eliminate. One way minorities break stereotypes is by acting against them. If every time they do so, people assume they are 'covering' some essential stereotypical identity, the stereotypes will never go away."

I have literally lost sleep over this criticism. But in my waking hours, I take it more as a caution than as a wholesale indictment. I agree that we must not assume that individuals behaving in "mainstream" ways are necessarily covering. My ultimate commitment is to autonomy as a means of achieving authenticity, rather than to a fixed conception of what authenticity might be. (Here I follow Winnicott, who observes the True Self is not susceptible to specific definition, as its nature differs for each of us.) In talking about classic civil rights groups, I have focused on the demand to conform to the mainstream because I think that for most groups (except women) these are the demands that most threaten our authenticity. But I am equally opposed to demands that individuals reverse cover, because such demands are also impingements on our autonomy, and therefore on our authenticity.

In practice, I expect the liberty paradigm to protect the authentic self better than the equality paradigm. While it need not do so, the equality paradigm is prone to essentializing the identities it protects. Under an equality paradigm, if a woman who wore a lot of makeup were protected by a court because makeup is an "essential" part of being a woman, this could reinforce the stereotype that women wear makeup. But if the same woman were given the liberty right to elaborate her own gender identity in ways that did not impinge on her job performance, she would be protected from demands to be either more "masculine" or more "feminine." Marsha Wislocki-Goin would be protected for wearing "too much makeup" and Darlene Jespersen would be protected for not wearing it at all. Each woman would then have the full panoply of options from which she could fashion her gender identity. And in protecting that range, the law would not articulate any presupposition about what an "authentic" or "essential" woman would look like. Authenticity would be something these women, and not the state or employer, would find for themselves.

Group-based identity politics is not dead. As I have argued, I still believe in a group-based accommodation model for existing civil rights groups. This is in part because I believe we have made a commitment to those groups to protect them from such covering demands. The statutory language of the Civil Rights Act and the Americans with Disabilities Act already protects racial minorities, religious minorities, women, and individuals with disabilities *as groups* against covering demands. It has been the courts that have erroneously limited the ambit of those protections. Such a group-based equality paradigm is completely consistent with the individual liberty paradigm. In fact, the equality and liberty strands of antidiscrimination law are inextricably intertwined.

Moreover, even if we shift the focus of civil rights law away from equality to liberty, identity politics will still be crucial. If it weren't for the gay rights movement, or the disability rights movement, cases like *Lawrence* or *Lane* would never have made it to the Court. But I'm sympathetic to the Court's desire to frame these cases not as "gay" or "disability" cases, but as cases touching on rights that, like a rising tide, will lift the boat of every person in America. Ironically, it may be the explosion of diversity in this country that will finally make us realize what we have in common. Multiculturalism has forced us to vary and vary the human being in the imagination until we discover what is invariable about her.

While I have great hopes for this new legal paradigm, I also believe law will be a relatively trivial part of the new civil rights. A doctor friend told me that in his first year of medical school, his dean described how doctors were powerless to cure the vast majority of human ills. People would get better, or they would not, but it would not be doctors who would cure them. Part of becoming a doctor, the dean said, was to surrender a layperson's awe for medical authority. I wished then that someone would give an analogous lecture to law students, and to Americans at large. My education in law has been in part an education in its limitations.

For starters, many covering demands are made by actors the law does not—and in my view should not—hold accountable, such as friends, family, neighbors, or people themselves. When I hesitate before engaging in a public display of same-sex affection, I am not thinking of the state or my employer, but of the strangers around me and my own internal censor. And while I am often tempted to sue myself, this is not my healthiest impulse.

Law is also an incomplete solution to coerced assimilation because it has yet to recognize the myriad groups subjected to covering demands outside traditional civil rights classifications like race, sex, orientation, religion, and disability. Whenever I speak about covering, I receive new instances of identities that can be covered. This is Winnicott's point—each one of us has a False Self that hides a True one. The law may someday move to protect some of these identities. But it will never protect them all.

Most important, law is incomplete in the qualitative remedies it provides. I confronted this recently when I became a plaintiff in a lawsuit against the Department of Defense. Under a congressional statute called the Solomon Amendment, the department threatened to cut off $350 million of federal funding from Yale University if the law school did not exempt the military from the law school's policy of protecting gays against discrimination by employers. Our suit argues that the statute is unconstitutional. I believe in this lawsuit, and was heartened that the vast majority of my law school colleagues signed on as plaintiffs. I was also elated when the district court judge, Judge Janet Hall, granted summary judgment in our favor. (As the government has taken an appeal, the case is still pending.) But there is nothing like being a plaintiff to realize that lawsuits occur between people who have no better way of talking to each other.

When I think about the elaboration of my gay identity, I am grateful to see litigation has had little to do with it. The department is the only entity I have ever wanted to sue. Even when I encountered demands for assimilation, my best response was to draw my interlocutor into a conversation. Just as important, framing the project of self-elaboration in purely legal—and therefore adversarial—terms would fail to honor all those who were not adversaries. I have described in these pages many individuals who helped me toward myself. But there were many more. I think here of my law professor Charles Reich, who wrote a memoir about coming out in 1976, when it was an act of real courage to do so, and who let me write the essay that begins this book in his class, though its relationship to the law was then entirely unclear. I think of the chair of my midtenure review committee, who sat me down when I was the only untenured member of the faculty and, unsurprisingly, a mass of nerves, to give me the verdict of the committee. He told me his only advice for the coming years was that I should be more myself, that instead of reasoning within the law as it existed, I should speak my truth and make the law shape itself around me. And I think of my parents, whose response to this manuscript was to say, with calm and conviction, that they were proud of the man I have become.

For these reasons, I am troubled that Americans seem increasingly to turn toward the law to do the work of civil rights precisely when they should be turning away from it. The real solution lies in all of us as citizens, not in the tiny subset of us who are lawyers. People who are not lawyers should have reason-forcing conversations outside the law. They should pull Goffman's term "covering" out of academic obscurity and press it into the popular lexicon, so that it has the same currency as terms like "passing" or "the closet." People confronted with demands to cover should feel emboldened to seek a reason for that demand, even if the law does not reach the actors making the demand, or recognize the group burdened by it. These reason-forcing conversations should happen outside courtrooms—in workplaces and restaurants, schools and playgrounds, chat rooms and living rooms, public squares and bars.

They should occur informally and intimately, where tolerance is made and unmade.

What will constitute a good enough reason to justify assimilation will obviously be controversial. But I want to underscore that we have come to some consensus that certain reasons are illegitimate—like white supremacy, patriarchy, homophobia, religious intolerance, and animus toward the disabled. I ask us to be true to the commitments we have made by never accepting such biases as legitimate grounds for covering demands. Beyond that, I have sought to engender a series of conversations, rather than a series of results—what reasons count, and for what purposes, will be for us to decide by facing one another as individuals. My personal inclination is always to privilege the claims of the individual against countervailing interests like "neatness" or "workplace harmony." But we should have that conversation.

Such conversations are the best—and perhaps the only—way to give both assimilation and authenticity their proper due. These conversations will help us chart and stay the course between the monocultural America suggested by conservative alarmists and the balkanized America suggested by the radical multiculturalists. They will reveal the true dimension of civil rights. The aspiration of civil rights has always been to permit people to pursue their human flourishing without limitations based on bias. Focusing on law prevents us from seeing the revolutionary breadth of that aspiration, as law has limited civil rights to particular groups. I am not faulting that limitation, as I think prioritization is necessary, and that the law's priorities are correct. But civil rights, which has always extended far beyond the law, may now need to do so more than ever. It is only when we leave the law that civil rights suddenly stops being about particular groups and starts to become a project of human flourishing in which we all have a stake.

We must use the relative freedom of adulthood to integrate the many selves we hold. This includes uncovering the selves we buried long ago because they were inconvenient, impractical, or even hated. Because they must pass the test of survival, most of the selves we hold, like most of our lives, are ordinary. Yet sometimes, what is consequential in us begins to shine.

# EPILOGUE

**THE BLUE STAR**

*"Show me the place," he said.*
*I removed my shirt and pointed*
*to a tiny star above my heart.*
*He leaned and listened. I could feel*
*his breath falling lightly, flattening*
*the hairs on my chest. He turned*
*me around, and his hands gently*
*plied my shoulder blades and then rose*
*to knead the twin columns forming*
*my neck. "You are an athlete?"*
*"No," I said, "I'm a working man."*

*"And you make?" he said. "I make*
*the glare for light bulbs." "Yes,*
*where would we be without them?"*
*"In the dark." I hear the starched*
*dress of the nurse behind me,*
*and then together they helped me*
*lie face up on his table, where blind*
*and helpless I thought of all*
*the men and women who had surrendered*
*and how little good it had done them.*
*The nurse took my right wrist*
*in her strong hands, and I*
*saw the doctor lean toward me,*
*a tiny chrome knife glinting in*
*one hand and tweezers in the other.*
*I could feel nothing, and then he said*
*proudly, "I have it!" and held up*
*the perfect little blue star, no*
*longer me and now bloodless. "And do*
*you know what we have under it?"*
*"No," I said. "Another perfect star."*
*I closed my eyes, but the lights*
*still swam before me in a sea*
*of golden fire. "What does it mean?"*
*"Mean?" he said, dabbing the place*
*with something cool and liquid,*
*and all the lights were blinking on*
*and off, or perhaps my eyes were*
*opening and closing. "Mean?" he said,*
*"It could mean this is who you are."*
    —Philip Levine

Because I know where to look, I can see the blue star even across the crowded ballroom. It smolders at the tip of Janet's left shoulder blade, above the wedding gown. It looks entirely of her body—at this distance like a birthmark. Only at a conversational closeness will its strict geometry reveal it to be a tattoo.

At thirty, Janet quips the tattoo is the best investment she has ever made. As this day approached, her conservative Korean parents offered her escalating sums of money to have it removed, or at least to hide it. But here it is, blue star on brown skin between bands of black hair and white gown. Like a painting of Bethlehem after Rothko.

As I watch her, a ripple passes over her back, meaning she is laughing. She grasps the hand of one of the aunts in *hanbuk,* who has flown in from Korea for the occasion. Janet's voice is wry and authoritative, surprisingly deep for her small fine-boned body. So while she laughs frequently, her laughter sounds like something bestowed. At the reception that has just ended, her maid of honor broke down in tears as she gave her speech. Janet hugged her with a tearless laugh. Why did this gesture—which would have seemed brusque in another—stir such warmth in me when made by her?

The summer between my two years at Oxford, in the midst of my great depression, I went to stay with her. Janet was living at the boarding school where she had finished a year of teaching English. She would start medical school in the fall. The term had ended long ago; the dormitory swelled with the silence of a structure not fulfilling its purpose. Janet had sent in grades for her students, boxed her 572 compact disks, and stored all her books except for the *Norton Anthology of Poetry,* from which we memorized a poem a day. Between us, we could name the nine muses.

Both of us knew that in the coming year we would change, that we would have to change, and that, as her father said on her answering machine, the road to hell was very wide. We packed it—black box of the future in a cardboard one of denial. So, while neither of us used the word "sanctuary," that was where we lived then. The outside world was a picture framed by the window, no more real than the neighboring photograph of zebras on the Serengeti.

I remember watching her as she fell asleep one night, her white shirt tied at the waist. The blue under-sheet of the futon showed her still as a continent against an oceanic expanse. I was a cartographer, student of her. I watched her and thought of her purple dress, her dreams of tigers in the trees, how she balanced on her heels as she stood in thought.

Janet wrote her undergraduate thesis on Milton. There is a moment in *Paradise Lost* where Adam asks the angel Raphael how angels have sex. Raphael blushes "celestial rosy red, Love's proper hue," and answers it is nothing so crude as human intercourse, as angels find no obstacle in "membrane, joint, or limb." Rather, he says: "Easier than Air with Air, if Spirits embrace / Total they mix, Union of Pure with Pure / Desiring nor restrain'd conveyance need / As Flesh to mix with Flesh." Since I heard them, these lines have limned my dream of sex—discorporation, clean mixing of molecules, no bodies or bedsprings, just a passing through.

I watched her and thought of these lines, wondering why I could not love her. If I wanted Milton's angelic mingling with her, why would a body be a barrier? I still return to this question without an answer. A friend speaks deeply to it when she says she became so ill in her adolescence she effectively did not have a body for a period of time. Since returning to it, she finds herself unable to care much for "shapes"—whether people's bodies are male or female, tall or short, large or small. As someone who aspires to read through the surface of texts, I am bemused at how my erotic readings of people snag so insistently on surfaces.

As she started medical school, Janet got the tattoo. She chose the blue star of a Philip Levine poem, in which the star appears on a man's chest, tiny and perfect. The man is a workingman who makes "the glare for light bulbs"—desirous of normalcy, he wants none of it. But after the surgeon cuts it off, he announces to his patient that underneath it is another perfect blue star. Presumably, under that one, another.

Janet and I fought over the tattoo. I told her she had misconstrued the nature of time. In thirty years, I said, she would be an entirely different person, but the tattoo would still be there to embarrass her. Who was she, at twenty-four, to bind that future self? Janet responded that I was the one who had misconstrued time. She agreed that over the next years, she would change, that she would have to change. Yet she said if her future self was embarrassed by the star, she wanted it to be embarrassed. She was entering a time in her life when her commitment to poetry would become more endangered than ever, and she wanted to protect that commitment by writing it on her body. If she became a doctor who stopped reading and writing poetry, she wanted to hear the reproach of this younger self. My mistake, she said, was that I assumed people got wiser as they got older.

So the star is still here, on her wedding day. I still dislike tattoos. Except for this one, which I love out of mind.

# NOTES

## EPIGRAPH

vii **"It is a fact"** Erving Goffman, *Stigma: Notes on the Management of Spoiled Identity* (Englewood Cliffs, N.J.: Prentice-Hall, 1963), p. 102.

## PREFACE

ix **Ramón Estévez covered** Reese Erlich, "A Star's Activism, On Screen and Off," *Christian Science Monitor,* December 28, 1990, p. 14.

ix **as did Krishna Bhanji** Angela Dawson, "Kingsley No Nice Guy in 'Sexy Beast,' " *Chicago Sun-Times,* June 29, 2001, p. 51.

ix **Margaret Thatcher covered** "Margaret Thatcher's rise from Finchley MP to Prime Minister was owed in no small part to hard work with a National Theatre voice coach who lowered her pitch by 46 Hertz to a point where it fell half-way between the range of male and female." Brenda Maddox, "The Woman Who Cracked the BBC's Glass Ceiling," *British Journalism Review* 13, no. 2 (2002): 69.

ix **Rosie O'Donnell**  CNN, *Larry King Weekend*, July 6, 2002.

ix **Mary Cheney still covered**  David D. Kirkpatrick, "Cheney Daughter's Political Role Disappoints Some Gay Activists," *New York Times*, August 30, 2004, p. P1.

x **Issur Danielovitch Demsky**  Anne Taubeneck, "Would a Star by Any Other Name Shine as Bright?" *Chicago Tribune*, April 11, 1999, p. C1.

x **as did Joseph Levitch**  Lloyd Grove, "Jerry Lewis, Seriously Funny: 'Damn Yankees' Star Cuts the Comedy, Then Your Necktie," *Washington Post*, December 11, 1996, p. D1.

x **Franklin Delano Roosevelt covered**  Goffman, *Stigma*, p. 21.

x **"get a name people could pronounce"**  Erlich, "A Star's Activism."

x **One of them has not**  Ibid.

x **Hector St. John de Crèvecoeur's**  "I could point out to you a family whose grandfather was an English-man, whose wife was Dutch, whose son married a French woman, and whose present four sons have now four wives of different nations. *He* is an American, who leaving behind him all his ancient prejudices and manners, receives new ones from the new mode of life he has embraced. . . . Here individuals of all nations are melted into a new race of men." J. Hector St. John de Crèvecoeur (Michel Guillaume Jean de Crèvecoeur), "Letter III," *Letters from an American Farmer* (1782; New York: Fox, Duffield, 1904), pp. 54–55.

x **Israel Zangwill's play**  "America is God's Crucible, the great Melting-Pot where all the races of Europe are melting and reforming!" Israel Zangwill, *The Melting Pot: A Drama in Four Acts*, Act I (New York: Macmillan Company, 1909), p. 33.

x **Only with the civil rights movement**  Rogers Brubaker, "The Return of Assimilation? Changing Perspectives on Immigration and Its Sequels in France, Germany, and the United States," *Ethnic and Racial Studies* 24 (July 2001): 531–48; Nathan Glazer and Daniel Patrick Moynihan, *Beyond the Melting Pot: The Negroes, Puerto Ricans, Jews, Italians, and Irish of New York City* (Cambridge: MIT Press, 1970), pp. 288–315.

xi **Fearful that we are spinning apart**  Arthur M. Schlesinger Jr., *The Disuniting of America* (Knoxville, Tenn.: Whittle Direct Books, 1991).

xi  the "return of assimilation"   Brubaker, "The Return of Assimilation?"

xii  I follow the Romantics here   Gerald N. Izenberg, *Impossible Individuality: Romanticism, Revolution, and the Origins of Modern Selfhood* (Princeton: Princeton University Press, 1992).


## AN UNCOVERED SELF

5  Impatient, he quoted Marvin Bell's line   "The growth of a poet sometimes seems to me to be related to his or her becoming less and less embarrassed about more and more." Marvin Bell, "Influences," in *Old Snow Just Melting: Essays and Interviews* (Ann Arbor: University of Michigan Press, 1983), p. 25.

7  Some say this commonality   "[The character for sexuality] literally meant 'color,' referring in Buddhist philosophy to the world of visually perceptible forms toward which lower beings, including humans, experienced desire, thus hindering their progress along the path of enlightenment." Gregory M. Pflugfelder, *Cartographies of Desire: Male-Male Sexuality in Japanese Discourse, 1600–1950* (Berkeley: University of California Press, 1999), p. 25.

14  He urged me to get   William B. Rubenstein, *Cases and Materials on Sexual Orientation and the Law,* 2nd ed. (St. Paul, Minn.: West Publishing Company, 1997).

14  I could see the difference   Ibid., p. xxii.

16  The published paper   Kenji Yoshino, "Suspect Symbols: The Literary Argument for Heightened Scrutiny for Gays," *Columbia Law Review* 96 (November 1996): 1753–1834. The paper was cited in *Boy Scouts of America v. Dale,* 530 U.S. 640, 696 (2000) (Stevens, J., dissenting); *Hernandez-Montiel v. INS,* 225 F.3d 1084, 1093 (9th Cir. 2000) (finding that gay men with female sexual identities in Mexico can constitute a particular social group for asylum purposes); *Able v. United States,* 968 F. Supp. 850, 852, 854, 861 (E.D.N.Y. 1997) (holding that classifications on the basis of sexual orientation are suspect), *rev'd on other grounds, Able v. United States,* 155 F.3d 628 (2d Cir. 1998).

18  After discussing passing, Goffman observes   Goffman, *Stigma,* p. 102.

18  Roosevelt was not passing   Ibid., p. 21.

19  Through the middle of the twentieth century   Jonathan Katz, *Gay American History: Lesbians and Gay Men in the U.S.A.; A Documentary* (New York:

Harper & Row, 1976), pp. 129–207. Methods such as drug therapy and electroshock therapy continue to be used (if rarely) in conversion therapy attempts. The Ninth Circuit Court of Appeals most recently addressed the practice in *Pitcherskaia v. INS*, 118 F.3d 641 (9th Cir. 1997).

19  **This shift can be seen**    *Policy Concerning Homosexuality in the Armed Forces, U.S. Code* 10 (1994), § 654; *Qualification Standards for Enlistment, Appointment, and Induction*, Department of Defense Directive 1304.2b.

19  **The contemporary resistance to gay marriage**    See, for instance, Pam Belluck, "Massachusetts Plans to Revisit Amendment on Gay Marriage," *New York Times*, May 10, 2005, p. A13; Charisse Jones, "Gay-marriage Debate Still Intense a Year Later," *USA Today*, May 17, 2005, p. 1A; Brian Virasami, "Coalition Criticizes Ruling Supporting Gay Marriage," *Newsday*, February 15, 2005, p. A19.

21  **All civil rights groups**    "Dress White" was the title of a report to African-American executives in Chicago. John T. Molloy, *New Dress for Success* (New York: Warner Books, 1988), p. 198. Paul Barrett notes the demand to abandon "street talk" for " 'proper' English." Paul M. Barrett, *The Good Black: A True Story of Race in America* (New York: Penguin Books, 1999). Frank Wu discusses the tension between assimilation and multiculturalism for Asian-Americans in *Yellow* (New York: Basic Books, 2002), pp. 234–38. Arlie Russell Hochschild writes about the demands on working women to minimize the needs of their children in *The Second Shift* (New York: Viking Penguin, 1989). A recent art exhibit organized by the Jewish Museum in New York toured the country under the exhibition title "Too Jewish?" See Norman L. Kleeblatt, ed., *Too Jewish? Challenging Traditional Identities* (New York: Jewish Museum; New Brunswick, N.J.: Rutgers University Press, 1996). Especially after 9/11, Muslims have been told to conceal religious emblems and religious dress and to refrain from speaking Arabic in public. See Leslie Goffe, "Not Responsible," *Middle East*, November 1, 2001, p. 46. Irving Kenneth Zola writes about how he refused a wheelchair for years to appear normal in *Missing Pieces: A Chronicle of Living with a Disability* (Philadelphia: Temple University Press, 1982), pp. 205–6.

22  **Alan Dershowitz writes**    Dershowitz attributes the observation to Alan Stone, and admits that it was "probably overstated." Alan M. Dershowitz, *Chutzpah* (Boston: Little, Brown, 1991), p. 79. Dershowitz also notes that Felix Frankfurter, the first Jew to become a professor at Harvard Law

School, went out of his way to describe himself as "a Harvard Law professor who happened to be a Jew," and not as "a Jewish professor at the Harvard Law School." Ibid., p. 79 n. *.

23   **As the sociologist Milton Gordon**   See Milton Gordon, *Assimilation in American Life: The Role of Race, Religion, and National Origins* (New York: Oxford University Press, 1964).

23   **To my chagrin**   *Civil Rights Act of 1964 tit. VII, U.S. Code* 42 (2000), § 2000e; U.S. Constitution, Amendment XIV. Although the Fourteenth Amendment applies on its face only to the states, it has been understood to apply with equal force to the federal government through the Fifth Amendment Due Process Clause. See *Bolling v. Sharpe*, 347 U.S. 497 (1954).

24   **courts will often not protect**   Speaking a language: *Garcia v. Gloor*, 618 F.2d 264, 270 (5th Cir. 1980) (see discussion pp. 137–39). Having a child: *Piantanida v. Wyman Center, Inc.*, 116 F.3d 340 (8th Cir. 1997) (see discussion pp. 163–64). Holding a same-sex commitment ceremony: *Shahar v. Bowers*, 70 F.3d 1218 (11th Cir. 1995) (see discussion pp. 93–101). Wearing religious garb: *Goldman v. Weinberger*, 475 U.S. 503 (1986) (see discussion pp. 174–75, 178–80). Refusing to "correct" a disability: *Sutton v. United Air Lines*, 527 U.S. 471 (1999) (see discussion pp. 174–75).

25   **As queer theorists have recognized**   See Michael Warner, *The Trouble with Normal: Sex, Politics, and the Ethics of Queer Life* (Cambridge: Harvard University Press, 1999), pp. 55–61.

26   **"poetry makes nothing happen"**   W. H. Auden, "In Memory of W. B. Yeats," in *Collected Poems: Auden*, ed. Edward Mendelson (New York: Vintage, 1991), p. 247.

26   **Now I see Auden meant**   Richard Posner makes this point in *Law and Literature: A Misunderstood Relation* (Cambridge: Harvard University Press, 1998), p. 305.


GAY CONVERSION

32   **his *Confessions***   "Let the last trump sound when it will, I shall come forward with this work in my hand, to present myself before my Sovereign Judge." Jean-Jacques Rousseau, *The Confessions*, trans. J. M. Cohen (1781; New York: Penguin Books, 1953), p. 17.

32   **Guy T. Olmstead**   E. S. Talbot and Havelock Ellis, "A Case of Developmen-

tal Degenerative Insanity, with Sexual Inversion, Melancholia, Following Removal of Testicle, Attempted Murder and Suicide," *Journal of Medical Science* 42 (April 1896): 341–44, reprinted in part in "1896–1897: Drs. Havelock Ellis and E. S. Talbot: Castration," in Katz, *Gay American History,* pp. 140–43.

32 "Since the operation"  Katz, *Gay American History,* p. 142.

33 **Kronemeyer**  Robert Kronemeyer, *Overcoming Homosexuality* (New York: Macmillan Publishing, 1980), p. 87.

33 **In a 1941 procedure**  Joseph Friedlander and Ralph S. Banay, "Psychosis Following Lobotomy in a Case of Sexual Psychopathology: Report of a Case," *Archives of Neurology and Psychiatry* 59 (1948): 303–11, 315, 321, reprinted in part in Katz, *Gay American History,* p. 177.

33 **The procedure was "repeated"**  Ibid., p. 181.

33 **The doctors reviewing the operation**  Ibid.

33 **A 1935 presentation**  Louis William Max, "Breaking Up a Homosexual Fixation by the Condition Reaction Technique: A Case Study," *Psychological Bulletin* 32 (1935): 734, reprinted in part in "1935: Dr. Louis W. Max: Aversion Therapy (Electric)," in Katz, *Gay American History,* p. 164.

33 **A patient describes**  Jonathan Katz, "1974: Anonymous: Electroshock," in Katz, *Gay American History,* pp. 203–4.

34 **A 1963 account**  Michael M. Miller, "Hypnotic-Aversion Treatment of Homosexuality," *Journal of the National Medical Association* 55 (1963): 411–13, 415, reprinted in part in "1963: Dr. Michael M. Miller: Aversion Therapy (Hypnotic)," in Katz, *Gay American History,* p. 194.

34 **A similar 1967 study**  Joseph R. Cautela, "Covert Sensitization," *Psychological Reports* 20 (1967): 464–65, reprinted in part in "1967: Joseph R. Cautela: Aversion Therapy ('Covert Sensitization')," in Katz, *Gay American History,* p. 198.

35 **In his introduction**  Jonathan Katz, "Treatment, 1884–1974: Introduction," in *Gay American History,* p. 131.

35 **As Timothy Murphy observes**  Timothy Murphy, *Gay Science: The Ethics of Sexual Orientation Research* (New York: Columbia University Press, 1997), pp. 82–83.

35 **Both proponents and opponents**  For reliance on Freud by proponents of conversion therapies, see Kronemeyer, *Overcoming Homosexuality;* Joseph Nicolosi, *Reparative Therapy of Male Homosexuality* (Northvale, N.J.: Jason

Aronson, 1997); Charles W. Socarides, *Homosexuality: A Freedom Too Far* (Phoenix: Adam Margrave Books, 1995). For reliance on Freud by opponents of conversion therapies, see Simon LeVay, *Queer Science: The Use and Abuse of Research into Homosexuality* (Cambridge: MIT Press, 1996); Murphy, *Gay Science.*

36  **Freud's answer was clear**   Freud notes "the universal bisexuality of human beings." Sigmund Freud, *The Psychogenesis of a Case of Homosexuality in a Woman* (1920), reprinted in *The Standard Edition of the Complete Psychological Works of Sigmund Freud,* vol. 18, ed. and trans. James Strachey (London: Hogarth Press, 1955), p. 157. "In all of us, throughout life, the libido normally oscillates between male and female objects." Ibid., p. 158. "Man is an animal organism with . . . an unmistakably bisexual disposition." Freud, *Civilization and Its Discontents* (1930), in *Standard Edition,* vol. 21, p. 105 n. 3. The term "bisexuality," however, had a much broader valence for Freud than it possesses for most contemporary readers. For Freud, bisexuality at least at times referred to the belief that human beings contained elements of both maleness and femaleness within them. Freud, *Three Essays on the Theory of Sexuality* (1905), in *Standard Edition,* vol. 7, p. 141; Freud, *A Child Is Being Beaten: A Contribution to the Study of the Origin of Sexual Perversion* (1919), in *Standard Edition,* vol. 17, p. 202. This is not to say that Freud believed all human beings were genitally hermaphroditic, but rather that he believed that "in every normal male or female individual, traces are found of the apparatus of the opposite sex." Freud, *Three Essays,* p. 141. Under this particular formulation, bisexuality described how individuals contained both men and women (a conceptualization I call sex-based bisexuality) rather than how they desired both men and women (the contemporary conceptualization of the term "bisexuality," which I here call orientation-based bisexuality). Yet in Freud's view, sex-based bisexuality entailed orientation-based bisexuality. If "every human being displayed both male and female instinctual impulses," and one of those instincts was sexual, then for Freud it followed that "each individual [sought] to satisfy both male and female wishes in his sexual life." Freud, *Civilization and Its Discontents,* pp. 105–6 n. 3. Put differently, if the psyche had both male and female aspects, the psyche must contain desire for both men and women, assuming, of course, that these male and female aspects were themselves heterosexual. Ironically, then, this belief in universal orientation-based bisexuality derived from an

unarticulated belief in the universal heterosexuality of the male and female aspects of the psyche. Through such machinations, Freud arrived at the conclusion that "every human being [was an orientation-based] bisexual" and that the "libido [was] distributed either in a manifest or latent fashion, over objects of both sexes." Freud, *Analysis Terminable and Interminable* (1937), in *Standard Edition,* vol. 23, p. 244.

36  **The belief that homosexuality**    See, for example, Richard Cohen, *Coming Out Straight: Understanding and Healing Homosexuality* (Winchester, Va.: Oakhill Press, 2000).

36  **His famous 1935 letter**    Sigmund Freud to Anonymous Mother (April 9, 1935), in "A Letter from Freud," *American Journal of Psychiatry* 107 (1951): 786–87.

36  **In *The Psychogenesis***    Freud, *The Psychogenesis of a Case of Homosexuality in a Woman,* p. 151.

36  **In his letter**    Freud, "Letter from Freud," p. 787.

37  **He put it more bluntly**    Kenneth Lewes, *The Psychoanalytic Theory of Male Homosexuality* (New York: Jason Aronson, 1988), p. 32, quoting Sigmund Freud, Brief, *Die Zeit* (Vienna), October 27, 1903.

37  **"produced by a certain arrest"**    Freud, "Letter from Freud," p. 787.

37  **Even more disturbingly**    Jack Drescher, "I'm Your Handyman: A History of Reparative Therapies," *Journal of Homosexuality* 36 (June 1998): 22.

37  **Insofar as homosexuality was concerned**    Lewes, *The Psychoanalytic Theory of Male Homosexuality,* p. 16.

37  **The new generation of therapists**    See, for example, Irving Bieber et al., *Homosexuality: A Psychoanalytic Study* (New York: Basic Books, 1962), pp. 44–117; Albert Ellis, *Homosexuality: Its Causes and Cure* (New York: Lyle Stuart, 1965); Sandor Rado, *Adaptational Psychodynamics: Motivation and Control* (New York: Science House, 1969); Charles W. Socarides, *The Overt Homosexual* (New York: Grune and Stratton, 1968).

37  **The year after Freud's death**    Sandor Rado, "A Critical Examination of the Concept of Bisexuality," in *Psychoanalysis of Behavior: Collected Papers* (New York: Grune and Stratton, 1956).

37  **His proof**    Ibid., pp. 145–46.

37  **He believed antisex views**    Rado, *Adaptational Psychodynamics,* p. 212.

38  **Bieber worked up the popular model**    Bieber observes that mothers "promoted homosexuality" by falling into a pattern described as "close-binding-

intimate." Bieber et al., *Homosexuality,* pp. 79–81. He also argues that "the pathologic seeking of need fulfillment from men has a clear point of origin in fathers who were detached." Ibid., p. 114.

38  **Socarides added**  Socarides observes that lesbianism derives from the subject's "dread of . . . a malevolent mother" and a conviction that the father "rejects and hates her." Charles W. Socarides, *Homosexuality* (New York: Jason Aronson, 1978), p. 188.

38  **The most systematic study**  Ronald Bayer, *Homosexuality and American Psychiatry* (Princeton: Princeton University Press, 1987), pp. 29–30.

38  **Published in 1962**  Bieber et al., *Homosexuality,* p. 319.

38  **Of the seventy-two**  Ibid., p. 276.

38  **the conversion therapists**  Rado, *Adaptational Psychodynamics,* p. 213.

38  **Ellis and Bieber**  Albert Ellis, *Reason and Emotion in Psychotherapy* (Secaucus, N.J.: Citadel Press, 1962), p. 242; Bieber et al., *Homosexuality,* p. 18.

38  **The first edition of the *Diagnostic***  The manual lists "homosexuality" as an instance of "pathologic behavior." Committee on Nomenclature and Statistics of the American Psychiatric Association, *Diagnostic and Statistical Manual of Mental Disorders* (New York: American Psychiatric Association, 1952), pp. 38–39.

38  **These therapists ushered in**  I take the term from Drescher, "I'm Your Handyman," pp. 25–26.

39  **In his memoir**  Martin Duberman, *Cures: A Gay Man's Odyssey* (New York: Dutton Books, 1991). Duberman discusses the first therapy on pp. 32–36, the second therapy on pp. 44–46, and the third therapy on pp. 93–115.

39  **Duberman describes**  Ibid., p. 31.

39  **Entomologist-turned-sexologist Alfred Kinsey**  Alfred C. Kinsey, Wardell B. Pomeroy, and Clyde E. Martin, *Sexual Behavior in the Human Male* (Philadelphia: W. B. Saunders, 1948); Alfred C. Kinsey et al., *Sexual Behavior in the Human Female* (Philadelphia: W. B. Saunders, 1953).

39  **Psychologist Evelyn Hooker**  See, for example, Evelyn Hooker, "The Adjustment of the Male Overt Homosexual," *Journal of Projective Techniques* 21 (1957): 18–31; Hooker, "Male Homosexuality in the Rorschach," *Journal of Projective Techniques* 22 (1958): 278–81.

39  **Hooker's test of clinical "gaydar"**  "Gay? or Eurotrash?" *Blair Magazine,* issue 3, http://www.blairmag.com/blair3/gaydar/euro.html.

39  **Thomas Szasz**  See, for example, Thomas Szasz, *Ideology and Insanity: Es-*

*says on the Psychiatric Dehumanization of Man* (New York: Doubleday, 1970); Szasz, *The Myth of Mental Illness: Foundations of a Theory of Personal Conduct* (New York: Harper & Row, 1961). Ronald Bayer describes Szasz's contribution in *Homosexuality and American Psychiatry,* pp. 54–55.

39 **Gays began agitating** Bayer, *Homosexuality and American Psychiatry,* p. 106.

40 **Guy Olmstead, castrated in 1894** Katz, *Gay American History,* p. 141.

40 **Rather than seeking to convert** The 1970 meeting of the American Psychiatric Association was held in San Francisco. "In the wake of the American Invasion of Cambodia in May 1970, the killings at Kent State, and the subsequent convulsion of protest that swept the nation, gay groups in alliance with feminists engaged in the first systematic effort to disrupt the annual meetings of the American Psychiatric Association." Bayer, *Homosexuality and American Psychiatry,* p. 102.

40 **As professor of public health** Ibid.

40 **In the 1970 meeting** The psychiatrist, Nathaniel McConaghy, was discussing the use of aversive conditioning techniques in the treatment of sexual deviation. Ibid., p. 103.

40 **The year after that** Ibid., p. 109.

40 **"Stop it"** Ibid., p. 125.

40 **Riffing off "Black is beautiful"** See Edmund White, *The Beautiful Room Is Empty* (1988; New York: Vintage, 1994), p. 197.

40 **The efforts of these activists** Bayer, *Homosexuality and American Psychiatry,* p. 138. The eighth printing of the *DSM* notes this change in the seventh printing. See Committee on Nomenclature and Statistics of the American Psychiatric Association, *Diagnostic and Statistical Manual of Mental Disorders,* 2nd ed., 8th prtg. (1975), p. vi.

41 **A 1952 congressional enactment** "Aliens afflicted with psychopathic personality, epilepsy, or a mental defect." § 212(4) of the *Immigration and Nationality Act of 1952, United States Code* 8 (1958), § 1182(a)(4). See *Boutilier v. INS,* 387 U.S. 118, 120–23 (1967).

41 **When the APA depathologized** William N. Eskridge Jr., *Gaylaw: Challenging the Apartheid of the Closet* (Cambridge: Harvard University Press, 1999), p. 133.

41 **Not until 1990** Ibid., p. 70, citing *Immigration and Nationality Act,* Pub. L. No. 82-414, 212(a)(4), 66 Stat. 163, 182 (1952) (repealed 1990).

41   **The major mental health associations**   See American Medical Association, House of Delegates Resolution 506: Policy Statement on Sexual Orientation Reparative (Conversion) Therapy (April 26, 2000), http://www.ama-assn. org/meetings/public/annual00/reports/refcome/506.rtf; Board of Trustees of the American Psychiatric Association, COPP Position Statement on Therapies Focused on Attempts to Change Sexual Orientation (Reparative or Conversion Therapies) (May 2000), http://www.psych.org/psych_pract/ copptherapyaddendum83100.cfm; American Psychological Association Council of Representatives, Resolution on Appropriate Therapeutic Responses to Sexual Orientation (August 14, 1997), http://www.apa.org/ pi/sexual.html; National Committee on Lesbian, Gay & Bisexual Issues, National Association of Social Workers, Position Statement: "Reparative" and "Conversion" Therapies for Lesbians and Gay Men (January 21, 2000), http://www.socialworkers.org/diversity/lgb/reparative.asp. Stephen C. Halpert lists organizations opposing conversion therapy in "If It Ain't Broke, Don't Fix It," *International Journal of Sexuality & Gender Studies* 5 (January 2000): 22 n. 2.

41   **Conversion therapists bemoan**   For the claim that Americans have been brainwashed into accepting homosexuality, see Charles W. Socarides, "How America Went Gay," available at http://www.leaderu.com/jhs/socarides.html.

41   **Responsibility for converting**   Douglas C. Haldeman, "The Practice and Ethics of Sexual Orientation Conversion Therapy," *Journal of Consulting & Clinical Psychology* 62 (April 1994): 224. David B. Cruz lists other religiously focused conversion groups in "Controlling Desires: Sexual Orientation Conversion and the Limits of Knowledge and Law," *Southern California Law Review* 72 (July 1999): 1309.

41   **These two groups**   See Haldeman, ibid., p. 224; Murphy, *Gay Science*, p. 85.

44   **At least eight states**   Alabama requires sex education course materials to emphasize "in a factual manner and from a public health perspective, that homosexuality is not a lifestyle acceptable to the general public and that homosexual conduct is a criminal offense under the laws of the state." *Ala. Code* § 16-40a-2(c)(8) (LexisNexis 2001). Arizona prohibits any course of study that (1) "[p]romotes a homosexual life-style," (2) "[p]ortrays homosexuality as a positive alternative life-style," or (3) "[s]uggests that some methods of sex are safe methods of homosexual sex." *Ariz. Rev. Stat. Ann.* § 15-716(C)(1) to (3) (2002). In Mississippi, state law requires educators

(1) to teach "the current state law related to sexual conduct, including forcible rape, statutory rape, paternity establishment, child support and homosexual activity" and (2) to teach that "a monogamous relationship in the context of marriage is the only appropriate setting for sexual intercourse." *Miss. Code Ann.* § 37-13-171(1)(e), (f) (West 1999). Sodomy is a crime in Mississippi under *Miss. Code Ann.* § 97-29-59 (West 1999), though such statutes are now unenforceable after *Lawrence v. Texas,* 539 U.S. 558 (2003). North Carolina requires (1) that education about AIDS include statements that a monogamous, heterosexual marriage is "the best lifelong means of avoiding diseases transmitted by sexual contact" and (2) that any instruction about diseases, such as AIDS, where "homosexual acts are a significant means of transmission . . . include the current legal status of those acts." *N.C. Gen. Stat. Ann.* § 115C-81(e1)(3) (West 2000). Sodomy is a felony under North Carolina law, see *N.C. Gen. Stat. Ann.* § 14-177 (West 2000), though as in the case of Mississippi, the sodomy statute is unenforceable. Under Oklahoma law, "AIDS prevention education" must "specifically teach students that . . . engaging in homosexual activity, promiscuous sexual activity, intravenous drug use or contact with contaminated blood products is now known to be primarily responsible for contact with the AIDS virus." *Okla. Stat. Ann.* tit. 70, § 11-103.3(D) (West 2005). South Carolina prohibits health education programs from discussing "alternate sexual lifestyles from heterosexual relationships" except in the context of sexually transmitted disease instruction. *S.C. Code Ann.* § 59-32-30(A)(5) (2004). Texas requires education programs for those eighteen and younger to "state that homosexual conduct is not an acceptable lifestyle and is a criminal offense." *Tex. Health & Safety Code Ann.* § 85.007 (Vernon 2001). In Utah, the laws governing public schools prohibit "instruction in . . . the advocacy of homosexuality." *Utah Code Ann.* § 53A-13-101(1)(c)(iii) (Supp. 2004); *Utah Admin. Code* r. 277-474-3(A) (2001).

44　**In some states**　In Arizona, for example, an executive order bars discrimination based on sexual orientation by state agencies. *Ariz. Exec. Order No.* 2003-22 (June 21, 2003). Any positive portrayal of homosexuality in the public schools of that state, however, is prohibited under *Ariz. Rev. Stat. Ann.* § 15-716(C)(1) to (3) (2002).

44　**As psychology professor E. L. Pattullo**　E. L. Pattullo, "Straight Talk About Gays," *Commentary,* December 1992, p. 22.

45  **Antigay psychologists**  Paul Cameron and Kirk Cameron, "Do Homosexual Teachers Pose a Risk to Pupils?" *Journal of Psychology* 130 (November 1996): 603.

45  **In 1978**  *Ratchford v. Gay Lib*, 434 U.S. 1080, 1084 (1978) (Rehnquist, J., dissenting from denial of certiorari).

47  **In the 1990s**  Simon LeVay, "A Difference in Hypothalamic Structure Between Heterosexual and Homosexual Men," *Science* 253 (August 1991): 1034–37; Dean H. Hamer et al., "A Linkage Between DNA Markers on the X Chromosome and Male Sexual Orientation," *Science* 261 (July 1993): 321–26; J. A. Y. Hall and D. Kimura, "Dermatoglyphic Asymmetry and Sexual Orientation in Men," *Behavioral Neuroscience* 108 (December 1994): 1023–26.

47  **One famous study**  J. Michael Bailey and Richard C. Pillard, "A Genetic Study of Male Sexual Orientation," *Archives of General Psychiatry* 48 (December 1991): 1089–96.

47  **Neuroanatomist Simon LeVay's brain study**  Simon LeVay, "A Difference in Hypothalamic Structure." For further limitations and confounding factors in the study, see Simon LeVay, *The Sexual Brain* (Cambridge: MIT Press, 1993), pp. 120–23; LeVay, *Queer Science*, pp. 143–47. For further challenges, see W. Byne and B. Parsons, "Human Sexual Orientation: The Biological Theories Reappraised," *Archives of General Psychiatry* 50 (March 1993): 228–39; W. Byne, "Is Homosexuality Biologically Influenced? The Biological Evidence Challenged," *Scientific American* 270 (May 1994): 50–55; W. Byne, "Science and Belief: Psychobiological Research on Sexual Orientation," *Journal of Homosexuality* 28 (June 1995): 303–44.

47  **The claim seemed too close**  For instance, Havelock Ellis described the adoption of "feminine" behaviors and affect by "inverted men." Havelock Ellis, *Studies in the Psychology of Sex: Sexual Inversion*, vol. 2 (London: University Press, 1897), p. 12.

47  **This was a disqualifying move**  LeVay's methods for determining sexual orientation are questionable. Of his forty-one subjects, he took nineteen of the thirty-five men to be "homosexual" ("one bisexual man was included in this group") based on information in their medical records. LeVay, "A Difference in Hypothalamic Structure," p. 1035. All had died of AIDS-related complications. Of the six "heterosexual" men who had died of AIDS-related complications, "two . . . had denied homosexual activity." Ibid., p. 1036 n. 7.

The records of the remaining fourteen "heterosexual" patients (four of whom died from AIDS-related complications) contained no information regarding sexual orientation, and were "assumed to have been mostly or all heterosexual on the basis of the numerical preponderance of heterosexual men in the population." Ibid. LeVay anticipated challenges based on the confounding influence of HIV, since all of his "homosexual" subjects had died of AIDS. See LeVay, *The Sexual Brain*, p. 121; LeVay, *Queer Science*, p. 320 n. 43. His response, however, is only to concede that "there is always the possibility that gay men who die of AIDS are not representative of the entire population of gay men." *The Sexual Brain*, p. 144.

47 **has sent up the twins study**   Michael Warner, *The Trouble with Normal*, pp. 9–10.

48 **Does this mean, Warner asks**   Ibid.

48 **Yet as literary critic Eve Sedgwick**   "[J]ust as it comes to seem questionable to assume that cultural constructs are peculiarly malleable ones, it is also becoming increasingly problematical to assume that grounding an identity in biology or 'essential nature' is a stable way of insulating it from societal interference. If anything, the gestalt of assumptions that undergird nature/nurture debates may be in the process of direct reversal. Increasingly, it is the conjecture that a particular trait is genetically or biologically based, *not* that it is 'only cultural,' that seems to trigger an estrus of manipulative fantasy in the technological institutions of the culture." Eve Kosofsky Sedgwick, *Epistemology of the Closet* (Berkeley: University of California Press, 1990), p. 43.

48 **As envisioned in Jonathan Tolins's play**   Jonathan Tolins, *The Twilight of the Golds* (New York: Samuel French, 1992). The play takes its name from the last opera in Richard Wagner's Ring Cycle, *Die Götterdämmerung*, "The Twilight of the Gods," in which the world is brought to an end by the pursuit of godly power in exchange for love. Suzanne, the daughter of the Gold family, learns that the child she is carrying will be homosexual, like her brother David. In deciding whether or not to abort, the family members struggle with the implications of Suzanne's decision for each of them, but particularly for David.

48 **Others have made subtler claims**   See, for example, Samuel Marcosson, "Constructive Immutability," *University of Pennsylvania Journal of Constitutional Law* 3 (May 2001): 646–721.

48  **Such a defense**   "Even an immutable bisexual is perceived to have a choice—he can choose to fit into the heterosexual matrix by selecting a partner of the opposite sex." Kenji Yoshino, "The Epistemic Contract of Bisexual Erasure," *Stanford Law Review* 52 (January 2000): 406. Janet Halley notes that immutability operates as an exoneration strategy because it eliminates choice. She then points out that the immutability theory "does not explain why bisexuals—by hypothesis capable of satisfactory sexual encounters with members of the so-called 'opposite' sex—should not be encouraged or forced to do so." Janet E. Halley, "Sexual Orientation and the Politics of Biology: A Critique of the Argument from Immutability," *Stanford Law Review* 46 (February 1994): 518–19, 528.

49  **As literature professor Leo Bersani**   Leo Bersani, *Homos* (Cambridge: Harvard University Press, 1995), p. 57.

GAY PASSING

50  **He instinctively knows**   Samuel Taylor Coleridge, *The Rime of the Ancient Mariner*, in *The Oxford Book of English Verse*, 2nd ed., ed. Arthur Quiller-Couch (New York: Oxford University Press, 1939), p. 562.

53  **The answer for when the movement**   See John D'Emilio, *Sexual Politics, Sexual Communities: The Making of a Homosexual Minority in the United States, 1940–70*, 2nd ed. (Chicago: University of Chicago Press, 1998), pp. 1–2. D'Emilio's work argues against that conventional wisdom. See ibid.

53  **The preceding decades are often described**   Ibid.

53  **Others came out**   Clendinen and Nagourney describe people coming out in bars in Dudley Clendinen and Adam Nagourney, *Out for Good: The Struggle to Build a Gay Rights Movement in America* (New York: Simon & Schuster, 1999), p. 17. D'Emilio describes people coming out in Communist-type cells in *Sexual Politics*, p. 64. Duberman describes people coming out during conversion therapy in *Cures*, pp. 93–115.

53  **"Another night two policemen came"**   Judy Grahn, "An Underground Bar," in *Another Mother Tongue: Gay Words, Gay Worlds* (Boston: Beacon Press, 1984), p. 32.

54  **Yet just as the years**   See George Chauncey, *Gay New York* (New York: Basic Books, 1994); D'Emilio, *Sexual Politics;* Faderman, *Odd Girls and Twilight*

*Lovers: A History of Lesbian Life in Twentieth-Century America* (New York: Columbia University Press, 1991).

54 **This world sustained bars** See ibid., pp. 29, 287 n. 3.

54 **Edward Sagarin** Donald Webster Cory, *The Homosexual in America: A Subjective Approach* (New York: Greenberg, 1951).

54 **One of the five founders of Mattachine** The Mattachine Society was founded by Harry Hay, Bob Hull, Dale Jennings, Chuck Rowland, and Rudi Gernreich ("R."). Konrad Stevens and John Gruber are often considered founders as well. Katz, *Gay American History,* p. 414. Historian John D'Emilio is among those who refer to Gernreich as "R." D'Emilio, *Sexual Politics,* p. 62.

55 **The Mattachine Society took its name** See Harry Hay, "The Homosexual and History . . . an Invitation to Further Study," in *Radically Gay: Gay Liberation in the Words of Its Founder,* ed. Will Roscoe (Boston: Beacon Press, 1996), pp. 92, 112.

55 **Its publication, *One*** "A mystic bond of brotherhood makes all men one," *One* 1 (1953), p. 1, quoting Thomas Carlyle.

55 **The Daughters of Bilitis** See *Ladder* 1 (1956), pp. 2–3.

57 **But when my father claimed me** "This thing of darkness I acknowledge mine," William Shakespeare, *The Tempest,* 5.1.275–76.

58 **In the midst of winter** "In the midst of winter, I at last discovered that there was in me an invincible summer." Albert Camus, "Return to Tipasa," in *The Myth of Sisyphus and Other Essays,* trans. Justin O'Brien (New York: Knopf, 1969), p. 202.

60 **The riots generated** John D'Emilio, "Cycles of Change, Questions of Strategy: The Gay and Lesbian Movement After Fifty Years," in *The Politics of Gay Rights,* ed. Craig A. Rimmerman, Kenneth Wald, and Clyde Wilcox (Chicago: University of Chicago Press, 2000), pp. 31, 35.

60 **Dudley Clendinen and Adam Nagourney** Clendinen and Nagourney, *Out for Good,* p. 31.

60 **Stonewall also birthed new publications** Rodger Streitmatter, *Unspeakable: The Rise of the Gay and Lesbian Press in America* (Boston: Faber & Faber, 1995), p. 117.

60 **As Cindy Patton describes it** Cindy Patton, foreword to *Lavender Culture,* ed. Karla Jay and Allen Young (New York: NYU Press, 1994), pp. ix, xiv.

62    **D. A. Miller**    D. A. Miller, *The Novel and the Police* (Berkeley: University of California Press, 1988), p. 206.

62    ***Bowers* was the 1986 case**    *Bowers v. Hardwick,* 478 U.S. 186 (1986).

62    **Until it was overruled**    *Bowers* was overruled by *Lawrence v. Texas,* 539 U.S. 558 (2003). For a description of how courts interpreted *Bowers* to foreclose various forms of protection for gays, see Joseph Landau, "Ripple Effect: Sodomy Statutes as Weapons," *New Republic,* June 23, 2003, p. 12.

63    **As described by his biographer**    John C. Jeffries Jr., *Justice Lewis F. Powell, Jr.* (New York: Fordham University Press, 1994), pp. 521–22.

63    **Though Powell didn't know it**    Ibid., p. 528. Whether Powell knew that Chinnis was gay or not is a source of some contention. See Jeffries, *Powell,* pp. 521–22. Powell approached Chinnis on several occasions to obtain information about homosexuality, despite the fact that the *Hardwick* case was assigned to another clerk, Michael Mosman. Mosman was a conservative Mormon from Idaho, married at the time with three children, and a graduate of Brigham Young University Law School. So it is unclear whether Powell, in turning to Chinnis, acted on a sense that Chinnis might be particularly helpful in providing information on homosexuality, or that Mosman was particularly unhelpful. See Joyce Murdoch and Deb Price, *Courting Justice: Gay Men and Lesbians v. the Supreme Court* (New York: Basic Books, 2001), pp. 272–74.

63    **In their discussion**    Powell reportedly told Chinnis that "I don't believe I've ever met a homosexual." Murdoch and Price, *Courting Justice,* p. 273. He reportedly told his colleagues in conference on *Hardwick* that he had never known a homosexual. Ibid., p. 307.

63    **The astonished Chinnis**    Ibid., pp. 305–6.

63    **After his story became known**    Ibid., pp. 335–36.

63    **But according to journalists**    Ibid., p. 335.

63    **Eve Sedgwick explains this anger**    Sedgwick, *Epistemology of the Closet,* pp. 75–76.

63    **"the holocaustal with the intimate"**    Ibid., p. 76.

64    **If Chinnis had put**    Jeffries, *Powell,* p. 522.

64    **Justice Powell later admitted**    Ibid., p. 530. He said, " 'I think I probably made a mistake in that one . . . so far as I'm concerned it's just a part of my past and not very important. . . . I don't suppose I've devoted half an hour'

to thinking about the decision since it was made." Ruth Marcus, "Powell Regrets Backing Sodomy Law," *Washington Post*, October 26, 1990, p. A3.

64 **Faderman recounts** Bunny MacCulloch interview with Johnnie Phelps, 1982, quoted in Faderman, *Odd Girls and Twilight Lovers*, p. 118.

65 **Powell was famous for hiring** Murdoch & Price, *Courting Justice*, pp. 275, 335–37.

66 **Not until the formulation** *Policy Concerning Homosexuality in the Armed Forces, U.S. Code* 10 (1994), § 654.

67 **Passing is often associated with death** See Henry Louis Gates Jr., *Figures in Black: Words, Signs, and the "Racial" Self* (New York: Oxford University Press, 1987), p. 202.

67 **Literal death was met with silence** By the end of 1986, 29,003 cases of AIDS in the United States had been reported to the CDC, and 16,301 deaths had been reported (though reporting was incomplete). Center for Infectious Diseases, Centers for Disease Control, "AIDS Weekly Surveillance Report 1—United States AIDS Program," December 29, 1986, p. 5, http://www.cdc.gov/hiv/stats/surveillance86.pdf. "In 1986 . . . the *Columbia Journalism Review* noted that the *New York Times* had cited AIDS as a cause of death in only a handful of obits; similar patterns were found in the *Miami Herald*, the *Los Angeles Times*, and most other large and small newspapers." Larry Gross, *Contested Closets: The Politics and Ethics of Outing* (Minneapolis: University of Minnesota Press, 1993), p. 53, citing Alexis Jetter, "AIDS and the Obits," *Columbia Journalism Review* (July/August 1986): 14–16. One notable exception to this trend was to be found in the *Bay Area Reporter* in San Francisco. During the explosion of AIDS cases in the mid-1980s, the paper averaged a dozen AIDS obituaries a week, and they covered two or three pages. One week, there were thirty-one obituaries. David Kligman, "No AIDS Obits Is Banner News for Gay Newspaper," *Austin American-Statesman*, August 15, 1998. See also C. Winick, "AIDS Obituaries in *The New York Times*," *AIDS & Public Policy Journal* 11 (1996): 148–52.

67 **Silence, in turn** Mark Barnes, "Toward Ghastly Death: The Censorship of AIDS Education," review of *Social Acts, Social Consequences: AIDS and the Politics of Public Health*, by Ronald Bayer and *Policing Desire: Pornography, AIDS, and the Media*, by Simon Watney, *Columbia Law Review* 89 (April 1989): 698–724.

67 **As AIDS closets became coffins** "With the advent of AIDS it became more

difficult to maintain the practice of inning, as more and more prominent men fell ill and died, but the media cooperated in turning celebrity coffins into permanent closets." Gross, *Contested Closets,* p. 53.

67  The AIDS-inspired slogans  "SILENCE=DEATH" is discussed in Douglas Crimp and Adam Rolston, *AIDS Demo Graphics* (Seattle: Bay Press, 1990), p. 14. "We're here, we're queer, get used to it!" is discussed in Bruce Bawer, "Notes on Stonewall," *New Republic,* June 13, 1994, pp. 24, 26.

68  The syndrome has left marks  Suzanne Young argues that Kaposi's sarcoma operates as a "visible [indicator] of a disease that remains severely stigmatizing and that is still associated with socially marginalized groups." Suzanne Young, "Speaking of the Surface: The Texts of Kaposi's Sarcoma," in *Homosexuality and Psychoanalysis,* ed. Tim Dean and Christopher Lane (Chicago: University of Chicago Press, 2001), pp. 322, 324.

68  In the early 1990s  For example, Rita Giordano describes the outing debate in the wake of an article outing a prominent Department of Defense official in "Gays Bitter in Division over Outing," *Newsday,* August 9, 1991, p. 17. Michelangelo Signorile, the originator of outing, is profiled in Renée Graham, "The Prince of Outing," *Boston Globe,* July 13, 1993, p. 25. Sally Jacobs describes the increasing popularity of outing tactics—such as a history professor's offer of $10,000 to anyone who successfully outed "a four-star officer serving in the military, a justice on the U.S. Supreme Court, or an American cardinal"—in " 'Outing' Seen as Political Tool," *Boston Globe,* April 3, 1993, p. 1. Beth Ann Krier describes the debate about outing among gay activists in "Whose Sex Secret Is It?" *Los Angeles Times,* March 22, 1990, p. E1. David Tuller describes rumors about the orientation of prominent government and business officials that have prompted journalists to wrestle with the outing issue in "Uproar over Gays Booting Others Out of the Closet," *San Francisco Chronicle,* March 12, 1990, p. A9. Articles from the mainstream press that exemplify the furor created by outing are reprinted in Gross, *Contested Closets,* pp. 219–30.

68  Long viewed as taboo  Gross, *Contested Closets,* pp. 283–303.

68  The pulpit was the gay magazine  For example, Michelangelo Signorile characterizes Malcolm Forbes as gay in "The Other Side of Malcolm," *Out-Week,* April 18, 1990, p. 40, reprinted in Gross, *Contested Closets,* p. 285. Signorile also characterizes David Geffen as gay in "Gossip Watch," *OutWeek,* December 26, 1990, p. 45, and characterizes Merv Griffin as gay in "Gossip

Watch," *OutWeek,* July 18, 1990, p. 45, reprinted in Gross, *Contested Closets,* p. 289.

68   **For many gays**   See, for example, C. Carr, "Why Outing Must Stop," *Village Voice,* March 18, 1991, p. 37; Ayofemi Folayan, "Whose Life Is It Anyway?" *OutWeek,* May 16, 1990, reprinted in Gross, *Contested Closets,* p. 248; Hunter Madsen, "Tattle Tale Traps," *OutWeek,* May 16, 1990, reprinted in Gross, *Contested Closets,* p. 237.

68   **The mainstream press**   See, for example, " 'Outing' Is Wrong Answer to Anti-Gay Discrimination," *USA Today,* March 30, 1992, p. 12A; Mike Royko, "Antsy Closet Crowd Should Think Twice," *Chicago Tribune,* April 2, 1990, p. 3.

68   *OutWeek* **closed its doors**   See James Cox, " 'OutWeek' Magazine Goes Out of Business," *USA Today,* July 1, 1991, p. 2B.

68   **The norm moved back**   Frank argued, "There is a right to privacy, but not hypocrisy. If politicians are gay or lesbian, and then use that against other people, they have forfeited their right to privacy. I resented very much that there were gay Republicans using gayness as an accusation." Dirk Johnson, "Privacy vs. the Pursuit of Gay Rights," *New York Times,* March 27, 1990, p. A21.

69   **The military used to be governed**   Enlisted Administrative Separations, Department of Defense Directive 1332.14, 47 *Fed. Reg.* 10,162, 10,178 (March 9, 1982).

69   **Under "Don't ask, don't tell"**   *U.S. Code* 10 (1994), § 654(b)(1).

70   **Or we could go further**   Janet E. Halley, *Don't: A Reader's Guide to the Military's Anti-Gay Policy* (Durham: Duke University Press, 1999), p. 1.

70   **While her contention**   A 1998 report to the secretary of defense notes that "although the trend from the early 1980s to the early 1990s reflected gradually decreasing numbers and rates of discharges, culminating in a historic low in Fiscal Year 1994, both the number and rate of discharges for homosexual conduct have increased each year since that time." Office of the Under Secretary of Defense (Pers. & Readiness), Report to the Secretary of Defense: Review of the Effectiveness of the Application and Enforcement of the Department's Policy on Homosexual Conduct in the Military (1998), http://www.defenselink.mil/pubs/rpt040798.html. The number of service members discharged for homosexuality in 1998 was double the number dismissed in 1993, when the policy was developed. Eric Schmitt,

"Close Quarters: How Is This Strategy Working? Don't Ask," *New York Times,* December 19, 1999, sec. 4, p. 1. But the number of service members discharged for homosexuality has dropped significantly since fighting began in Afghanistan and Iraq, and "gay discharge numbers have dropped every time America has entered a war, from Korea to Vietnam to the Persian Gulf to the present conflicts." Servicemembers Legal Defense Network, Conduct Unbecoming: 10th Annual Report on "Don't Ask, Don't Tell" (2004), p. 1, http://www.sldn.org/binary-data/SLDN_ARTICLES/pdf_file/1411.pdf.

70 **In 1984, a federal court**   *Rowland v. Mad River Local School District,* 730 F.2d 444, 446-47 (6th Cir. 1984).

70 **Under controlling precedents**   The test was set out by the Supreme Court in *Pickering v. Board of Education,* 391 U.S. 563 (1968), and elaborated in subsequent cases such as *Givhan v. Western Line Consolidated School District,* 439 U.S. 410 (1979).

70 **The court found Rowland's "coming out"**   *Rowland,* 730 F.2d at 449.

71 **The court upheld**   Ibid., p. 452.

71 **More recently, a lower court**   *Weaver v. Nebo School District,* 29 F. Supp. 2d 1279 (C.D. Utah 1998).

71 **When it does**   See *Rowland v. Mad River Local School District,* 470 U.S. 1009 (1985) (Brennan, J., dissenting from denial of certiorari).

71 **Dissenting from the Supreme Court's refusal**   Ibid., p. 1016 n. 11.

72 **After telling me how she passes**   "The genealogy of the term passing in American history associates it with the discourse of racial difference and especially with the assumption of a fraudulent 'white' identity by an individual culturally and legally defined as 'Negro' or black by virtue of a percentage of African ancestry." Elaine K. Ginsberg, "Introduction: The Politics of Passing," in *Passing and the Fictions of Identity,* ed. Elaine K. Ginsberg (Durham: Duke University Press, 1996), pp. 1, 2–3. William Craft describes the antebellum practice of slaves passing as white in *Running a Thousand Miles for Freedom; or, The Escape of William and Ellen Craft from Slavery* (1860; Miami: Mnemosyne Publishing, 1969). Jerry Kang discusses the recent phenomenon of racial passing on the Internet in "Cyber-Race," *Harvard Law Review* 113 (March 2000): 1131–1208.

76 As sociologist Steven Seidman observes   Steven Seidman, *Beyond the Closet: The Transformation of Gay and Lesbian Life* (New York: Routledge, 2002), p. 6.

77 Should gays "act straight"   Francisco Valdes observes that gender-atypical behavior and minority sexual orientation are bundled in popular consciousness. See Francisco Valdes, "Queers, Sissies, Dykes, and Tomboys: Deconstructing the Conflation of 'Sex,' 'Gender,' and 'Sexual Orientation' in Euro-American Law and Society," *California Law Review* 83 (January 1995): 51–55.

77 At least since his influential 1993   Andrew Sullivan, "The Politics of Homosexuality," *New Republic,* May 10, 1993, p. 34.

77 Because he believes gays have become   Andrew Sullivan, *Virtually Normal: An Argument About Homosexuality* (New York: Vintage Books, 1995).

77 "Following legalization of same-sex"   Quoted in Warner, *The Trouble with Normal,* pp. 60–61, citing David Groff, ed., *Out Facts: Just About Everything You Need to Know About Gay and Lesbian Life* (New York: Universe, 1997).

77 By *queers,* I mean gays who   Warner, *The Trouble with Normal.*

77 Warner exhorts queers to resist   Ibid., p. 59.

78 For this reason, Warner believes   Ibid., p. 74.

78 Writer Bruce Bawer inveighs against   Bruce Bawer, "Truth in Advertising," in *Beyond Queer: Challenging Gay Left Orthodoxy,* ed. Bruce Bawer (Columbus, Ohio: Free Press, 1996), p. 43.

78 Warner criticizes normals   Warner, *Trouble with Normal,* p. 19.

80 Foucault writes   Michel Foucault, *The History of Sexuality: An Introduction,* vol. 1, trans. Robert Hurley (1976; New York: Random House, 1978), p. 43.

80 I recently came across   The website is http://www.straightacting.com.

80 the gay plaintiffs   *Steffan v. Perry,* 41 F.3d 677 (D.C. Cir. 1994) (en banc); *Boy Scouts of America v. Dale,* 530 U.S. 640 (2000).

80 We see less of Perry Watkins   *Watkins v. United States Army,* 875 F.2d 699 (9th Cir. 1989) (en banc). For a description of the *Watkins* case, see William N. Eskridge Jr., "Gaylegal Narratives," *Stanford Law Review* 46 (1994): 607–46.

80 A 1993 *New York Times* profile   Jeffrey Schmalz, "On the Front Lines with

Joseph Steffan: From Midshipman to Gay Advocate," *New York Times,* February 4, 1993, p. C1.

81  **As Goffman observes**   Goffman, *Stigma,* p. 108.

81  **"I like to see it Lap the Miles"**   Emily Dickinson, "I like to see it Lap the Miles," *The Complete Poems of Emily Dickinson,* ed. Thomas H. Johnson (1960; New York: Back Boy Books, 1976), p. 286.

81  **"the experience of repetition as Death"**   Adrienne Rich, "A Valediction Forbidding Mourning," *The Fact of a Doorframe* (1984; New York, W. W. Norton, 1994), pp. 136–37.

84  **Historically, the practice of alluding**   "Men commonly described one gay man's efforts to drop hints to another man that he was gay, often in an effort to determine whether the second man was also, as 'dropping [hair] pins.' " Chauncey, *Gay New York,* p. 289. Armistead Maupin depicts a fictional conversation in which one gay man asks another, "Did he drop any hairpins?" to allude to this practice. Armistead Maupin, *Sure of You* (New York: HarperCollins, 1989), p. 109.

85  **I have come to Boston**   Kristin Eliasberg, "Making a Case for the Right to Be Different," *New York Times,* June 16, 2001, p. B11.

86  **homosexuality in Japan**   For English-language discussions of the history of same-sex sexuality in Japan, see generally Gary P. Leupp, *Male Colors: The Construction of Homosexuality in Tokugawa Japan* (Berkeley: University of California Press, 1995); Pflugfelder, *Cartographies of Desire.*

86  **In his widely sold 1687 book**   Ihara Saikaku, *The Great Mirror of Male Love,* trans. Paul Gordon Schalow (1687; Stanford: Stanford University Press, 1990), p. 53.

86  **The first gay pride march**   "Asia's trailblazer is Japan which held its first Gay Pride Parade on August 28, 1994, when 1,500 marchers walked the three miles from the Shinjuku district, which has about 400 gay bars, to neighboring Shibuya." "Queer, Asian/Pacific Islander & Proud," *Pride.01,* June 2001.

86  **In 1997, a Tokyo appellate court**   "World Datelines," *San Francisco Examiner,* September 16, 1997, p. B8. For a discussion of the trial court's decision, see James D. Wilets, "International Human Rights and Sexual Orientation," *Hastings International and Comparative Law Review* 18 (1994): 87 nn. 391–92.

88 **I went, in James Baldwin's** Richard Goldstein, " 'Go the Way Your Blood Beats': An Interview with James Baldwin," in Rubenstein, *Sexual Orientation and the Law,* p. 71.

90 **Foucault** Bersani, *Homos,* p. 77, translating an interview by Jean Le Bitoux, "Michel Foucault, le gai savoir," *Mec* 5 (June 1988): 35.

91 **Along the axis of affiliation** Paula L. Ettelbrick attacks marriage as a craven act of covering in "Since When Is Marriage a Path to Liberation?" *Out/Look,* autumn 1989, p. 8, reprinted in part in William N. Eskridge Jr. and Nan D. Hunter, *Sexuality, Gender, and the Law* (New York: Foundation Press, 1997), p. 818. Thomas B. Stoddard praises same-sex marriage as a healthy act of covering in "Why Gay People Should Seek the Right to Marry," *Out/Look,* autumn 1989, p. 8, reprinted in part in Eskridge and Hunter, *Sexuality.*

91 **Along the axes of appearance** For instance, Robin Shahar was fired from the Georgia attorney general's office for flaunting her homosexuality by engaging in a same-sex commitment ceremony. See *Shahar v. Bowers,* 114 F.3d 1097 (11th Cir. 1997).

92 **As Goffman observes** Goffman, *Stigma,* p. 102.

93 **I know of only one legal context** In a sexual-orientation-based asylum case an applicant was denied asylum because "his appearance, his dress, his manner, his demeanor, his gestures, his voice" were not "gay enough." Fadi Hanna discusses this decision and criticizes the judge's decision to "reward those who 'reverse cover,' or act more visibly 'gay'" with a grant of asylum in "Punishing Masculinity in Gay Asylum Claims," *Yale Law Journal* 114 (January 2005): 913–14.

93 **Robin Shahar** Unless otherwise specified, facts regarding the *Shahar* case are drawn from the author's interview with Robin Shahar, conducted on June 11, 2002.

97 **Shahar lost all her claims** *Shahar v. Bowers,* 836 F. Supp. 859 (N.D. Ga. 1993); *Shahar v. Bowers,* 70 F.3d 1218 (11th Cir. 1995).

97 **At this point, a majority** *Shahar v. Bowers,* 78 F.3d 499 (11th Cir. 1996).

97 **This twelve-member body** *Shahar v. Bowers,* 114 F.3d 1097 (11th Cir. 1997) (en banc).

97 **As the trial court** *Shahar,* 836 F. Supp. at 867.

97 **Bowers also stated** Ibid., p. 867.

97   **Indeed, in a letter written**   See *Shahar,* 114 F.3d at 1116 n. 9 (Tjoflat, J., concurring). Judge Tjoflat also noted, "The record in this case supports an inference that the Attorney General withdrew Shahar's offer of employment because he thought Shahar had 'set him up'; once ensconced in the Department of Law office, she would use her position to advance a homosexual-rights agenda among her co-employees." Ibid., p. 1111 n. 1.

98   **In the 1996 case**   *Romer v. Evans,* 517 U.S. 620 (1996).

98   **The Court's opinion suggested**   The Court wrote that Amendment 2 "is a status-based enactment divorced from any factual context from which we could discern a relationship to legitimate state interests; it is a classification of persons undertaken for its own sake, something the Equal Protection Clause does not permit." Ibid., p. 635.

98   **The court cited a precedent**   *Shahar,* 114 F.3d at 1108 (citing *McMullen v. Carson,* 754 F.2d 936 [11th Cir. 1985]).

98   **It observed that** *Romer* **was**   *Shahar,* 114 F.3d at 1110.

98   **Bowers's claim that retaining**   The court described Bowers's interest: "When the Attorney General viewed Shahar's decision to 'wed' openly— complete with changing her name—another woman (in a large 'wedding') . . . he saw her acts as having a realistic likelihood to . . . interfere with the Department's ability to handle certain kinds of controversial matters . . . such as claims to same-sex marriage licenses." Ibid., pp. 1104–5.

99   **Bowers's statement**   The court noted Bowers's claim that the "wedding" would "interfere with the Department's efforts to enforce Georgia's laws against homosexual sodomy." Ibid., p. 1105.

99   **Georgia's sodomy statute**   *Official Code of Ga. Ann.* § 16-6-2 (2004) (rendered unconstitutional by *Lawrence v. Texas,* 539 U.S. 558 [2003]).

99   **Because the statute**   In *Gordon v. State,* for instance, the court noted that the statute "applies equally to homosexual and heterosexual intimate relationships." *Gordon v. State,* 360 S.E.2d 253, 254 (Ga. 1987).

100   **The Supreme Court**   *Shahar v. Bowers,* 522 U.S. 1049 (1998).

100   **Although he was the runaway**   James Salzer, "Governor-Hopeful Bowers Admits Decade-Long Affair," *Florida Times-Union,* June 6, 1997, p. A1.

100   **Bowers confessed**   Bill Rankin, "Irony in Georgia: Bowers Wins Case, Admits Adultery," *National Law Journal,* June 16, 1997, p. A6.

100   **As adultery has long been a crime**   Georgia's code classifies adultery—

defined as a "married person . . . voluntarily ha[ving] sexual intercourse with a person other than his spouse"—as a misdemeanor. *Official Code of Ga. Ann.* § 16-6-19 (2004).

100 **"Mr. Bowers penalized me"** See ABC News, *Sex, Drugs, and Consenting Adults: Should People Be Able to Do Whatever They Want?*, May 26, 1998; transcript available at http://www.mapinc.org/drugnews/v98/n389/a07.html.

101 **"It's still awful"** Shahar interview.

102 **"Had the evidence revealed"** *Teegarden v. Teegarden*, 642 N.E.2d 1007, 1010 (Ind. Ct. App. 1994).

102 **"Appellant does not merely say"** *Chaffin v. Frye*, 45 Cal. App. 3d 39, 46–47 (Cal. Ct. App. 1975).

102 **In reaching a similar result** *Charpentier v. Charpentier*, 536 A.2d 948, 950 (Conn. 1988).

103 **A Missouri court of appeals** *Delong v. Delong*, No. WD 52726, 1998 WL 15536, at *12 (Mo. Ct. App. Jan. 20, 1998), *rev'd in part sub nom. J.A.D. v. F.J.D.*, 978 S.W.2d 336 (Mo. 1998).

103 **Applying the same standard** *Lundin v. Lundin*, 563 So. 2d 1273, 1277 (La. Ct. App. 1990).

103 **Notice as well *why*** Ibid.

103 **In 1974, a New Jersey court** *In re J. S. & C.*, 324 A.2d 90, 95 (N.J. Super. Ct. Ch. Div. 1974), *aff'd*, 362 A.2d 54 (N.J. Super. Ct. App. Div. 1976).

103 **Based on these findings** Ibid., p. 97.

104 **a Missouri court of appeals** *J.L.P.(H.) v. D.J.P.*, 643 S.W.2d 865, 872 (Mo. Ct. App. 1982).

104 **An Indiana appellate court** *Marlow v. Marlow*, 702 N.E.2d 733, 736 (Ind. Ct. App. 1998).

104 **Sex columnist Dan Savage** See Dan Savage, "Sunday Lives: Role Reversal," *New York Times Magazine*, March 11, 2001, p. 104.

105 **As I sat in the Supreme Court** *Lawrence v. Texas*, 539 U.S. 558 (2003).

105 **A few rows behind me** Brief of Amici Curiae Mary Robinson et al. in Support of Petitioners, 2003 WL 164151 (Jan. 16, 2003), *Lawrence v. Texas*, 539 U.S. 558 (2003) (No. 02-102).

106 **that no-promo-homo argument** Most basically, this means "argu[ing] that progay changes in law or norms would encourage homosexuality or homosexual conduct." William N. Eskridge Jr., "No Promo Homo: The Sedi-

mentation of Antigay Discourse and the Channeling Effect of Judicial Review," *NYU Law Review* 75 (November 2001): 1327, 1329.

106 **"Since in a net I seek"** *Sir Thomas Wyatt: Selected Poems* (New York: Routledge, 2003), p. 21.

106 **In his firsthand account** White writes, "Someone beside me called out 'Gay is good,' in imitation of the new slogan, 'Black is beautiful,' and we all laughed." White, *The Beautiful Room Is Empty*, p. 197.

106 **In 1986, the *Bowers* Court** The Court wrote, "To claim that a right to engage in [sodomy] is 'deeply rooted in this Nation's history and tradition' or 'implicit in the concept of ordered liberty' is, at best, facetious." *Bowers v. Hardwick*, 478 U.S. 186, 194 (1986).

## RACIAL COVERING

116 **The Japan scholar** Reischauer notes, "An unkind commentator has likened the Japanese to a school of small fish, progressing in orderly fashion in one direction until a pebble dropped into the water breaks this up and sets them off suddenly in the opposite direction, but again in orderly rows." Edwin Reischauer and Marius B. Jansen, *The Japanese Today: Change and Continuity* (1977; Cambridge: Harvard University Press, 1995), p. 136. He also discusses the idea that "Japanese are much more likely than Westerners to operate in groups" and will often "be quite content to conform." Ibid., p. 128.

120 **"like gold to airy thinness beat"** John Donne, "A Valediction: Forbidding Mourning," in *The Complete Poetry and Selected Prose of John Donne*, ed. Charles M. Coffin (New York: Modern Library, 2001), p. 38.

122 **I am large** Walt Whitman, "Song of Myself," chapter 51, *Leaves of Grass* (1855; New York: Bantam Books, 1983), p. 22.

123 **like the Escher** M. C. Escher, *Verbum*, in J. L. Locker, *The Magic of M. C. Escher* (New York: Abrams, 2000), p. 136.

123 **During my college years** In *USA Today*, for instance, one Asian man described his family as "one of those amazing Asian families that the media likes to look at" because "we all went to either Stanford or MIT." Mark Hazard Osmun, "Asian Says Whites Are Hurt by Quotas," *USA Today*, February 6, 1990, p. 2A.

124 **"Here are some"** Eric Liu, *The Accidental Asian: Notes of a Native Speaker* (New York: Random House, 1998), p. 33.

125 Liu stresses his "yellow skin" Ibid., p. 34.

126 Jean, also an Asian-American Liu admits as much, saying that he has "been described as an 'honorary white,' by other whites, and as a 'banana' by other Asians." Ibid., p. 34.

126 She retorts that Ibid., p. 46.

127 In this class, she will begin Jean Shin, "The Asian American Closet," *Asian Law Journal* 11 (May 2004): 1–29.

127 Later in the seminar Barrett, *The Good Black.*

128 "You are a human" Ibid., p. 24.

128 "street talk" Ibid., p. 26.

128 "get past" his race Ibid., p. 25.

128 He laughed Ibid., p. 66.

128 After graduating from Harvard Ibid., pp. 84–94.

128 With respect to appearance Ibid., p. 105.

128 Mungin also engaged Ibid., p. 41.

129 As Mungin stated Ibid., p. 6.

129 Believing his predicament *Mungin v. Katten Muchin & Zavis,* 941 F. Supp. 153 (1996), *rev'd,* 116 F.3d 1549 (D.C. Cir. 1997).

129 "I was going to have to" Barrett, *The Good Black,* p. 163.

130 "Times have changed" Liu, *The Accidental Asian,* p. 35.

130 As in the orientation context In *Rogers v. American Airlines, Inc.,* 527 F. Supp. 229 (S.D.N.Y. 1981), a federal district court in New York found that an employer's policy prohibiting employees from wearing cornrows did not constitute racial discrimination (see discussion pp. 131–36). In *Hernandez v. New York,* 500 U.S. 352 (1991), the Supreme Court held that a prosecutor's decision to strike jurors based on their ability to speak Spanish did not violate the Equal Protection Clause. In *Dimaranan v. Pomona Valley Hospital Medical Center,* 775 F. Supp. 338 (C.D. Cal. 1991), a federal district court in California held that a hospital policy prohibiting the speaking of Tagalog by Filipina nurses did not constitute discrimination on the basis of national origin. The court later withdrew its opinion pursuant to a settlement. See *Dimaranan v. Pomona Valley Hospital Medical Center,* No. 89 4299 ER (JRX), 1993 WL 326559 (C.D. Cal. March 17, 1993).

131 *Rogers v. American Airlines* *Rogers v. American Airlines, Inc.,* 527 F. Supp. 229.

131 Rogers was an African-American Ibid., p. 231.

131  Yet the policy disproportionately burdened  Paulette Caldwell, "A Hair Piece: Perspectives on the Intersection of Race and Gender," *Duke Law Journal* (April 1991): 365, 379.

131  Rogers, who wore cornrows  *Rogers*, 527 F. Supp. at 231.

132  It pointed out that Rogers  Ibid., p. 232.

132  This defense, of course, turns back  Caldwell, "A Hair Piece," p. 379.

132  The court posited that an "Afro/bush"  *Rogers*, 527 F. Supp. at 232.

132  The court then maintained that  Ibid.

132  The court observed that  Ibid., quoting *Garcia v. Gloor*, 618 F.2d 264, 269 (5th Cir. 1980).

133  "historical essence of Black"  Ibid., quoting Plaintiff's Memorandum in Opposition to Motion to Dismiss at 4-5.

133  That answer has been elaborated  Caldwell, "A Hair Piece."

133  When her hair is long  Ibid., p. 382.

133  When she wears an Afro  Ibid., p. 370.

133  When she wears cornrows  Caldwell recounts how "the student [who]. . . publicly introduced the subject of braided hair . . . stopped in mid-sentence and covered her mouth in embarrassment," because Caldwell "appeared at each class meeting wearing a neatly-braided pageboy"; and she reflects that she "resented being the unwitting object of one in thousands of law school hypotheticals." Ibid., p. 368.

134  Caldwell concludes from these experiences  Ibid., p. 391.

134  She notes that virtually all novels  Ibid., pp. 391–92.

134  "Blacks selling to whites"  Molloy, *New Dress for Success*, p. 211.

135  "It is an undeniable fact"  Ibid., p. 234.

135  After conducting research  Ibid., p. 233.

136  "Doing the things a white"  Ariela J. Gross, "Litigating Whiteness: Trials of Racial Determination in the Nineteenth-Century South," *Yale Law Journal* 108 (October 1998): 112.

137  And they do: the Molloy book  See Mike Bruton, "Eagles Radio Employee Wouldn't Go by the Book," *Philadelphia Inquirer*, March 19, 2002, p. C1.

137  Economics professors  Marianne Bertrand and Sendhil Mullainathan, "Are Emily and Greg More Employable Than Lakisha and Jamal? A Field Experiment on Labor Market Discrimination," *American Economic Review* 94 (September 2004): 991–1013. For press coverage of their findings, see, for example, Alan B. Krueger, "Sticks and Stones Can Break Bones, but the

Wrong Name Can Make a Job Hard to Find," *New York Times*, December 12, 2002, p. C2.

137 **The "white" résumés** Bertrand and Mullainathan report, "Resumes with White names have a 9.65 percent chance of receiving a callback. Equivalent resumes with African American names have a 6.45 percent chance of being called back. This represents a difference in callback rates of 3.20 percentage points, or 50 percent, that can solely be attributed to the name manipulation." Bertrand and Mullainathan, "Emily and Greg," pp. 997–98.

137 **"To a person who speaks"** *Garcia v. Gloor,* 618 F.2d 264, 270 (5th Cir. 1980).

138 **As sociolinguist Joshua Fishman** Joshua A. Fishman, "Language and Ethnicity," in *Language, Ethnicity and Intergroup Relations,* ed. Howard Giles (Oxford: Pergamon Press, 1977), pp. 25–26.

138 **In 1988, a federal appellate** *Gutierrez v. Municipal Court of Southeast Judicial District,* 838 F.2d 1031 (9th Cir.), *reh'g denied,* 861 F.2d 1187 (9th Cir. 1988), *vacated as moot,* 490 U.S. 1016 (1989).

139 **Dissenting from the court's decision** *Gutierrez,* 861 F.2d at 1193 (Kozinski, J., dissenting from denial of rehearing en banc).

140 **He aspires to compose** Zangwill, *The Melting Pot,* p. 33.

140 **Then David's own commitment** Ibid.

140 **the massacre of his parents in Russia** Ibid., pp. 148–53.

140 **Sitting on a roof garden** Ibid., p. 184.

140 **"Celt and Latin"** Ibid.

140 **"the great Alchemist"** Ibid., p. 185.

140 **My reaction was akin to** Schlesinger, *The Disuniting of America,* p. 39.

140 **to whom the published version** The dedication reads, "To Theodore Roosevelt: in respectful recognition of his strenuous struggle against the forces that threaten to shipwreck the great republic which carries mankind and its fortunes, this play is, by his kind permission, cordially dedicated." Zangwill, *The Melting Pot.*

140 **I shared Roosevelt's vision** Niall Ferguson, *The Pity of War* (New York: Basic Books, 1999), p. 192.

140 **This, after all, was the ideal** Stephen T. Wagner, "America's Non-English Heritage," *Society* 19 (November/December 1981): 37, 41.

142   **In 2001, when this meeting**   See, for example, Jonathan D. Glater, "Women Are Close to Being Majority of Law Students," *New York Times,* March 26, 2001, p. A1; Jane Stancill, "Women in Law Schools Find Strength in Rising Numbers," *News & Observer* (Raleigh, N.C.), April 18, 2001, p. B1; Susan C. Thomson, "Women Are Poised to Outnumber Men in Law School," *St. Louis Post-Dispatch,* September 19, 2001, p. C1.

143   **According to the American Bar Association**   Deborah L. Rhode, *The Unfinished Agenda: Women and the Legal Profession* (Chicago: ABA Commission on Women in the Profession, 2001), p. 14. The report is available at http://www.abanet.org/ftp/pub/women/unfinishedagenda.pdf.

143   **While some believe**   A study by the National Association for Law Placement found that many firms attribute their low percentage of women to a " 'pipeline' issue, reasoning that the number will increase as more females enter the profession." Stephanie Francis Ward, "Few Women Get Partnerships," *ABA Journal E-Report,* February 6, 2004. A chairman of the Massachusetts Judicial Nominating Commission similarly argued, "We do not get a high proportion of women in the pipeline compared to men." Eileen McNamara, "Backtracking on the Bench," *Boston Globe,* February 6, 2005, p. B1. Deborah Rhode notes that "the most common explanation is that women's underrepresentation is the product of cultural lag; current inequalities are viewed as a legacy of discriminatory practices that are no longer legal, and it is only a matter of time until us girls catch up. However, this pipeline theory cannot explain the extent of underrepresentation of women leaders in fields like law, where they have long constituted over a third of new entrants." Deborah L. Rhode, "Keynote Address: The Difference 'Difference' Makes," *Maine Law Review* 55 (2003): 17.

143   **law professor Deborah Rhode**   Rhode, *The Unfinished Agenda,* p. 14.

143   **A 2000 *ABA Journal* poll**   Terry Carter, "Paths Need Paving," *American Bar Association Journal* 86 (September 2000): 34.

145   **I'm most struck by**   Lani Guinier, Michelle Fine, and Jane Balin, *Becoming Gentlemen: Women, Law School, and Institutional Change* (Boston: Beacon Press, 1997).

145   **In a study**   Ibid., pp. 37–38.

145   **In the words of one**   Ibid., p. 29.

145 **Women who did not conform** Ibid., p. 68.

145 **The literature on sex equality** On the "double bind," see Cynthia Fuchs Epstein et al., "Glass Ceilings and Open Doors: Women's Advancement in the Legal Profession," *Fordham Law Review* 64 (November 1995): 352; Rhode, "The Difference 'Difference' Makes." On the "Catch-22," see Vicki Schultz, "Telling Stories About Women and Work: Judicial Interpretations of Sex Segregation in the Workplace in Title VII Cases Raising the Lack of Interest Argument," *Harvard Law Review* 103 (June 1990): 1839; Joan C. Williams and Nancy Segal, "Beyond the Maternal Wall: Relief for Family Caregivers Who Are Discriminated Against on the Job," *Harvard Women's Law Journal* 26 (spring 2003): 95–101. On the "tightrope," see Katharine T. Bartlett, "Only Girls Wear Barrettes: Dress and Appearance Standards, Community Norms, and Workplace Equality," *Michigan Law Review* 92 (August 1994): 2552–53; Charlotte L. Miller, "Checklist for Improving the Workplace Environment (or Dissolving the Glass Ceiling)," *Utah Bar Journal* (February 1996): 7.

147 **Recent literature on African-American** See, for example, Gary Peller, "Notes Toward a Postmodern Nationalism," *University of Illinois Law Review* (1992): 1099; Carolyn Edgar, "Black and Blue," *Reconstruction* (1994): 16.

147 **More generally, negative epithets** For a discussion of this phenomenon in the African-American community, see Peller, "Notes Toward a Postmodern Nationalism"; Edgar, "Black and Blue." For a discussion of this phenomenon in the Asian-American community, see Liu, *The Accidental Asian,* p. 34.

147 **The mind-set through which** See, for example, Nancy F. Cott, *The Bonds of Womanhood* (New Haven: Yale University Press, 1977), pp. 63–100; Frances E. Olsen, "The Family and the Market: A Study of Ideology and Legal Reform," *Harvard Law Review* 96 (May 1983): 1497–1578; Barbara Welter, "The Cult of True Womanhood: 1820–1860," *American Quarterly* 18 (summer 1966): 151–74.

147 **"I have no hesitation in saying"** Alexis de Tocqueville, *Democracy in America,* ed. J. P. Mayer, trans. George Lawrence (1835; New York: HarperCollins, 1969), p. 603.

148 **In 1872, the Supreme Court** *Bradwell v. Illinois,* 83 U.S. 130 (1872).

148 **Concurring in that judgment** Ibid., p. 141 (Bradley, J., concurring).

148 **In the 1973 opinion** *Frontiero v. Richardson,* 411 U.S. 677, 684 (1973).

149  **Grooming manuals**    See, for example, Susan Bixler and Nancy Nix-Rice, *The New Professional Image: From Business Casual to the Ultimate Power Look* (Avon, Mass.: Adams Media Corp., 1997); Sherry Maysonave, *Casual Power: How to Power Up Your Nonverbal Communication and Dress Down for Success* (Austin: Bright Books, 1999); John T. Molloy, *New Women's Dress for Success* (New York: Warner Books, 1996); Victoria A. Seitz, *Your Executive Image: The Art of Self-Packaging for Men and Women* (Avon, Mass.: Adams Media Corp., 1992).

149  **They instruct women**    Victoria Seitz writes, "Avoid pastels. Pastels are perceived as weak, extremely feminine, and not really business oriented." Seitz, *Your Executive Image*, p. 63. Sherry Maysonave cautions, "Wearing sweet prints, especially small floral designs, in the workplace conveys that you have little-girl attitudes or that you are uncomfortable asserting yourself in a competitive business setting." Maysonave, *Casual Power*, p. 39. Susan Bixler and Nancy Nix-Rice instruct, "Avoid floral prints or pictures of animals, scenes, or the like." Bixler and Nix-Rice, *The New Professional Image*, p. 153. On makeup, John Molloy writes, "All women should wear lipstick. We are so used to seeing women with lipstick that a woman without lipstick usually looks washed out." Molloy, *New Women's Dress for Success*, p. 202. Maysonave argues, "To exude casual power, women must wear makeup." Maysonave, *Casual Power*, p. 184. Bixler and Nix-Rice insist, "There is no such thing as a woman who doesn't look better with makeup. Makeup conceals flaws, accents attractive features, creates a creamy, polished look, and should be worn by every businesswoman every day." Bixler and Nix-Rice, *The New Professional Image*, p. 115.

149  **They recommend shoulder pads**    Sherry Maysonave writes, "Shoulder pads are necessary to add power to a woman's physique, but not Shoulder Pads on Steroids! Avoid the huge extended pads of the '80s." Maysonave, *Casual Power*, p. 118. Victoria Seitz argues, "Earrings are a must, to give shine to a woman's face," but she cautions to "stay away from dangling earrings, multiple rings, and noisy bracelets." Seitz, *Your Executive Image*, p. 91. Maysonave concurs, "Dressed down or up, a woman needs earrings for a completed, polished image." Maysonave, *Casual Power*, p. 127. On hairstyle, Susan Bixler and Nancy Nix-Rice write, "Hairstyles convey messages. Excessively long hair says 'sex goddess' or 'little girl.' Severely short may say 'masculine,' unless a woman has an extremely feminine face. Full, tousled, big

hair says 'pageant contestant.' But a wide range of clean-cut short to shoulder-length styles say 'businesswoman.' " Bixler and Nix-Rice, *The New Professional Image*, p. 108. Seitz agrees: "Your hairstyle should be a conservative cut that is easy to manage. . . . The style should not be too short or tailored, or long and overly feminine." Seitz, *Your Executive Image*, p. 67.

149 **She encourages women**   Gail Evans, *Play Like a Man, Win Like a Woman: What Men Know About Success That Women Need to Learn* (New York: Broadway Books, 2000), p. 8.

149 **At the same time**   Ibid., pp. 119–34.

149 **In her book**   Jean Hollands, *Same Game, Different Rules: How to Get Ahead Without Being a Bully Broad, Ice Queen, or "Ms. Understood"* (New York: McGraw-Hill, 2002), p. 13.

149 **She cautions that**   Ibid., p. 20.

150 **Her twenty-five rules**   Ibid., pp. 6–7.

150 **As writer Sylvia Ann Hewlett**   Sylvia Ann Hewlett, *Creating a Life: Professional Women and the Quest for Children* (New York: Talk Mirimax Books, 2002), pp. 3, 50.

150 **For her, "one pair"**   Ibid., p. 42.

150 **Women who do have children**   Joan Williams, *Unbending Gender: Why Family and Work Conflict and What to Do About It* (New York: Oxford University Press, 2000), pp. 69–70.

150 **Williams adduces the testimony**   Ibid., p. 69.

150 **Williams also quotes**   Ibid.

151 **Sue Shellenbarger, author**   These columns appear respectively as "How to Look Like a Workaholic While Still Having a Life," *Wall Street Journal*, December 28, 1994, p. B1; "Go Mobile and Wreck Your Sense of Balance," February 22, 1995, p. B1; "Some Top Executives Are Finding a Balance Between Job and Home," April 23, 1997, p. B1.

151 **Sociologist Arlie Hochschild**   For instance, after having her first child, personnel manager Nina Tanagawa tried to maintain her managerial image by arriving half an hour earlier than her staff in the morning and staying half an hour later at night, as well as reading reports and writing memoranda after her child was in bed. Hochschild, *The Second Shift*, p. 80. Hochschild also describes her own attempt to build up stores of goodwill before having a child: "Before having David, I saw students all the time, took every com-

mittee assignment, worked evenings and nights writing articles, and had in this way accumulated a certain amount of departmental tolerance." Ibid., p. viii. Hochschild discusses women's choice not to display photographs of their children in a later book, *The Time Bind: When Work Becomes Home and Home Becomes Work* (New York: Henry Holt, 1997), pp. 85–88.

151  **Hochschild's study of a major**    Hochschild, *The Time Bind*, pp. 85–86.

151  **As one female manager put it**    Ibid., p. 87.

151  **Sociologist Cynthia Epstein describes**    Epstein et al., "Glass Ceilings and Open Doors," p. 425.

151  **Hochschild discusses how men**    Hochschild discusses the "mother identity" in *The Second Shift*, p. 92. The mortgage comment appears in *The Time Bind*, p. 107.

152  **In her study of women lawyers**    Rhode, *The Unfinished Agenda*, p. 18.

154  **As law professor Susan Estrich**    Lynda Gorov, "Marcia's Makeover—Oh the Injustice of It All: Women Lawyers Bemoan Clark's Softer Look," *Boston Globe*, October 12, 1994, p. 69.

154  **In 1982, when seven**    *Price Waterhouse v. Hopkins*, 490 U.S. 228, 233 (1989) (plurality opinion).

154  **Of the nominees**    Ibid., pp. 233–34.

155  **When the partners refused**    *Hopkins v. Price Waterhouse*, 618 F. Supp. 1109 (D.D.C. 1985).

155  **The partners in her office**    *Price Waterhouse v. Hopkins*, 490 U.S. at 234.

155  **At trial, one State Department**    Ibid.

155  **One partner advised her**    Ann Branigar Hopkins, *So Ordered: Making Partner the Hard Way* (Amherst: University of Massachusetts Press, 1996), p. 148.

155  **Another suggested Hopkins**    Ibid., p. 202.

155  **Others described Hopkins**    *Price Waterhouse v. Hopkins*, 490 U.S. at 235.

155  **Still others complained of**    Hopkins, *So Ordered*, p. 209.

155  **Previous female candidates**    Ibid., p. xiii.

155  **When Hopkins first perceived**    Ibid., p.139.

156  **Only one partner**    Ibid., p. 221.

156  **As the trial judge observed**    *Hopkins v. Price Waterhouse*, 618 F. Supp. at 1117.

156  **An expert witness for Hopkins**    Hopkins, *So Ordered*, p. 236.

156  **Fiske first explained stereotyping**    Ibid., p. 234.

156  Fiske maintained that because  Ibid., p. 236.

156  In 1989, six justices  Justice Brennan's plurality opinion was joined by Justices Marshall, Blackmun, and Stevens. Justices White and O'Connor each wrote a concurring opinion. *Price Waterhouse v. Hopkins,* 490 U.S. at 228.

156  This opinion first articulated  Ibid., p. 251.

157  In *Dillon v. Frank*  *Dillon v. Frank,* 952 F.2d 403, 1992 WL 5436 (6th Cir. Jan. 15, 1992).

157  Dillon claimed that  Ibid., p. *5.

157  In rejecting Dillon's argument  Ibid., p. *10.

158  The plurality notes that  *Price Waterhouse v. Hopkins,* 490 U.S. at 251.

158  In a more recent case  In *Nichols v. Azteca,* a male employee alleged he was harassed by his male coworkers and supervisor because he did not conform to a male stereotype. The court agreed with the employee's contention "that the holding in *Price Waterhouse* applies with equal force to a man who is discriminated against for acting too feminine." *Nichols v. Azteca Restaurant Enterprises, Inc.,* 256 F.3d 864 (9th Cir. 2001). In a subsequent case, the same court held that sexual harassment of an employee on the basis of sexual orientation violated Title VII; a concurring opinion argued that the case was one of "gender stereotyping harassment" and was strikingly similar to *Nichols. Rene v. MGM Grand Hotel, Inc.,* 305 F.3d 1061, 1068 (9th Cir. 2002) (en banc) (Pregerson, J., concurring).

159  In 2004, an appellate court  *Jespersen v. Harrah's Operating Co.,* 392 F.3d 1076 (9th Cir. 2004), *reh'g granted,* 409 F.3d 1061 (2005).

159  Darlene Jespersen, who began  Ibid., p. 1077.

159  In 2000, Harrah's implemented  Ibid., p. 1078.

159  Under the Personal Best program  Ibid., p. 1077.

159  Later that year, Harrah's  Ibid., p. 1078 n. 2.

160  The district court rejected  *Jespersen v. Harrah's Operating Co.,* 280 F. Supp. 2d 1189 (D. Nev. 2002); *Jespersen,* 392 F.3d 1076.

160  As the dissenting judge  *Jespersen,* 392 F.3d at 1084 (Thomas, J., dissenting).

160  Male beverage servers were  Ibid., p. 1077.

160  The majority disagrees, asserting  Ibid., p. 1082.

160  The *Price Waterhouse* decision  *Price Waterhouse v. Hopkins,* 490 U.S. at 235.

160  As law professor Catharine MacKinnon  Catharine A. MacKinnon, "Re-

flections on Sex Equality Under Law," *Yale Law Journal* 100 (March 1991): 1292 n. 50.

161 **Law professor Mary Anne Case**    Mary Anne C. Case, "Disaggregating Gender from Sex and Sexual Orientation: The Effeminate Man in the Law and Feminist Jurisprudence," *Yale Law Journal* 105 (October 1995): 1–105.

161 **In 1987, the Seventh Circuit**    *Wislocki-Goin v. Mears*, 831 F.2d 1374 (7th Cir. 1987).

161 **It was uncontested**    Ibid.

161 **in 1983, Wislocki-Goin**    In addition to wearing her hair down and wearing excessive makeup, Wislocki-Goin cried during the deposition hearing of a disturbed juvenile and, for a Christmas party, wrote a "Dear Santa" letter that Judge Mears considered offensive. Ibid., p. 1377.

162 **As Joan Williams**    Williams and Segal, "Beyond the Maternal Wall," p. 88.

162 **Indeed, as my students**    Jennifer A. Kingson, "Women in the Law Say Path Is Limited by 'Mommy Track,' " *New York Times*, August 8, 1988, p. A1.

162 **A related article describes**    Mary C. Hickey, "The Dilemma of Having It All," *Washington Lawyer*, May/June 1988, p. 59.

163 **The Supreme Court delivered**    *Geduldig v. Aiello*, 417 U.S. 484 (1974).

163 **The Court held that discrimination**    Ibid., p. 496.

163 **As law professor Dan Danielsen**    Dan Danielsen, "Representing Identities: Legal Treatment of Pregnancy and Homosexuality," *New England Law Review* 26 (summer 1992): 1458.

164 **By passing the Pregnancy Discrimination Act**    *Pregnancy Discrimination Act of 1978, U.S. Code* 42 (2000), § 2000e(k).

164 **Courts have gone both ways**    Cases in which courts have held that discrimination against mothers is sex discrimination include *Santiago-Ramos v. Centennial P.R. Wireless Corp.*, 217 F.3d 46 (1st Cir. 2000); *Sheehan v. Donlen Corp.*, 173 F.3d 1039 (7th Cir. 1999); *Coble v. Hot Springs School District No. 6*, 682 F.2d 721 (8th Cir. 1982); *Harper v. Thiokol Chemical Corp.*, 619 F.2d 489 (5th Cir. 1980); *Moore v. Alabama State University*, 980 F. Supp. 426 (M.D. Ala. 1997); and *Trezza v. The Hartford, Inc.*, No. 98 Civ. 2205, 1998 WL 912101 (S.D.N.Y. Dec. 30, 1998). Cases in which courts have held that discrimination against mothers is not sex discrimination include *Piantanida v. Wyman Center, Inc.*, 116 F.3d 340 (8th Cir. 1997); *Troupe v. May Department Store*, 20 F.3d 734 (7th Cir. 1994); *Maganuco v. Leyden Community High School District 212*, 939 F.2d 440 (7th Cir. 1991); *Martinez v. NBC, Inc.*, 49 F.

Supp. 2d 305 (S.D.N.Y. 1999); *Fuller v. GTE Corp.*, 926 F. Supp. 653 (M.D. Tenn. 1996); and *McNill v. N.Y. City Department of Correction*, 950 F. Supp. 564 (S.D.N.Y. 1994).

## THE END OF CIVIL RIGHTS

168  **In the nineteenth century, Mormons**   Congress passed a series of increasingly severe laws aimed at curtailing polygamy, including measures banning polygamy in the territories, barring polygamists from jury service and political office, and invalidating the corporation of the Mormon church. In 1890, when over one thousand polygynists were imprisoned, the president of the Mormon church issued a manifesto stating that the church would submit to the law and he would use his influence to discourage polygamy. See David L. Chambers, "Polygamy and Same-Sex Marriage," *Hofstra Law Review* 26 (fall 1997): 63-65; Sarah Barringer Gordon, *The Mormon Question: Polygamy and Constitutional Conflict in Nineteenth-Century America* (Chapel Hill: University of North Carolina Press, 2002).

168  **Those who refused**   For instance, small groups of polygamist families split off from the Mormon church and settled in rural communities in southern Utah and Arizona. In the early twentieth century there were several raids on these communities. Martha Sonntag Bradley, *Kidnapped from That Land: The Government Raids on the Short Creek Polygamists* (Salt Lake City: University of Utah Press, 1993).

169  **More recently, authorities have turned**   Polygamist Tom Green was prosecuted and sentenced to five years in prison. *State v. Green*, No. 001600036 at 2 (4th Dist. Ct. Utah July 10, 2000) (memorandum decision). As one newspaper reported, "Polygamy is an open secret in Utah and elsewhere in the West, where an estimated 30,000 people practice plural marriage. But Green practically dared prosecutors to go after him by appearing on television talk shows to discuss his lifestyle." "Brazen Polygamist Gets 5-Year Jail Term," *Chicago Tribune*, August 25, 2001, p. 12. The prosecution is also discussed in Julie Cart, "Polygamy Verdict Set Precedent," *Los Angeles Times*, May 20, 2001, p. A18; Michael Janofsky, "Conviction of a Polygamist Raises Fears Among Others," *New York Times*, May 24, 2001, p. A14.

169  For many American Jews   Norman L. Kleeblatt, ed., *Too Jewish?*

169  Riv-Ellen Prell describes   Riv-Ellen Prell, *Fighting to Become Americans: Jews, Gender, and the Anxiety of Assimilation* (Boston: Beacon Press, 1999), p. 216.

169  Abraham Korman recounts   Abraham K. Korman, *The Outsiders: Jews and Corporate America* (Lexington, Mass.: Lexington Books, 1988), pp. 38–39.

169  Academics like Phyllis Chesler   Phyllis Chesler, *The New Anti-Semitism: The Current Crisis and What We Must Do About It* (San Francisco: Jossey-Bass, 2003), pp. 18–19, 149–50.

169  And journalism professor   Samuel Freedman, *Jew vs. Jew: The Struggle for the Soul of American Jewry* (New York: Simon & Schuster, 2000), p. 25.

169  The idea of closeting ethnic   East European poet J. L. Gordon told his community, "Be a Jew in your own tent and a *mensch* when you go out." Elliott Abrams, "Judaism or Jewishness," *First Things*, June/July 1997, p. 21.

169  The idea of covering to avoid   Dershowitz, *Chutzpah*, pp. 18–19.

169  Like queers who seek   Ibid., p. 9.

170  The piece reports that   Leslie Goffe, "Not Responsible," *Middle East*, November 1, 2001, p. 46.

170  Other sources reveal similar   See, for example, Alan Cooperman, "In U.S., Muslims Alter Their Giving: Those Observing Islamic Tenet Want to Aid Poor but Fear Persecution," *Washington Post*, December 7, 2002, p. A1; Jessica Heslam, "Arab Students Feel Pressure to Return Home or Stay Quiet," *Boston Herald*, September 30, 2001, p. 17.

170  I could multiply examples   See, respectively, *Hamilton v. Schriro*, 74 F.3d 1545 (8th Cir. 1996); *Sherbert v. Verner*, 374 U.S. 398 (1963); *West Virginia State Board of Education v. Barnette*, 319 U.S. 624 (1943).

172  In her memoir   Georgina Kleege, *Sight Unseen* (New Haven: Yale University Press, 1999), pp. 11–12.

172  Steven Kuusisto writes   Steven Kuusisto, *Planet of the Blind* (New York: Dial Press, 1998), pp. 23–43.

172  The most famous instance   Cynthia Ozick, "What Helen Keller Saw," *New Yorker*, June 16 & 23, 2003, p. 196.

172  Jenny Morris notes   Jenny Morris, *Pride Against Prejudice: Transforming Attitudes to Disability* (Philadelphia: New Society Publishers, 1991), p. 36.

172  Others describe pressure   Lois Keith, "Encounters with Strangers: The Public's Responses to Disabled Women and How This Affects Our Sense of

Self," in *Encounters with Strangers: Feminism and Disability*, ed. Jenny Morris (London: Women's Press, 1996), p. 81.

172  **Irving Zola writes**   Zola, *Missing Pieces*, pp. 205–6.

173  **Under this model, courts**   On skin color versus language, compare *McDonald v. Santa Fe Trail Transportation Co.*, 427 U.S. 273 (1976), and *Abdulrahim v. Gene B. Glick Co.*, 612 F. Supp. 256 (N.D. Ind. 1985), with *Hernández v. New York*, 500 U.S. 352 (1991), and *Garcia v. Gloor*, 618 F.2d 264 (5th Cir. 1980). On chromosomes versus pregnancy, compare *Frontiero v. Richardson*, 411 U.S. 677 (1973), and *Los Angeles Department of Water & Power v. Manhart*, 435 U.S. 702 (1978), with *Geduldig v. Aiello*, 417 U.S. 484 (1974), and *General Electric Co. v. Gilbert*, 429 U.S. 125 (1976). The Supreme Court suggested in the 1996 case of *Romer v. Evans*, 517 U.S. 620 (1996), that discrimination based on sexual orientation alone might violate the Constitution's equality guarantee. In *Lawrence v. Texas*, 539 U.S. 558 (2003), the Supreme Court also struck down a Texas statute that criminalized same-sex sodomy, but it has not addressed same-sex marriage. Massachusetts is the only state to recognize same-sex marriages. See *Goodridge v. Department of Public Health*, 798 N.E.2d 941 (Mass. 2003). Vermont recognizes same-sex civil unions. See *Baker v. State*, 744 A.2d 864 (Vt. 1999). Cases upholding prohibitions on same-sex marriages include *Standhardt v. Superior Court*, 77 P.3d 451 (Ariz. Ct. App. 2003); *Dean v. District of Columbia*, 653 A.2d 307 (D.C. 1995); *Jones v. Hallahan*, 501 S.W.2d 588 (Ky. 1973); *Baker v. Nelson*, 191 N.W.2d 185 (Minn. 1971); *Storrs v. Holcomb*, 645 N.Y.S.2d 286 (Sup. Ct. 1996); and *Singer v. Hara*, 522 P.2d 1187 (Wash. Ct. App. 1974).

173  **As Justice O'Connor put it**   *Employment Division, Department of Human Resources of Oregon v. Smith*, 494 U.S. 872, 893 (1990) (O'Connor, J., concurring in the judgment).

173  **The 1972 case**   *Wisconsin v. Yoder*, 406 U.S. 205 (1972).

173  **They were prosecuted**   Ibid., pp. 207–8.

174  **The Court, however, found**   Ibid., p. 220.

174  **Accommodation is also a key**   *Americans with Disabilities Act of 1990*, U.S. Code 42 (2000), §§ 12,101–12,213. The "reasonable accommodation" provision appears at § 12,112(b)(5)(A).

174  **Employers can refuse only**   Ibid., § 12111(10)(A).

174   In a case litigated   *Fitzgerald v. Green Valley Area Education Agency*, 589 F. Supp. 1130 (S.D. Iowa 1984).

174   As law professor Linda Krieger   Linda Hamilton Krieger, "Foreword—Backlash Against the ADA: Interdisciplinary Perspectives and Implications for Social Justice Strategies," *Berkeley Journal of Employment and Labor Law* 21 (2000): 3.

174   In 1986, the Court   *Goldman v. Weinberger*, 475 U.S. 503 (1986).

175   In 1990, however   *Employment Division v. Smith*, 494 U.S. at 872.

175   So the Court ingeniously   *Sutton v. United Air Lines, Inc.*, 527 U.S. 471 (1999).

175   But some people with disabilities   Jacqueline Vaughn Switzer, *Disabled Rights: American Disability Policy and the Fight for Equality* (Washington, D.C.: Georgetown University Press, 2003), pp. 156–60.

175   Once it found Sutton's   *Sutton*, 527 U.S. at 488-89.

176   "The life of the law"   Oliver Wendell Holmes Jr., *The Common Law* (1881; Mineola, N.Y.: Dover Publications, 1991), p. 1.

176   That explosion has raised   Schlesinger, *The Disuniting of America*.

176   Schlesinger argues from   Ibid., p. 19.

176   His prescription, made most recently   Brubaker, "The Return of Assimilation?"

176   Looking at the United States   Ibid., p. 532.

176   The early cases   Respectively *Sherbert v. Verner*, 374 U.S. 398 (1963), and *Wisconsin v. Yoder*, 406 U.S. 205 (1972).

177   In the yarmulke case   *Goldman*, 475 U.S. at 512–13.

177   In the 1990 peyote case   *Employment Division v. Smith*, 494 U.S. at 888.

178   In a 2003 case   *Freeman v. State*, 2003 WL 21338619 (Fla. Cir. Ct. June 6, 2003).

178   In the fall of 2003   See "Muslim Girl Can Wear Head Scarf to School," *Associated Press*, May 20, 2004; Curt Anderson, "Muslim Girl in Oklahoma Can Wear Head Scarf to School Under Federal Settlement," *Contra Costa Times*, May 20, 2004, p. 4.

179   France and some German states   On February 10, 2004, the French National Assembly voted 494 to 36 to ban the wearing of an Islamic head scarf, or any other conspicuous religious symbol, within French public schools. The legislation reads: "Dans les écoles, les collèges et les lycées publics, le

port de signes ou tenues par lesquels les élèves manifestent ostensiblement une appartenance religieuse est interdit. Le règlement intérieur rappelle que la mise en oeuvre d'une procédure disciplinaire est précédée d'un dialogue avec l'élève." Assembleé Nationale, Douzième Législature, Projet de Loi Encadrant, en Application du Principe de Laïcité, le Port de Signes ou de Tenues Manifestant une Appartenance Religieuse dans les Écoles, Collèges et Lycées Publics, No. 253 (2004). On September 24, 2003, the German Constitutional Court held that an Afghani-born German citizen could not be denied a teaching position in the public schools because she wore a head scarf; the court also held that Germany's sixteen states could each decide whether to ban head scarves. *Kopftuch-Urteil [Head Scarf Decision]*, 2 BvR 1436/02 (BVerfGE Sept. 24, 2003). On subsequent state legislation see Bertrand Benoit, "Germans Wake Up to the Call of the Muezzin," *Financial Times,* November 4, 2003, p. 9; Jon Henley, "Europe Faces Up to Islam and the Veil: Muslims Claim Discrimination in Legal Battles over Religious Symbol," *Guardian,* February 4, 2004, p. 15.

179 **The 1994 instruction**   François Bayrou, Circulaire no. 1649 du 20 Septembre 1994, available at http://www.assemblee-nat.fr/12/dossiers/documents-laicite/document-3.pdf.

179 **Proponents of the ban**   For a discussion of this position, see Jane Kramer, "Taking the Veil: How France's Public Schools Became the Battleground in a Culture War," *New Yorker,* November 22, 2004, p. 60.

180 **Opponents of the law**   See Elaine Sciolino, "Ban on Head Scarves Takes Effect in a United France," *New York Times,* September 3, 2004, p. A8.

180 **Proponents of the French prohibition**   See "Scarf Wars: Banning the Muslim Headscarf in Schools," *Economist,* December 13, 2003, p. 47.

181 **Brennan dryly observed**   *McCleskey v. Kemp,* 481 U.S. 279, 339 (1987) (Brennan, J., dissenting).

181 **Based in part on our**   Race Relations Act, 1965, c. 73.

181 **Under the 1976 version**   Race Relations Act, 1976, c. 74.

181 **In a 1983 case**   *Mandla v. Dowell Lee,* [1983] 2 A.C. 548.

181 **As Lord Fraser stated**   Ibid., pp. 565–66.

182 **In 2003, amendments**   Race Relations Act 1976 (Amendment) Regulations, 2003. Under the new regulations, any provision, criterion, or practice that puts members of one racial or ethnic group at a disadvantage and cannot be shown to be a proportionate means of achieving a legitimate aim is

unlawful discrimination. The amended regulations can be found at http://www.legislation.hmso.gov.uk/si/si2003/20031626.htm.

182  **The House of Lords similarly**  Sex Discrimination Act, 1975, c. 65.

182  **In 1978, women challenged**  *Price v. Civil Service Commission,* [1978] 1 All E.R. 1228.

182  **The court rejected this**  Ibid., p. 1231.

182  **Justice has been blindfolded**  On the iconography of Justice, see Dennis E. Curtis and Judith Resnik, "Images of Justice," *Yale Law Journal* 96 (July 1987), p. 1742 n. 39.

## THE NEW CIVIL RIGHTS

184  **The object-relations theorist**  D. W. Winnicott, "Ego Distortion in Terms of True and False Self," in *The Maturational Processes and the Facilitating Environment* (New York: International Universities Press, 1965), pp. 140–52.

185  **The True Self is the self**  Winnicott, "Mirror-Role of Mother and Family in Child Development," in *Playing and Reality* (1971; New York: Routledge, 1989), p. 117.

185  **The True Self is associated**  Winnicott, "Ego Distortion," p. 148.

185  **To the contrary, Winnicott**  Ibid., pp. 146–47.

185  **In a less extreme case**  Ibid., p. 143.

185  **The individual approaches health**  Ibid.

186  **Based on extensive clinical research**  Carol Gilligan, *The Birth of Pleasure: A New Map of Love* (New York: Knopf, 2002), pp. 89–91, 223–25. In other works, Gilligan has explored the unique problems girls' voices face during development. In *Meeting at the Crossroads,* she notes that while men often talk as if they are autonomous and free to speak as they please, women describe "a relational crisis: a giving up of voice, an abandonment of self, for the sake of becoming a good woman and having relationships." Lyn Mikel Brown and Carol Gilligan, *Meeting at the Crossroads: Women's Psychology and Girls' Development* (Cambridge: Harvard University Press, 1992), p. 2.

187  **In the 2003 case**  *Lawrence v. Texas,* 539 U.S. 558 (2003).

187  **Similarly, in the 2004 case**  *Tennessee v. Lane,* 541 U.S. 509 (2004).

188  **Rather, it held that all persons**  Ibid., p. 533.

188  **I worked on a friend-of-the-court brief**  Brief of Amici Curiae Mary Robinson et al., *Lawrence v. Texas,* 539 U.S. 558 (2003) (No. 02-102).

188 **We knew this argument** For instance, Justice Scalia has argued that "the practices of the 'world community,' whose notions of justice are (thankfully) not always those of our people," are "irrelevant" to the Court's decisions. *Atkins v. Virginia*, 536 U.S. 304, 347–48 (2002) (Scalia, J., dissenting). He has similarly maintained, "Where there is not first a settled consensus among our own people, the views of other nations, however enlightened the Justices of this Court may think them to be, cannot be imposed upon Americans through the Constitution." *Thompson v. Oklahoma*, 487 U.S. 815, 868–69 n. 4 (1998) (Scalia, J., dissenting).

188 **But to our surprise** *Lawrence*, 539 U.S. at 576–77.

189 **As Stewart Burns** Stewart Burns, *To the Mountaintop: Martin Luther King Jr.'s Sacred Mission to Save America, 1955–1968* (New York: Harper, 2004), p. 322.

189 **Similarly, Malcolm X** Malcolm X, "The Ballot or the Bullet" (speech, Cory Methodist Church, Cleveland, Ohio, April 3, 1964).

189 **German Constitution's** Article 2(1) of the German Constitution provides: "Everyone shall have the right to free development of his personality in so far as he does not violate the rights of others or offend against the constitutional order or against morality." Grundgesetz [Constitution] [GG] art. 2, para. 1 (F.R.G.) (official translation of the Grundgesetz provided by the German Ministry of Foreign Affairs).

190 **The coup de grâce** For thoughtful academic commentary on the danger that civil rights law might itself engage in and lead to stereotyping, see Richard Ford, *Racial Culture: A Critique* (Princeton: Princeton University Press, 2004), and Roberto J. Gonzalez, "Cultural Rights and the Immutability Requirement in Disparate Impact Doctrine," *Stanford Law Review* 55 (June 2003): 2195–227.

190 **Here I follow Winnicott** Winnicott, "Ego Distortion."

191 **The statutory language** See *Civil Rights Act of 1964, U.S. Code* 42 (2000), §§ 2000e–2000e-2; *Americans with Disabilities Act of 1990, U.S. Code* 42 (2000), §§ 12,101–12,213.

193 **Under a congressional statute** *Solomon Amendment, U.S. Code* 10 (2004), § 983.

193 **I was also elated when** *Burt v. Rumsfeld*, No. CIV.A.3-03-CV-1777 (JCH), 2005 WL 273205 (D. Conn. Jan. 31, 2005). On January 31, 2005, Judge Janet C. Hall granted summary judgment to the plaintiffs upon finding that

the statute violates the faculty's free speech and expressive association rights. The Supreme Court has granted a writ of certiorari in a separate case challenging the same statute. See *Forum for Academic and Institutional Rights v. Rumsfeld*, 390 F.3d 219 (3d Cir. 2004), *cert. granted*, 125 S. Ct. 1977 (2005) (No. 04-1152).

194 **I think here of** Charles Reich, *The Sorcerer of Bolinas Reef* (New York: Random House, 1976).

EPILOGUE

197 **" 'Show me the place' "** Philip Levine, "The Doctor of Starlight," *One for the Rose* (Pittsburgh: Carnegie-Mellon University Press, 1999), p. 57.

200 **Raphael blushes** Milton, *Paradise Lost*, book 7, lines 1256–66.

Wilbur, and Toby B. Bieber. *Homosexuality: A Psychoanalytic Study.* New York: Basic Books, 1962.

Bixler, Susan, and Nancy Nix-Rice. *The New Professional Image: From Business Casual to the Ultimate Power Look.* Avon, Mass.: Adams Media Corp., 1997.

Bradley, Martha Sonntag. *Kidnapped from That Land: The Government Raids on the Short Creek Polygamists.* Salt Lake City: University of Utah Press, 1993.

Brown, Lyn Mikel, and Carol Gilligan. *Meeting at the Crossroads: Women's Psychology and Girls' Development.* Cambridge: Harvard University Press, 1992.

Burns, Stewart. *To the Mountaintop: Martin Luther King Jr.'s Sacred Mission to Save America, 1955–1968.* New York: Harper, 2004.

Camus, Albert. *The Myth of Sisyphus and Other Essays.* Translated by Justin O'Brien. New York: Knopf, 1969.

Chauncey, George. *Gay New York.* New York: Basic Books, 1994.

Chesler, Phyllis. *The New Anti-Semitism: The Current Crisis and What We Must Do About It.* San Francisco: Jossey-Bass, 2003.

Clendinen, Dudley, and Adam Nagourney. *Out for Good: The Struggle to Build a Gay Rights Movement in America.* New York: Simon & Schuster, 1999.

Cohen, Richard. *Coming Out Straight: Understanding and Healing Homosexuality.* Winchester, Va.: Oakhill Press, 2000.

Coleridge, Samuel Taylor. *The Rime of the Ancient Mariner.* In *The Oxford Book of English Verse.* 2nd ed. Edited by Arthur Quiller-Couch. New York: Oxford University Press, 1939.

Committee on Nomenclature and Statistics of the American Psychiatric Association. *Diagnosis and Statistical Manual: Mental Disorders.* New York: American Psychiatric Association, 1952.

Cory, Donald Webster. *The Homosexual in America: A Subjective Approach.* New York: Greenberg, 1951.

Cott, Nancy F. *The Bonds of Womanhood.* New Haven: Yale University Press, 1977.

Craft, William. *Running a Thousand Miles for Freedom; or, The Escape of William and Ellen Craft from Slavery.* 1860. Miami: Mnemosyne Publishing, 1969.

Crèvecoeur, J. Hector St. John de (Michel Guillaume Jean de Crèvecoeur). *Letters from an American Farmer.* 1782. New York: Fox, Duffield, 1904.

Crimp, Douglas, and Adam Rolston. *AIDS Demo Graphics.* Seattle: Bay Press, 1990.

# BIBLIOGRAPHY

BOOKS

Auden, W. H. *Collected Poems: Auden.* Edited by Edward Mendelson. New York: Vintage, 1991.

Barrett, Paul M. *The Good Black: A True Story of Race in America.* New York: Penguin Books, 1999.

Bayer, Ronald. *Homosexuality and American Psychiatry.* Princeton: Princeton University Press, 1987.

Bell, Marvin. *Old Snow Just Melting: Essays and Interviews.* Ann Arbor: University of Michigan Press, 1983.

Bersani, Leo. *Homos.* Cambridge: Harvard University Press, 1995.

Bieber, Irving, Harvey J. Dain, Paul R. Dince, Marvin G. Drellich, Henry G. Grand, Ralph H. Gundlach, Malvina W. Kremer, Alfred H. Rifkin, Cornelia B.

Dean, Tim, and Christopher Lane, eds. *Homosexuality and Psychoanalysis.* Chicago: University of Chicago Press, 2001.

D'Emilio, John. *Sexual Politics, Sexual Communities: The Making of a Homosexual Minority in the United States, 1940–70.* 2nd ed. Chicago: University of Chicago Press, 1998.

Dershowitz, Alan M. *Chutzpah.* Boston: Little, Brown, 1991.

Dickinson, Emily. *The Complete Poems of Emily Dickinson.* 1960. Edited by Thomas H. Johnson. New York: Back Bay Books, 1976.

Donne, John. *The Complete Poetry and Selected Prose of John Donne.* Edited by Charles M. Coffin. New York: Modern Library, 2001.

Duberman, Martin. *Cures: A Gay Man's Odyssey.* New York: Dutton Books, 1991.

Ellis, Albert. *Homosexuality: Its Causes and Cure.* New York: Lyle Stuart, 1965.

———. *Reason and Emotion in Psychotherapy.* Secaucus, N.J.: Citadel Press, 1962.

Ellis, Havelock. *Studies in the Psychology of Sex: Sexual Inversion.* Vol. 2. London: University Press, 1897.

Eskridge, William N., Jr. *Gaylaw: Challenging the Apartheid of the Closet.* Cambridge: Harvard University Press, 1999.

Eskridge, William N., Jr., and Nan D. Hunter. *Sexuality, Gender, and the Law.* New York: Foundation Press, 1997.

Evans, Gail. *Play Like a Man, Win Like a Woman: What Men Know About Success That Women Need to Learn.* New York: Broadway Books, 2000.

Faderman, Lillian. *Odd Girls and Twilight Lovers: A History of Lesbian Life in Twentieth-Century America.* New York: Columbia University Press, 1991.

Ferguson, Niall. *The Pity of War.* New York: Basic Books, 1999.

Ford, Richard T. *Racial Culture: A Critique.* Princeton: Princeton University Press, 2004.

Foucault, Michel. *The History of Sexuality: An Introduction.* Vol. 1. 1976. Translated by Robert Hurley. New York: Random House, 1978.

Freedman, Samuel. *Jew vs. Jew: The Struggle for the Soul of American Jewry.* New York: Simon & Schuster, 2000.

Freud, Sigmund. *Analysis Terminable and Interminable.* 1937. In *The Standard Edition of the Complete Psychological Works of Sigmund Freud.* Edited and translated by James Strachey. 24 vols. London: Hogarth Press, 1953–66. Vol. 23.

———. *A Child Is Being Beaten.* 1919. In *Standard Edition,* vol. 17.

———. *Civilization and Its Discontents.* 1930. In *Standard Edition,* vol. 21.

———. *The Psychogenesis of a Case of Homosexuality in a Woman.* 1920. In *Standard Edition,* vol. 18.

———. *Three Essays on the Theory of Sexuality.* 1905. In *Standard Edition,* vol. 7.

Gates, Henry Louis, Jr. *Figures in Black: Words, Signs, and the "Racial" Self.* New York: Oxford University Press, 1987.

Gilligan, Carol. *The Birth of Pleasure: A New Map of Love.* New York: Knopf, 2002.

Ginsberg, Elaine K., ed. *Passing and the Fictions of Identity.* Durham: Duke University Press, 1996.

Glazer, Nathan, and Daniel Patrick Moynihan. *Beyond the Melting Pot: The Negroes, Puerto Ricans, Jews, Italians, and Irish of New York City.* 1963. Cambridge: MIT Press, 1970.

Goffman, Erving. *Stigma: Notes on the Management of Spoiled Identity.* Englewood Cliffs, N.J.: Prentice-Hall, 1963.

Gordon, Milton. *Assimilation in American Life: The Role of Race, Religion, and National Origins.* New York: Oxford University Press, 1964.

Gordon, Sarah Barringer. *The Mormon Question: Polygamy and Constitutional Conflict in Nineteenth-Century America.* Chapel Hill: University of North Carolina Press, 2002.

Grahn, Judy. *Another Mother Tongue: Gay Words, Gay Worlds.* Boston: Beacon Press, 1984.

Gross, Larry. *Contested Closets: The Politics and Ethics of Outing.* Minneapolis: University of Minnesota Press, 1993.

Guinier, Lani, Michelle Fine, and Jane Balin. *Becoming Gentlemen: Women, Law School, and Institutional Change.* Boston: Beacon Press, 1997.

Halley, Janet E. *Don't: A Reader's Guide to the Military's Anti-Gay Policy.* Durham: Duke University Press, 1999.

Hewlett, Sylvia Ann. *Creating a Life: Professional Women and the Quest for Children.* New York: Talk Miramax Books, 2002.

Hochschild, Arlie Russell. *The Second Shift.* New York: Viking Penguin, 1989.

———. *The Time Bind: When Work Becomes Home and Home Becomes Work.* New York: Henry Holt, 1997.

Hollands, Jean. *Same Game, Different Rules: How to Get Ahead Without Being a Bully Broad, Ice Queen, or "Ms. Understood."* New York: McGraw-Hill, 2002.

Holmes, Oliver Wendell, Jr. *The Common Law.* 1881. Mineola, N.Y.: Dover Publications, 1991.

Hopkins, Ann Branigar. *So Ordered: Making Partner the Hard Way.* Amherst: University of Massachusetts Press, 1996.

Izenberg, Gerald N. *Impossible Individuality: Romanticism, Revolution, and the Origins of Modern Selfhood.* Princeton: Princeton University Press, 1992.

Jay, Karla, and Allen Young, eds. *Lavender Culture.* New York: NYU Press, 1994.

Jeffries, John C., Jr. *Justice Lewis F. Powell, Jr.* New York: Fordham University Press, 1994.

Johnson, Suzanne M. *The Gay Baby Boom.* New York: NYU Press, 2002.

Katz, Jonathan. *Gay American History: Lesbians and Gay Men in the U.S.A.; A Documentary.* New York: Harper & Row, 1976.

Kinsey, Alfred C., Wardell B. Pomeroy, and Clyde E. Martin. *Sexual Behavior in the Human Male.* Philadelphia: W. B. Saunders, 1948.

Kinsey, Alfred C., Wardell B. Pomeroy, Clyde E. Martin, and Paul H. Gebhard. *Sexual Behavior in the Human Female.* Philadelphia: W. B. Saunders, 1953.

Kleeblatt, Norman L., ed., *Too Jewish? Challenging Traditional Identities.* New York, Jewish Museum. New Brunswick, N.J.: Rutgers University Press, 1996.

Kleege, Georgina, *Sight Unseen.* New Haven: Yale University Press, 1999.

Korman, Abraham K. *The Outsiders: Jews and Corporate America.* Lexington, Mass.: Lexington Books, 1988.

Kronemeyer, Robert. *Overcoming Homosexuality.* New York: Macmillan Publishing, 1980.

Kuusisto, Steven. *Planet of the Blind.* New York: Dial Press, 1998.

Leupp, Gary P. *Male Colors: The Construction of Homosexuality in Tokugawa Japan.* Berkeley: University of California Press, 1995.

LeVay, Simon. *Queer Science: The Use and Abuse of Research into Homosexuality.* Cambridge: MIT Press, 1996.

———. *The Sexual Brain.* Cambridge: MIT Press, 1993.

Levine, Philip. *One for the Rose.* Pittsburgh: Carnegie-Mellon University Press, 1999.

Lewes, Kenneth. *The Psychoanalytic Theory of Male Homosexuality.* New York: Jason Aronson, 1988.

Liu, Eric. *The Accidental Asian: Notes of a Native Speaker.* New York: Random House, 1998.

Locker, J. L. *The Magic of M.C. Escher.* New York: Abrams, 2000.

Maupin, Armistead. *Sure of You.* New York: HarperCollins, 1989.

Maysonave, Sherry. *Casual Power: How to Power Up Your Nonverbal Communication and Dress Down for Success.* Austin: Bright Books, 1999.

Miller, D. A. *The Novel and the Police.* Berkeley: University of California Press, 1988.

Molloy, John T. *New Dress for Success.* New York: Warner Books, 1988.

———. *New Women's Dress for Success.* New York: Warner Books, 1996.

Morris, Jenny. *Pride Against Prejudice: Transforming Attitudes to Disability.* Philadelphia: New Society Publishers, 1991.

Murdoch, Joyce, and Deb Price. *Courting Justice: Gay Men and Lesbians v. the Supreme Court.* New York: Basic Books, 2001.

Murphy, Timothy. *Gay Science: The Ethics of Sexual Orientation Research.* New York: Columbia University Press, 1997.

Nicolosi, Joseph. *Reparative Therapy of Male Homosexuality.* Northvale, N.J.: Jason Aronson, 1997.

Pflugfelder, Gregory M. *Cartographies of Desire: Male-Male Sexuality in Japanese Discourse, 1600–1950.* Berkeley: University of California Press, 1999.

Posner, Richard A. *Law and Literature: A Misunderstood Relation.* Cambridge: Harvard University Press, 1998.

Prell, Riv-Ellen. *Fighting to Become Americans: Jews, Gender, and the Anxiety of Assimilation.* Boston: Beacon Press, 1999.

Rado, Sandor. *Adaptational Psychodynamics: Motivation and Control.* New York: Science House, 1969.

———. *Psychoanalysis of Behavior: Collected Papers.* New York: Grune and Stratton, 1956.

Reich, Charles. *The Sorcerer of Bolinas Reef.* New York: Random House, 1976.

Reischauer, Edwin, and Marius B. Jansen. *The Japanese Today: Change and Continuity.* 1977. Cambridge: Harvard University Press, 1995.

Rhode, Deborah L. *The Unfinished Agenda: Women and the Legal Profession.* Chicago: ABA Commission on Women in the Profession, 2001.

Rich, Adrienne. *The Fact of a Doorframe.* 1984. New York: W. W. Norton, 1994.

Rimmerman, Craig A., Kenneth D. Wald, and Clyde Wilcox, eds. *The Politics of Gay Rights.* Chicago: University of Chicago Press, 2000.

Roscoe, Will, ed. *Radically Gay: Gay Liberation in the Words of Its Founder.* Boston: Beacon Press, 1996.

Rousseau, Jean-Jacques. *The Confessions.* 1781. Translated by J. M. Cohen. New York: Penguin Books, 1953.

Rubenstein, William B. *Cases and Materials on Sexual Orientation and the Law.* 2nd ed. St. Paul, Minn.: West Publishing Company, 1997.

Saikaku, Ihara. *The Great Mirror of Male Love.* 1687. Translated by Paul Gordon Schalow. Stanford: Stanford University Press, 1990.

Schlesinger, Arthur M., Jr. *The Disuniting of America.* Knoxville, Tenn.: Whittle Direct Books, 1991.

Sedgwick, Eve Kosofsky. *Epistemology of the Closet.* Berkeley: University of California Press, 1990.

Seidman, Steven. *Beyond the Closet: The Transformation of Gay and Lesbian Life.* New York: Routledge, 2002.

Seitz, Victoria A. *Your Executive Image: The Art of Self-Packaging for Men and Women.* Avon, Mass.: Adams Media Corp., 1992.

Socarides, Charles W. *Homosexuality.* New York: Jason Aronson, 1978.

———. *Homosexuality: A Freedom Too Far.* Phoenix: Adam Margrave Books, 1995.

———. *The Overt Homosexual.* New York: Grune and Stratton, 1968.

———. *The Preoedipal Origin and Psychoanalytic Therapy of Sexual Perversions.* Madison, Conn.: International Universities Press, 1988.

Streitmatter, Rodger. *Unspeakable: The Rise of the Gay and Lesbian Press in America.* Boston: Faber & Faber, 1995.

Sullivan, Andrew. *Virtually Normal: An Argument About Homosexuality.* New York: Vintage Books, 1995.

Switzer, Jacqueline Vaughn. *Disabled Rights: American Disability Policy and the Fight for Equality.* Washington, D.C.: Georgetown University Press, 2003.

Szasz, Thomas. *Ideology and Insanity: Essays on the Psychiatric Dehumanization of Man.* New York: Doubleday, 1970.

———. *The Myth of Mental Illness: Foundations of a Theory of Personal Conduct.* New York: Harper & Row, 1961.

Tocqueville, Alexis de. *Democracy in America.* 1835. Edited by J. P. Mayer. Translated by George Lawrence. New York: HarperCollins, 1969.

Tolins, Jonathan. *The Twilight of the Golds.* New York: Samuel French, 1992.

Warner, Michael. *The Trouble with Normal: Sex, Politics, and the Ethics of Queer Life.* Cambridge: Harvard University Press, 1999.

White, Edmund. *The Beautiful Room Is Empty.* 1988. New York: Vintage, 1994.

Whitman, Walt. *Leaves of Grass.* 1855. New York: Bantam Books, 1983.

Williams, Joan. *Unbending Gender: Why Family and Work Conflict and What to Do About It.* New York: Oxford University Press, 2000.

Winnicott, D. W. *The Maturational Processes and the Facilitating Environment.* New York: International Universities Press, 1965.

————. *Playing and Reality.* 1971. New York: Routledge, 1989.

Wordsworth, William. *The Prelude.* Edited by Jonathan Wordsworth et al. New York: W. W. Norton, 1979.

Wu, Frank. *Yellow.* New York: Basic Books, 2002.

Wyatt, Thomas. *Sir Thomas Wyatt: Selected Poems.* New York: Routledge, 2003.

Zangwill, Israel. *The Melting Pot: A Drama in Four Acts.* New York: Macmillan Company, 1909.

Zola, Irving Kenneth. *Missing Pieces: A Chronicle of Living with a Disability.* Philadelphia: Temple University Press, 1982.

SCHOLARLY ARTICLES

Bailey, J. Michael, and Richard C. Pillard. "A Genetic Study of Male Sexual Orientation." *Archives of General Psychiatry* 48 (December 1991): 1089–96.

Bartlett, Katharine T. "Only Girls Wear Barrettes: Dress and Appearance Standards, Community Norms, and Workplace Equality." *Michigan Law Review* 92 (August 1994): 2541–82.

Bawer, Bruce. "Truth in Advertising." In *Beyond Queer: Challenging Gay Left Orthodoxy.* Edited by Bruce Bawer. Columbus, Ohio: Free Press, 1996.

Bertrand, Marianne, and Sendhil Mullainathan. "Are Emily and Greg More Employable Than Lakisha and Jamal? A Field Experiment on Labor Market Discrimination." *American Economic Review* 94 (September 2004): 991–1013.

Brubaker, Rogers. "The Return of Assimilation? Changing Perspectives on Immigration and Its Sequels in France, Germany, and the United States." *Ethnic and Racial Studies* 24 (July 2001): 531–48.

Byne, W. "Is Homosexuality Biologically Influenced? The Biological Evidence Challenged." *Scientific American* 270 (May 1994): 50–55.

————. "Science and Belief: Psychobiological Research on Sexual Orientation." *Journal of Homosexuality* 28 (June 1995): 303–44.

Byne, W., and B. Parsons. "Human Sexual Orientation: The Biological Theories Reappraised." *Archives of General Psychiatry* 50 (March 1993): 228–39.

Caldwell, Paulette. "A Hair Piece: Perspectives on the Intersection of Race and Gender." *Duke Law Journal* (April 1991): 365–96.

Cameron, Paul, and Kirk Cameron. "Do Homosexual Teachers Pose a Risk to Pupils?" *Journal of Psychology* 130 (November 1996): 603–13.

Carter, Terry. "Paths Need Paving." *American Bar Association Journal* 86 (September 2000): 34–39.

Case, Mary Anne C. "Disaggregating Gender from Sex and Sexual Orientation: The Effeminate Man in the Law and Feminist Jurisprudence." *Yale Law Journal* 105 (October 1995): 1–105.

Chambers, David L. "Polygamy and Same-Sex Marriage." *Hofstra Law Review* 26 (fall 1997): 53–83.

Cruz, David B. "Controlling Desires: Sexual Orientation Conversion and the Limits of Knowledge and Law." *Southern California Law Review* 72 (July 1999): 1297–400.

Curtis, Dennis E., and Judith Resnik. "Images of Justice." *Yale Law Journal* 96 (July 1987): 1727–72.

Danielsen, Dan. "Representing Identities: Legal Treatment of Pregnancy and Homosexuality." *New England Law Review* 26 (summer 1992): 1453–508.

Drescher, Jack. "I'm Your Handyman: A History of Reparative Therapies." *Journal of Homosexuality* 36 (June 1998): 19–42.

Edgar, Carolyn. "Black and Blue." *Reconstruction* (1994): 13–16.

Epstein, Cynthia Fuchs, Robert Saute, Bonnie Oglensky, and Martha Gever. "Glass Ceilings and Open Doors: Women's Advancement in the Legal Profession." *Fordham Law Review* 64 (November 1995): 291–449.

Eskridge, William N., Jr. "Gaylegal Narratives." *Stanford Law Review* 46 (1994): 607–46.

———. "No Promo Homo: The Sedimentation of Antigay Discourse and the Channeling Effect of Judicial Review," *NYU Law Review* 75 (November 2001): 1327–411.

Fishman, Joshua A. "Language and Ethnicity." In *Language, Ethnicity and Intergroup Relations.* Edited by Howard Giles, 15–57. Oxford: Pergamon Press, 1977.

Freud, Sigmund. "A Letter from Freud." *American Journal of Psychiatry* 107 (1951): 786–87.

Gonzalez, Roberto J. "Cultural Rights and the Immutability Requirement in Disparate Impact Doctrine." *Stanford Law Review* 55 (June 2003): 2195–227.

Gross, Ariela J. "Litigating Whiteness: Trials of Racial Determination in the Nineteenth-Century South." *Yale Law Journal* 108 (October 1998): 109–86.

Haldeman, Douglas C. "The Practice and Ethics of Sexual Orientation Conversion Therapy." *Journal of Consulting and Clinical Psychology* 62 (April 1994): 221–27.

Hall, J. A. Y., and D. Kimura. "Dermatoglyphic Asymmetry and Sexual Orientation in Men." *Behavioral Neuroscience* 108 (December 1994): 1203–26.

Halley, Janet E. "Sexual Orientation and the Politics of Biology: A Critique of the Argument from Immutability." *Stanford Law Review* 46 (February 1994): 503–68.

Halpert, Stephen C. "If It Ain't Broke, Don't Fix It." *International Journal of Sexuality and Gender Studies* 5 (January 2000): 19–35.

Hamer, Dean H., Stella Hu, Victoria L. Magnuson, Nan Hu, and Angela M. L. Pattatucci. "A Linkage Between DNA Markers on the X Chromosome and Male Sexual Orientation." *Science* 261 (July 1993): 321–26.

Hanna, Fadi. "Punishing Masculinity in Gay Asylum Claims." *Yale Law Journal* 114 (January 2005): 913–20.

Hooker, Evelyn. "The Adjustment of the Male Overt Homosexual." *Journal of Projective Techniques* 21 (1957): 18–31.

———. "Male Homosexuality in the Rorschach." *Journal of Projective Techniques* 22 (1958): 278–81.

Jetter, Alexis. "AIDS and the Obits." *Columbia Journalism Review* (July/August 1986): 14–16.

Kang, Jerry. "Cyber-Race." *Harvard Law Review* 113 (March 2000): 1131–208.

Keith, Lois. "Encounters with Strangers: The Public's Responses to Disabled Women and How This Affects Our Sense of Self." In *Encounters with Strangers: Feminism and Disability.* Edited by Jenny Morris, 68–88. London: Women's Press, 1996.

Krieger, Linda Hamilton. "Foreword—Backlash Against the ADA: Interdisciplinary Perspectives and Implications for Social Justice Strategies." *Berkeley Journal of Employment and Labor Law* 21 (2000): 1–18.

LeVay, Simon. "A Difference in Hypothalamic Structure Between Heterosexual and Homosexual Men." *Science* 253 (August 1991): 1034–37.

MacKinnon, Catharine A. "Reflections on Sex Equality Under Law." *Yale Law Journal* 100 (March 1991): 1281–328.

Maddox, Brenda. "The Woman Who Cracked the BBC's Glass Ceiling." *British Journalism Review* 13:2 (2002): 69–72.

Marcosson, Samuel. "Constructive Immutability." *University of Pennsylvania Journal of Constitutional Law* 3 (May 2001): 646–721.

Miller, Charlotte L. "Checklist for Improving the Workplace Environment (or Dissolving the Glass Ceiling)." *Utah Bar Journal* (February 1996): 6–9.

Olsen, Frances E. "The Family and the Market: A Study of Ideology and Legal Reform." *Harvard Law Review* 96 (May 1983): 1497–578.

Peller, Gary. "Notes Toward a Postmodern Nationalism." *University of Illinois Law Review* (1992): 1095–102.

Rhode, Deborah L. "Keynote Address: The Difference 'Difference' Makes." *Maine Law Review* 55 (2003): 15–21.

Schultz, Vicki. "Telling Stories About Women and Work: Judicial Interpretations of Sex Segregation in the Workplace in Title VII Cases Raising the Lack of Interest Argument." *Harvard Law Review* 103 (June 1990): 1749–843.

Shin, Jean. "The Asian American Closet." *Asian Law Journal* 11 (May 2004): 1–29.

Valdes, Francisco. "Queers, Sissies, Dykes, and Tomboys: Deconstructing the Conflation of 'Sex,' 'Gender,' and 'Sexual Orientation' in Euro-American Law and Society." *California Law Review* 83 (January 1995): 1–377.

Wagner, Stephen T. "America's NonEnglish Heritage." *Society* 19 (November/ December 1981): 37–44.

Welter, Barbara. "The Cult of True Womanhood: 1820–1860." *American Quarterly* 18 (summer 1966): 151–74.

Wilets, James D. "International Human Rights and Sexual Orientation." *Hastings International and Comparative Law Review* 18 (1994): 1–120.

Williams, Joan C., and Nancy Segal. "Beyond the Maternal Wall: Relief for Family Caregivers Who Are Discriminated Against on the Job." *Harvard Women's Law Journal* 26 (spring 2003): 77–162.

Winick, C. "AIDS Obituaries in *The New York Times.*" *AIDS & Public Policy Journal* 11 (1996): 148–52.

Yoshino, Kenji. "Assimilationist Bias in Equal Protection: The Visibility Presumption and the Case of 'Don't Ask, Don't Tell.' " *Yale Law Journal* 108 (December 1998): 485–571.

———. "Covering." *Yale Law Journal* 111 (January 2002): 769–939.

————. "The Epistemic Contract of Bisexual Erasure." *Stanford Law Review* 52 (January 2000): 353–461.

————. "Suspect Symbols: The Literary Argument for Heightened Scrutiny for Gays." *Columbia Law Review* 96 (November 1996): 1753–834.


MAGAZINE AND NEWSPAPER ARTICLES

Abrams, Elliott. "Judaism or Jewishness." *First Things,* June/July 1997.

Anderson, Curt. "Muslim Girl in Oklahoma Can Wear Head Scarf to School Under Federal Settlement." *Contra Costa Times,* May 20, 2004.

Bawer, Bruce. "Notes on Stonewall." *New Republic,* June 13, 1994.

Belluck, Pam. "Massachusetts Plans to Revisit Amendment on Gay Marriage." *New York Times,* May 10, 2005.

Benoit, Bertrand. "Germans Wake Up to the Call of the Muezzin." *Financial Times,* November 4, 2003.

"Brazen Polygamist Gets 5-Year Jail Term." *Chicago Tribune,* August 25, 2001.

Bruton, Mike. "Eagles Radio Employee Wouldn't Go by the Book." *Philadelphia Inquirer,* March 19, 2002.

Carr, C. "Why Outing Must Stop." *Village Voice,* March 18, 1991.

Cart, Julie. "Polygamy Verdict Sets Precedent." *Los Angeles Times,* May 20, 2001.

Cooperman, Alan. "In U.S., Muslims Alter Their Giving: Those Observing Islamic Tenet Want to Aid Poor but Fear Persecution." *Washington Post,* December 7, 2002.

Cox, James. " 'OutWeek' Magazine Goes Out of Business." *USA Today,* July 1, 1991.

Daughters of Bilitis. *Ladder* 1 (1956).

Dawson, Angela. "Kingsley No Nice Guy in 'Sexy Beast.' " *Chicago Sun-Times,* June 29, 2001.

Eliasberg, Kristin. "Making a Case for the Right to Be Different." *New York Times,* June 16, 2001.

Erlich, Reese. "A Star's Activism, On Screen and Off." *Christian Science Monitor,* December 28, 1990.

"Gay? or Eurotrash?" *Blair Magazine,* issue 3, http://www.blairmag.com/blair3/gaydar/euro.html.

Giordano, Rita. "Gays Bitter in Division over Outing." *Newsday,* August 9, 1991.

Glater, Jonathan D., "Women Are Close to Being Majority of Law Students." *New York Times,* March 26, 2001.

Goffe, Leslie. "Not Responsible." *Middle East,* November 1, 2001.

Gorov, Lynda. "Marcia's Makeover—Oh the Injustice of It All: Women Lawyers Bemoan Clark's Softer Look." *Boston Globe,* October 12, 1994.

Graham, Renée. "The Prince of Outing." *Boston Globe,* July 13, 1993.

Grove, Lloyd. "Jerry Lewis, Seriously Funny: 'Damn Yankees' Star Cuts the Comedy, Then Your Necktie." *Washington Post,* December 11, 1996.

Henley, Jon. "Europe Faces Up to Islam and the Veil: Muslims Claim Discrimination in Legal Battles over Religious Symbol." *Guardian,* February 4, 2004.

Heslam, Jessica. "Arab Students Feel Pressure to Return Home or Stay Quiet." *Boston Herald,* September 30, 2001.

Hickey, Mary C. "The Dilemma of Having It All." *Washington Lawyer,* May/June 1988.

Jacobs, Sally. " 'Outing' Seen as Political Tool." *Boston Globe,* April 3, 1993.

Janofsky, Michael. "Conviction of a Polygamist Raises Fears Among Others." *New York Times,* May 24, 2001.

Johnson, Dirk. "Privacy vs. the Pursuit of Gay Rights." *New York Times,* March 27, 1990.

Jones, Charisse. "Gay-marriage Debate Still Intense a Year Later." *USA Today,* May 17, 2005.

Kingson, Jennifer A. "Women in the Law Say Path Is Limited by 'Mommy Track.' " *New York Times,* August 8, 1988.

Kirkpatrick, David D. "Cheney Daughter's Political Role Disappoints Some Gay Activists." *New York Times,* August 30, 2004.

Kligman, David. "No AIDS Obits Is Banner News for Gay Newspaper." *Austin American-Statesman,* August 15, 1998.

Kramer, Jane. "Taking the Veil: How France's Public Schools Became the Battleground in a Culture War." *New Yorker,* November 22, 2004.

Krier, Beth Ann. "Whose Sex Secret Is It?" *Los Angeles Times,* March 22, 1990.

Krueger, Alan B. "Sticks and Stones Can Break Bones, but the Wrong Name Can Make a Job Hard to Find." *New York Times,* December 12, 2002.

Landau, Joseph. "Ripple Effect: Sodomy Statutes as Weapons." *New Republic,* June 23, 2003, p. 12.

Marcus, Ruth. "Powell Regrets Backing Sodomy Law." *Washington Post,* October 26, 1990.

Mattachine Society. *One* 1 (1953).

McNamara, Eileen. "Backtracking on the Bench." *Boston Globe*, February 6, 2005.

"Muslim Girl Can Wear Head Scarf to School." *Associated Press*, May 20, 2004.

Osmun, Mark Hazard. "Asian Says Whites Are Hurt by Quotas." *USA Today*, February 6, 1990.

" 'Outing' Is Wrong Answer to Anti-Gay Discrimination." *USA Today*, March 30, 1992.

Ozick, Cynthia. "What Helen Keller Saw." *New Yorker*, June 16 & 23, 2003.

Pattullo, E. L. "Straight Talk About Gays." *Commentary*, December 1992.

Rankin, Bill. "Irony in Georgia: Bowers Wins Case, Admits Adultery." *National Law Journal*, June 16, 1997.

Royko, Mike. "Antsy Closet Crowd Should Think Twice." *Chicago Tribune*, April 2, 1990.

Salzer, James. "Governor-Hopeful Bowers Admits Decade-Long Affair." *Florida Times-Union*, June 6, 1997.

Savage, Dan. "Sunday Lives: Role Reversal." *New York Times Sunday Magazine*, March 11, 2001.

"Scarf Wars: Banning the Muslim Headscarf in Schools." *Economist*, December 13, 2003.

Schmalz, Jeffrey. "On the Front Lines with Joseph Steffan: From Midshipman to Gay Advocate," *New York Times*, February 4, 1993.

Schmitt, Eric. "Close Quarters: How Is This Strategy Working? Don't Ask." *New York Times*, December 19, 1999.

Sciolino, Elaine. "Ban on Head Scarves Takes Effect in a United France." *New York Times*, September 3, 2004.

Shellenbarger, Sue. "Go Mobile and Wreck Your Sense of Balance." *Wall Street Journal*, February 22, 1995.

―――. "How to Look Like a Workaholic While Still Having a Life." *Wall Street Journal*, December 28, 1994.

―――. "Some Top Executives Are Finding a Balance Between Job and Home." *Wall Street Journal*, April 23, 1997.

Signorile, Michelangelo. "Gossip Watch." *OutWeek*, February 20, 1991; December 26, 1990; July 18, 1990.

―――. "The Other Side of Malcolm." *OutWeek*, April 18, 1990.

Stancill, Jane. "Women in Law Schools Find Strength in Rising Numbers." *News & Observer* (Raleigh, N.C.), April 18, 2001.

Sullivan, Andrew. "The Politics of Homosexuality." *New Republic,* May 10, 1993.

Taubeneck, Anne. "Would a Star by Any Other Name Shine as Bright?" *Chicago Tribune,* April 11, 1999.

Thomson, Susan C. "Women Are Poised to Outnumber Men in Law School." *St. Louis Post-Dispatch,* September 19, 2001.

Tuller, David. "Uproar over Gays Booting Others Out of the Closet." *San Francisco Chronicle,* March 12, 1990.

Virasami, Brian. "Coalition Criticizes Ruling Supporting Gay Marriage." *Newsday,* February 15, 2005.

Ward, Stephanie Francis. "Few Women Get Partnerships." *ABA Journal E-Report,* February 6, 2004.

"World Datelines." *San Francisco Examiner,* September 16, 1997, B8.

CASES

*Abdulrahim v. Gene B. Glick Co.,* 612 F. Supp. 256 (N.D. Ind. 1985).

*Able v. United States,* 968 F. Supp. 850 (E.D.N.Y., 1997).

*Able v. United States,* 155 F.3d 628 (2d Cir. 1998).

*Atkins v. Virginia,* 536 U.S. 304 (2002).

*Baker v. Nelson,* 191 N.W.2d 185 (Minn. 1971).

*Baker v. State,* 744 A.2d 864 (Vt. 1999).

*Bolling v. Sharpe,* 347 U.S. 497 (1954).

*Boutilier v. INS,* 387 U.S. 118 (1967).

*Bowers v. Hardwick,* 478 U.S. 186 (1986).

*Boy Scouts of America v. Dale,* 530 U.S. 640 (2000).

*Bradwell v. Illinois,* 83 U.S. 130 (1872).

*Burt v. Rumsfeld,* No. CIV.A.3-03-CV-1777(JCH), 2005 WL 273205 (D. Conn. Jan. 31, 2005).

*Chaffin v. Frye,* 45 Cal. App. 3d 39 (Cal. Ct. App. 1975).

*Charpentier v. Charpentier,* 536 A.2d 948, 950 (Conn. 1988).

*Coble v. Hot Springs School District No. 6,* 682 F.2d 721 (8th Cir. 1982).

*Dean v. District of Columbia,* 653 A.2d 307 (D.C. 1995).

*Delong v. Delong,* No. WD 52726, 1998 WL 15536, at 12 (Mo. Ct. App. Jan. 20, 1998), *rev'd in part sub nom. J.A.D. v. F.J.D.,* 978 S.W.2d 336 (Mo. 1998).

*Dillon v. Frank,* 952 F.2d 403, 1992 WL 5436 (6th Cir. Jan. 15, 1992).

*Dimaranan v. Pomona Valley Hospital Medical Center,* 775 F. Supp. 338 (C.D. Cal. 1991), *withdrawn,* No. 89 4299 ER (JRX), 1993 WL 326559 (C.D. Cal. March 17, 1993).

*Employment Division, Department of Human Resources of Oregon v. Smith,* 494 U.S. 872 (1990).

*Fitzgerald v. Green Valley Area Education Agency,* 589 F. Supp. 1130 (S.D. Iowa 1984).

*Forum for Academic and Institutional Rights v. Rumsfeld,* 390 F.3d 219 (3d Cir. 2004), *cert. granted,* 125 S. Ct. 1977 (2005) (No. 04-1152).

*Freeman v. State,* 2003 WL 21338619 (Fla. Cir. Ct. June 6, 2003).

*Frontiero v. Richardson,* 411 U.S. 677 (1973).

*Fuller v. GTE Corp.,* 926 F. Supp. 653 (M.D. Tenn. 1996).

*Garcia v. Gloor,* 618 F.2d 264 (5th Cir. 1980).

*Geduldig v. Aiello,* 417 U.S. 484 (1974).

*General Electric Co. v. Gilbert,* 429 U.S. 125 (1976).

*Givhan v. Western Line Consolidated School District,* 439 U.S. 410 (1979).

*Goldman v. Weinberger,* 475 U.S. 503 (1986).

*Goodridge v. Department of Public Health,* 798 N.E.2d 941 (Mass. 2003).

*Gordon v. State,* 360 S.E.2d 253 (Ga. 1987).

*Gutierrez v. Municipal Court of Southeast Judicial District,* 838 F.2d 1031 (9th Cir. 1988), *vacated as moot,* 490 U.S. 1016 (1989).

*Gutierrez v. Municipal Court of Southeast Judicial District,* 861 F.2d 1187 (9th Cir. 1988).

*Hamilton v. Schriro,* 74 F.3d 1545 (8th Cir. 1996).

*Harper v. Thiokol Chemical Corp.,* 619 F.2d 489 (5th Cir. 1980).

*Hernández v. New York,* 500 U.S. 352 (1991).

*Hernandez-Montiel v. INS,* 225 F.3d 1084 (9th Cir. 2000).

*Hopkins v. Price Waterhouse,* 618 F. Supp. 1109 (D.D.C. 1985), *rev'd,* 490 U.S. 228 (1989).

*In re J. S. & C.,* 324 A.2d 90 (N.J. Super. Ct. Ch. Div. 1974), *aff'd,* 362 A.2d 54 (N.J. Super. Ct. App. Div. 1976).

*J.L.P.(H.) v. D.J.P.,* 643 S.W.2d 865, 872 (Mo. Ct. App. 1982).

*Jespersen v. Harrah's Operating Co.,* 280 F. Supp. 2d 1189 (D. Nev. 2002).

*Jespersen v. Harrah's Operating Co.,* 392 F.3d 1076 (9th Cir. 2004), *reh'g granted,* 409 F.3d 1061 (2005).

*Jones v. Hallahan,* 501 S.W.2d 588 (Ky. 1973).

*Kopftuch-Urteil [Head Scarf Decision],* 2 BvR 1436/02 (BVerfGE Sept. 24, 2003).

*Lawrence v. Texas,* 539 U.S. 558 (2003).

*Los Angeles Department of Water & Power v. Manhart,* 435 U.S. 702 (1978).

*Lundin v. Lundin,* 563 So. 2d 1273 (La. Ct. App. 1990).

*Maganuco v. Leyden Community High School District 212,* 939 F.2d 440 (7th Cir. 1991).

*Mandla v. Dowell Lee,* [1983] 2 A.C. 548.

*Marlow v. Marlow,* 702 N.E.2d 733 (Ind. Ct. App. 1998).

*Martinez v. NBC, Inc.,* 49 F. Supp. 2d 305 (S.D.N.Y. 1999).

*McCleskey v. Kemp,* 481 U.S. 279 (1987).

*McDonald v. Santa Fe Trail Transportation Co.,* 427 U.S. 273 (1976).

*McNill v. N.Y. City Department of Correction,* 950 F. Supp. 564 (S.D.N.Y. 1994).

*Moore v. Alabama State University,* 980 F. Supp. 426 (M.D. Ala. 1997).

*Mungin v. Katten Muchin & Zavis,* 941 F. Supp. 153 (1996), *rev'd,* 116 F.3d 1549 (D.C. Cir. 1997).

*Nichols v. Azteca Restaurant Enterprises, Inc.,* 256 F.3d 864 (9th Cir. 2001).

*Piantanida v. Wyman Center, Inc.,* 116 F.3d 340 (8th Cir. 1997).

*Pickering v. Board of Education,* 391 U.S. 563 (1968).

*Pitcherskaia v. INS,* 118 F.3d 641 (9th Cir. 1997).

*Price v. Civil Service Commission,* [1978] 1 All E.R. 1228.

*Price Waterhouse v. Hopkins,* 490 U.S. 228 (1989).

*Ratchford v. Gay Lib,* 434 U.S. 1080 (1978).

*Rene v. MGM Grand Hotel, Inc.,* 305 F.3d 1061 (9th Cir. 2002) (en banc).

*Rogers v. American Airlines, Inc.,* 527 F. Supp. 229 (S.D.N.Y. 1981).

*Romer v. Evans,* 517 U.S. 620 (1996).

*Rowland v. Mad River Local School District,* 730 F.2d 444 (6th Cir. 1984).

*Rowland v. Mad River Local School District,* 470 U.S. 1009 (1985).

*Santiago-Ramos v. Centennial P.R. Wireless Corp.,* 217 F.3d 46 (1st Cir. 2000).

*Shahar v. Bowers,* 836 F. Supp. 859 (N.D. Ga. 1993).

*Shahar v. Bowers,* 70 F.3d 1218 (11th Cir. 1995).

*Shahar v. Bowers,* 78 F.3d 499 (11th Cir. 1996).

*Shahar v. Bowers,* 114 F.3d 1097 (11th Cir. 1997) (en banc).

*Shahar v. Bowers,* 522 U.S. 1049 (1998).

*Sheehan v. Donlen Corp.,* 173 F.3d 1039 (7th Cir. 1999).

*Sherbert v. Verner,* 374 U.S. 398 (1963).

*Singer v. Hara,* 522 P.2d 1187 (Wash. Ct. App. 1974).

*Standhardt v. Superior Court,* 77 P.3d 451 (Ariz. Ct. App. 2003).

*State v. Green,* No. 001600036 at 2 (4th Dist. Ct. Utah July 10, 2000).

*Steffan v. Perry,* 41 F.3d 677 (D.C. Cir. 1994) (en banc).

*Storrs v. Holcomb,* 645 N.Y.S.2d 286 (Sup. Ct. 1996).

*Sutton v. United Air Lines, Inc.,* 527 U.S. 471 (1999).

*Teegarden v. Teegarden,* 642 N.E.2d 1007 (Ind. Ct. App. 1994).

*Tennessee v. Lane,* 541 U.S. 509, 124 S.Ct. 1978 (2004).

*Thompson v. Oklahoma,* 487 U.S. 815 (1998).

*Trezza v. The Hartford, Inc.,* No. 98 Civ. 2205, 1998 WL 912101 (S.D.N.Y. Dec. 30, 1998).

*Troupe v. May Department Store,* 20 F.3d 734 (7th Cir. 1994).

*Watkins v. United States Army,* 875 F.2d 699 (9th Cir. 1989) (en banc).

*Weaver v. Nebo School District,* 29 F. Supp. 2d 1279 (C.D. Utah 1998).

*West Virginia State Board of Education v. Barnette,* 319 U.S. 624 (1943).

*Wisconsin v. Yoder,* 406 U.S. 205 (1972).

*Wislocki-Goin v. Mears,* 831 F.2d 1374 (7th Cir. 1987).

## CONSTITUTIONS, STATUTES, AND REGULATIONS

*Ala. Code* § 16-40a-2 (LexisNexis 2001).

*Americans with Disabilities Act of 1990. U.S. Code* 42 (2000), §§ 12,101–12,213.

*Ariz. Exec. Order* No. 2003-22 (June 21, 2003).

*Ariz. Rev. Stat. Ann.* § 15-716 (2000).

*Civil Rights Act of 1964, tit. VII, U.S. Code* 42 (2000), § 2000e et seq.

Enlisted Administrative Separations, Department of Defense Directive 1331.14.

*Official Code of Ga. Ann.* § 16-6-2, § 16-6-19 (2004).

Grundgesetz [Constitution] [GG] art. 2, para. 1 (F.R.G.).

*Immigration and Nationality Act of 1952, United States Code* 8 (1958), § 1182.

*Miss. Code Ann.* § 37-13-171 (West 1999).

*Miss. Code Ann.* § 97-29-59 (West 1999).

*N.C. Gen. Stat. Ann.* § 14-177 (West 2000).

*N.C. Gen. Stat. Ann.* § 115C-81 (West 2000).

*Okla. Stat. Ann.* tit. 70, § 11-103.3 (West 2005).

*Policy Concerning Homosexuality in the Armed Forces, U.S. Code* 10 (1994), § 654.

*Pregnancy Discrimination Act of 1978. U.S. Code* 42 (2000), § 2000e(k).

*Qualification Standards for Enlistment, Appointment, and Induction,* Department of Defense Directive 1304.26.

Race Relations Act, 1965, c. 73 (Eng.).

Race Relations Act, 1976, c. 74 (Eng.).

Sex Discrimination Act, 1975, c. 65 [UK].

*Solomon Amendment, U.S. Code* 10 (2004), § 983.

*S.C. Code Ann.* § 59-32-30 (2004).

*Tex. Health & Safety Code Ann.* 85.007 (Vernon 2001).

U.S. Constitution, amends. I, V, XIV.

*Utah Code Ann.* § 53A-13-101 (Supp. 2004).

*Utah Admin. Code* r. 277-474-3 (2001).


OTHER

ABC News, *Sex, Drugs & Consenting Adults: Should People Be Able to Do Whatever They Want?* May 26, 1998. Transcript available at http://www.mapinc.org/drugnews/v98/n389/a07.html.

American Medical Association. House of Delegates Resolution 506: Policy Statement on Sexual Orientation Reparative (Conversion) Therapy (April 26, 2000), http://www.ama-assn.org/meetings/public/annual00/reports/refcome/506.rtf.

American Psychological Association Council of Representatives. Resolution on Appropriate Therapeutic Responses to Sexual Orientation (August 14, 1997).

Assembleé Nationale, Douzième Législature, Projet de Loi Encadrant, en Application du Principe de Laïcité, le Port de Signes ou de Tenues Manifestant une Appartenance Religieuse dans les Écoles, Collèges et Lycées Publics. No. 253 (2004).

Bayrou, François. Circulaire no. 1649 du 20 Septembre 1994, http://www.assemblee-nat.fr/12/dossiers/documents-laicite/document-3.pdf.

Board of Trustees of the American Psychiatric Association. COPP Position Statement on Therapies Focused on Attempts to Change Sexual Orientation (Reparative or Conversion Therapies) (May 2000).

Brief of Amici Curiae Mary Robinson et al., *Lawrence v. Texas,* 539 U.S. 558 (2003) (No. 02-102).

Center for Infectious Diseases, Centers for Disease Control, AIDS Weekly Surveillance Report, "1—United States AIDS Program," December 29, 1986.

CNN, *Larry King Weekend,* July 6, 2002.

http://www.straightacting.com.

National Committee on Lesbian, Gay & Bisexual Issues, National Association of Social Workers. Position Statement: "Reparative" and "Conversion" Therapies for Lesbians and Gay Men (January 21, 2000).

Office of the Under Secretary of Defense (Pers. & Readiness). Report to the Secretary of Defense: Review of the Effectiveness of the Application and Enforcement of the Department's Policy on Homosexual Conduct in the Military (1998), http://www.defenselink.mil/pubs/rpt040798.html.

Servicemembers Legal Defense Network, Conduct Unbecoming: 10th Annual Report on "Don't Ask, Don't Tell" (2004).

Socarides, Charles W. "How America Went Gay," available at http://www.leaderu.com/jhs/socarides.html.

X, Malcolm. "The Ballot or the Bullet." Speech, Cory Methodist Church, Cleveland, Ohio, April 3, 1964.

# ACKNOWLEDGMENTS

I am indebted to the following friends and colleagues: Bruce Ackerman, Matt Alsdorf, Ian Ayres, Ina Bort, Bo Burt, Iain Campbell, Janet Choi, Amy Chua, Gene Coakley, Ariela Dubler, Elizabeth Emens, Robert Ferguson, Paul Festa, George Fisher, Owen Fiss, Cary Franklin, Adam Freed, Maureen Freed, Adam Haslett, Michael Kavey, Gia Kim, Harold Koh, Oren Izenberg, Christopher Jewell, Kenneth Katz, Anthony Light, Robert Post, Tom Pulham, Sonya Rasminsky, Carol Rose, Bill Rubenstein, Lisa Rubin, Catherine Sharkey, Reva Siegel, and Robert Wintemute. At Random House, Jon Karp, Jane von Mehren, Jonathan Jao, and Jillian Quint gave me tireless support. My agent Betsy Lerner supplied wisdom and friendship. Jessica Bulman-Pozen, Mike Gottlieb, and Fadi Hanna provided sterling research assistance.

# INDEX

## ABOUT THE AUTHOR

KENJI YOSHINO is Deputy Dean for Intellectual Life and
Professor of Law at Yale Law School. He lives in New Haven,
Connecticut.

## ABOUT THE TYPE

This book was set in Minion, a 1990 Adobe Originals typeface by Robert Slimbach. Minion is inspired by classical, old-style typefaces of the late Renaissance, a period of elegant, beautiful, and highly readable type designs. Created primarily for text setting, Minion combines the aesthetic and functional qualities that make text type highly readable with the versatility of digital technology.